THE FABER BOOK OF THE THEATRE

The Faber Book
of the
Theatre

EDITED BY

Ronald Harwood

faber and faber
LONDON · BOSTON

First published in 1993
by Faber and Faber Limited
3 Queen Square London WC1N 3AU

Photoset by Wilmaset Ltd, Wirral
Printed in England by Clays Ltd, St Ives plc

A CIP record for this book is
available from the British Library.

ISBN 0–571–16480–3

2 4 6 8 10 9 7 5 3 1

Contents

This book would not have been possible without the assistance of a brilliant young actor, Nick Hutchison. His knowledge of the literature of the theatre is immense and I thank him for sharing it so generously with me.

R. H.

I

Purposes
Plays & Playwrights

The theatre, as we now recognize it, developed out of religious ritual in Athens two and a half thousand years ago. No one really knows how this transformation took place, but suddenly there it was, fully developed and wonderful, with theatres, actors, audiences and, most important of all, the playwright, whose personal vision was the driving force. Since then the theatre has flourished all over the world, serving various purposes, its most potent being as an agent for change – social, political, moral. A clue to this power may lie in the medium's religious origins.

For the mystery to work, both actors and audience must lose a sense of themselves and of their surroundings. Samuel Taylor Coleridge's oft-quoted phrase concerning 'the willing suspension of disbelief . . . which constitutes poetic faith' misses the point: what is in fact asked of the audience is that it makes believe just as, in a more obvious sense, the actors make believe.

The theatre is influential when it needs to be influential. It may lie dormant for long periods and then suddenly assert itself and identify social ills or capture the mood and preoccupations of an age. In that, it is unique. The theatre at its best entertains and beguiles while it does its more serious work. Its secret target is our subconscious.

The genesis of most theatrical activity begins with the writing of a play.

MARGARETE BIEBER, from The History of the Greek and Roman Theatre, 1939:

The performance of a Greek tragedy is apt to make a markedly deep impression on an educated audience. It may almost be described as miraculous that the works of Aeschylus, Sophocles and Euripides, belonging as they do to the very beginning of the drama in the fifth century BC, should be works of art so lofty as to retain their heroic greatness and eternal life even today. We shall never be able to explain this miracle fully . . .

There is perhaps no more moving example of the theatre's power to make people lose a sense of themselves and their surroundings than the following observations recorded in the Vilna Ghetto during the Second World War:

18 January 1942
People laughed and cried. They cast off the depression that had been weighing on their spirits. The alienation that had hitherto existed among the Ghetto population seemed to have been thrown off . . . people awoke from a long difficult dream.
(DR LAZAR EPSTEIN on the opening of the Ghetto theatre)

Saturday 27 March 1943
In a hall filled to capacity, the première of *Der Oytser* took place. Outside, the police were guarding the arrivals from Swieciany. Here in the theatre, as if nothing were happening – a première! The performance is smooth, the play is unblemished, the sets really beautiful – as if this were not the Ghetto.
(From HERMANN KRUK's diary)

KENNETH TYNAN (1927–80), from *Pausing on the Stairs*; 1957:

Show me a congenital eavesdropper with the instincts of a peeping Tom and I will show you the makings of a dramatist.

AUGUST STRINDBERG (1849–1912), 1888:

I do not believe in simple characters on stage . . . My souls are conglomerations from past and present stages of civilization; they are excerpts from books and newspapers, scraps of humanity, pieces torn from festive garments which have become rags – just as the soul itself is a piece of patchwork.

PETER BROOK (b. 1925), from *The Empty Space*, 1968:

In theory few men are as free as a playwright. He can bring the whole world on to his stage. But in fact he is strangely timid. He looks at the whole of life, and like all of us he only sees a tiny fragment; a fragment, one aspect of which catches his fancy. Unfortunately he rarely searches to relate his detail to any larger structure – it is as though he accepts without question his intuition as complete, his reality as all of reality. It is as though his belief in his subjectivity as his instrument and his strength precludes him from any dialectic between what he sees and what he apprehends. So there is either the author who explores his inner experience in depth and darkness, or else the author who shuns these areas, exploring the outside world – each one thinks his world is complete. If Shakespeare had never existed we would quite understandably theorize that the two can never combine. The Elizabethan Theatre did exist, though – and awkwardly enough we have this example constantly hanging over our heads. Four hundred years ago it was possible for a dramatist to wish to bring the pattern of events in the outside world, the inner events of complex men isolated as individuals, the vast tug of their fears and aspirations, into open conflict. Drama was exposure, it was confrontation, it was contradiction and it led to analysis, involvement, recognition and, eventually, to an awakening of understanding. Shakespeare was not a peak without a base, floating magically on a cloud: he was supported by scores of lesser dramatists, naturally with lesser and lesser talents – but sharing the same ambition for wrestling with what Hamlet calls the forms and pressures of the age.

JOHN DRYDEN (1631–1700), Preface to *An Evening's Love*, 1671:

Tragedy fulfils one great part of its institution; which is, by example, to instruct. But in comedy it is not so; for the chief end of it is divertissement and delight. . . . The business of the poet is to make you laugh: when he writes humour, he makes folly ridiculous; when wit, he moves you, if not always to laughter, yet to a pleasure that is more noble. And if he works a cure on folly, and the small imperfections in mankind, by exposing them to public view, that cure is not performed by an immediate operation: for it works first on the ill-nature of the audience; they are moved to laugh by the representation of deformity; and the shame of that laughter teaches us to amend what is ridiculous in our manners. This being then established, that the first end of comedy is delight, and instruction only the second; it may reasonably be inferred, that comedy is not so much obliged to the punishment of faults which it represents, as tragedy.

MOLIÈRE (1622–73), from *Critique de l'Ecole des femmes*, 1663:

. . . if you were to put a plus for difficulty on the side of comedy, perhaps you would be making no mistake. For, after all, I think it would be much easier to strike a lofty pose upon grand sentiments, to brave fortune in rhyme, accuse destiny, and hurl insults at the gods, than to enter into the ridiculous side of men and represent everybody's defects agreeably on stage. When you paint heroes, you do what you like . . . But when you paint men, you must paint from nature . . . In a word, in serious plays, to avoid blame it is enough to say things that are sensible and well written; but in the other kind this is not enough, you have to be funny; and it's quite an undertaking to make people of breeding laugh.

GEOFFREY CHAUCER (c. 1343–1400), from the Prologue to *The Monk's Tale*:

> Tragedie is to seyn a certeyn storie,
> As olde bookes maken us memorie,
> Of hym that stood in greet prosperitee
> And is yfallen out of heigh degree
> Into myserie, and endeth wrecchedly.

RICHARD BRINSLEY SHERIDAN (1751–1816), from a letter to his father-in-law, November 1774, with news of *The Rivals*:

There will be a comedy of mine in rehearsal at Covent Garden within a few days. It will be very well played and Harris tells me that the least shilling I shall get (if it succeeds) will be £600. I had not written a line of it two months ago . . .

JEAN ANOUILH (1910–87), from *Antigone*, 1942:

The spring is wound up tight. It will uncoil of itself. That is what is so convenient in tragedy. The least little turn of the wrist will do the job . . .

The rest is automatic. You don't need to lift a finger. The machine is in perfect order; it has been oiled ever since time began, and it runs without friction. Death, treason and sorrow are on the march; and they move in the wake of storm, of tears, of stillness. Every kind of stillness. The hush when the executioner's axe goes up at the end of the last act. The unbreathable silence when, at the beginning of the play, the two lovers, their hearts bared, their bodies naked, stand for the first time face to face in the darkened room, afraid to stir . . .

Tragedy is clean, it is restful, it is flawless. It has nothing to do with melodrama – with wicked villains, persecuted maidens, avengers, sudden revelations and eleventh-hour repentances. Death, in a melodrama, is really horrible because it is never inevitable . . .

In a tragedy, nothing is in doubt and everyone's destiny is known. That makes for tranquillity. There is a sort of fellow-feeling among characters in a tragedy: he who kills is as innocent as he who gets killed: it's all a matter of what part you are playing. Tragedy is restful; and the reason is that hope, that foul, deceitful thing, has no part in it. There isn't any hope. You're trapped. The whole sky has fallen on you, and all you can do about it is to shout.

Don't mistake me: I said 'shout': I did not say groan, whimper, complain. That, you cannot do. But you can shout aloud; you can get all those things said that you never thought you'd be able to say – or never even knew you had it in you to say. And you don't say these things because it will do any good to say them: you know better than that. You say them for their own sake; you say them because you learn a lot from them.

Anton Chekhov (1860–1904), writes to Maxim Gorky, 16 October 1900:

I found the writing of *Three Sisters* terribly difficult. You must remember it has three heroines and each of them has to be made according to her own pattern and all three of them daughters to a general. The action takes place in a provincial town like Perm: the environment is military – artillery.

RICHARD BRINSLEY SHERIDAN, from the Epilogue to *The Rivals*, 1775:

> Through all drama – whether damn'd or not –
> Love gilds the scene, and women guide the plot.

APHRA BEHN (1640–89), from the Epilogue to *Sir Patient Fancy*, 1678:

> MRS GWIN: I here and there o'erheard a Coxcomb cry,
> 'Ah, Rot it – 'tis a Women's Comedy,
> One, who because she lately chanc'd to please us.
> With her damn'd Stuff, will never cease to teeze us.'
> What has poor Woman done, that she must be
> Debar'd from Sense, and sacred Poetry?
> Why in this Age has Heaven allow'd you more,
> And Women less of Wit than heretofore?
> We once were fam'd in story, and could write
> Equal to Men; cou'd govern, nay, cou'd fight.
> We still have passive Valour, and can show,
> Wou'd Custom give us leave, the active too,
> Since we no Provocations want from you.
> For who but we cou'd your dull Fopperies bear,
> Your saucy Love, and your brisk Nonsense hear;
> Indure your worse than womanish Affectation,
> Which renders you the Nusance of the Nation;
> Scorn'd even by all the Misses of the Town,
> A Jest to Vizard Mask, the *Pit-Buffoon*;
> A Glass by which the admiring Country Fool
> May learn to dress himself *en Ridicule*:
> In Leudness, Foppery, Nonsense, Noise and Show.

And yet to these fine things we must submit
Our Reason, Arms, our Laurels, and our Wit.
Because we do not laugh at you, when leud,
And scorn and cudgel ye when ye are rude.
That we have nobler Souls than you, we prove,
By how much more we're sensible of Love;
Quickest in finding all the subtlest ways
To make your Joys, why not to make your Plays?
We best can find your foibles, know your own,
And Jilts and Cuckolds now best please the Town;
Your way of Writing's out of fashion grown.
Method and Rule – you only understand;
Pursue that way of Fooling and be damn'd.
Your learned Cant of Action, Time and Place,
Must all give way to the unlabour'd Farce.
To all the Men of Wit we will subscribe –
But for your half Wits, ye unthinking Tribe
We'll let you see, whate'er besides we do,
How artfully we copy some of you –
And if you're drawn to th' Life pray tell me then,
Why Women should not write as well as Men.

ARISTOTLE (384–322 BC), from *Poetics*:

Plots are either simple or complex, since the actions they represent are naturally of this twofold description. The action, proceeding in the way defined, as one continuous whole, I call simple, when the change in the hero's fortunes takes place without Peripety or Discovery; and complex when it involves one or the other or both. These should each of them arise out of the structure of the plot itself, so as to be the consequence, necessary or probable, of the antecedents. There is a great difference between a thing happening *propter hoc* and *post hoc*.

RICHARD BRINSLEY SHERIDAN from *The Critic*, 1779:

MR PUFF: O Lord, yes – ever while you live have two plots to your tragedy. The grand point in managing them is only to let your underplot have as little connexion with your main plot as possible. I flatter myself nothing can be more distinct than mine, for as in my chief plot the characters are all great people, I have laid my underplot in low life; and as the former is to end in deep distress, I make the other end as happy as a farce.

SIMON GRAY (b. 1936), from *An Unnatural Pursuit and Other Pieces*, 1985:

I finished the play at six this morning, having worked through half the night. I'd also worked through three packages of cigarettes and half a bottle of malt whisky. But the main thing is that it's finished. Olé. I numbered the pages, packed and shaped them into a completed looking pile, toasted myself with a further gulp of whisky and a few more cigarettes, gloated. This for me is the only moment of pure happiness I ever experience in the play-writing business.

SACHA GUITRY (1885–1957), actor and playwright, 1957:

If a playwright is funny, the English look for the serious message, and if he is serious they look for the joke.

MARTY FELDMAN, comedian, quoted in *The Times*:

Comedy, like sodomy, is an unnatural act.

RANJIT BOLT, translator, 'When Fame is the Spur' (the *Guardian*), 1991:

Then I remember the great advantage a translator has over a 'writer proper'. If people like your work, you lap up the praise quietly. If they don't, you intimate, with as much modesty as possible, that a translator can only be as good as the material he or she is given to work with.

GEORGE BERNARD SHAW (1856–1950), from *The Problem Play*, 1895:

At all events, we find Ibsen, after producing, in *Brand*, *Peer Gynt*, and *Emperor and Galilean*, dramatic poems on the grandest scale, deliberately turning to comparatively prosaic topical plays on the most obviously transitory social questions, finding in their immense magnitude under modern conditions the stimulus which, a hundred years ago, or four thousand, he would only have received from the eternal strife of man with his own spirit. *A Doll's House* will be as flat as ditchwater when *A Midsummer Night's Dream* will still be as fresh as paint; but it will have done more work in the world; and that is enough for the highest genius, which is always intensely utilitarian . . .

I need not elaborate the matter further. The conclusions to be drawn are:
1. Every social question, arising as it must from a conflict between human feeling and circumstances, affords material for drama.
2. The general preference of dramatists for subjects in which the conflict is between man and his apparently inevitable and eternal rather than his political and temporal circumstances, is due in the vast majority of cases to the dramatist's political ignorance (not to

mention that of his audience), and in a few to the comprehensiveness of his philosophy.

3. The hugeness and complexity of modern civilizations and the development of our consciousness of them by means of the press, have the double effect of discrediting comprehensive philosophies by revealing more facts than the ablest man can generalize, and at the same time intensify the urgency of social reforms sufficiently to set even the poetic faculty in action on their behalf.

T. S. ELIOT (1888–1965), from 'Whispers of Immortality':

> Webster was much possessed by death
> And saw the skull beneath the skin;
> And breastless creatures underground
> Leaned backwards with a lipless grin.

SIR THOMAS BODLEY (1545–1613), collector of medieval manuscripts, to the keeper of his library, a letter of 1 January 1611:

Sir, I would you had forborne to catalogue our London books, until I had been privy to your purpose. There are many idle books, and riff-raffs among them, which shall never come to the library, and I fear me that little, which you have done already, will raise a scandal upon it, when it shall be given out by such as would disgrace it, that I have made up a number with almanacs, plays, and proclamations: of which I will have none, but such as are singular.

And 4 January 1611:

I can see no good reason to alter my opinion for excluding such books as almanacs, plays, and an infinite number, that are daily printed, of very unworthy matters and handling, such as, methinks, both the keeper and the underkeeper should disdain to seek out, to deliver unto any man. Haply some plays may be worth the keeping: but hardly one in forty . . . Thus is my opinion, wherein if I err, I think I shall err with infinite others: and the more I think upon it, the more it doth distaste me, that such kind of books, should be vouchsafed a room, in so noble a library . . .

KONSTANTIN STANISLAVSKY (1863–1938) and Vladimir Nemirovich-Danchenko (1858–1943) were the co-founders of the Moscow Art and Popular Theatre in 1897. (The word Popular was later dropped from the title.) After their first meeting they wrote down a set of ethics that they hoped to apply to their theatre of the future. From Stanislavsky's *The Seagull produced by Stanislavsky,* 1925:

There are no small parts, there are only small actors.
One must love art, and not one's self in art.
Today Hamlet, tomorrow a walk-on, but even as a walk-on you must
    become an artist.
The poet, the actor, the artist, the costumier, the stage-hand serve one
    goal, which is placed by the poet in the very basis of his play.
All disobedience to the creative life of the theatre is a crime.
Lateness, laziness, caprice, hysterics, bad character, ignorance of the
    role, the need to repeat anything twice are all harmful to our
    enterprise and must be rooted out.

The first precept of the two Russians would never find favour, for timeless reasons best described by WILLIAM CHARLES MACREADY (1793–1873), a great actor and diarist. After playing the supporting part of Friar Lawrence in *Romeo and Juliet,* he wrote in his diary on 30 April 1838:

I find playing a part of this sort, with no direct character to sustain, no effort to make, no power of perceiving an impression made, to be a very disagreeable and unprofitable task. Having required many of the actors to do what they considered beneath them, perhaps it was only a just sacrifice to their opinions to conclude so far – but it is for the first and last time.

ELEONORA DUSE (1859–1924), Italian actress:

To save the Theatre, the Theatre must be destroyed, the actors and actresses all die of the plague . . . they make art impossible.

JAPANESE NOH THEATRE instruction:

> Forget the theatre and look at the Noh.
> Forget the Noh and look at the actor.
> Forget the actor and look at the idea.
> Forget the idea and you understand Noh.

Extract from a letter written by the LORD MAYOR OF LONDON to the Privy Council, 1597:

1. They [the plays] are a special cause of corrupting youth, containing nothing but unchaste matters, lascivious devices, shifts of cozenage, and other lewd and ungodly practises, being so as that they impress the very quality and corruption of manners which they represent, contrary to the rules and art prescribed for the making of comedies even among the heathen, who used them seldom and at certain set times, and not all the year long as our manner is. Whereby such as frequent them, being of the base and refuse sort of people or such young gentlemen as have small regard of credit or conscience, draw the same into imitation and not to the avoiding the like vices which they represent.

2. They are the ordinary places for vagrant persons, masterless men, thieves, horse-stealers, whoremongers, cozeners, coney-catchers, contrivers of treason and other idle and dangerous persons to meet together and to make their matches to the great displeasure of Almighty God and the hurt and annoyance of her Majesty's people: which cannot be prevented nor discovered by the governors of the city for that they are out of the city's jurisdiction.

3. They maintain idleness in such persons as have no vocation, and draw apprentices and other servants from their ordinary works and all sorts of people from the resort unto sermons and other Christian exercises to the great hindrance of trades and profanation of religion established by her Highness within this realm.

4. In the time of sickness is to be found by experience that many, having sores and yet not heart-sick, take occasion hereby to walk abroad and to recreate themselves by hearing a play. Whereby others are infected, and themselves also many things miscarry.

THOMAS HEYWOOD (c. 1570–1641), from *An Apology for Actors*, 1612:

Plays are writ with this aim . . . to teach their subjects obedience to their king, to show the people the untimely ends of such as have moved insurrections, to present them with the flourishing estate of such as live in obedience, exhorting them to allegiance, dehorting them from all felonious stratagems.

A. C. BRADLEY (1851–1935), from *Shakespearean Tragedy*, 1920:

Shakespeare was not attempting to justify the ways of God to men, or to show the universe a divine Comedy. He was writing tragedy, and tragedy would not be tragedy if it were not a painful mystery.

W. B. YEATS (1865–1939), from *Windlestraws*, 1901:

Let us learn construction from the masters, and dialogue from ourselves. A relation of mine has just written me a letter, in which he says: 'It is natural to an Irishman to write plays, he has an inborn love of dialogue and sound about him, of a dialogue as lively, gallant, and passionate as in the times of great Eliza. In these days an Englishman's dialogue is that of an amateur, that is to say, it is never spontaneous. I mean in *real life*. Compare it with an Irishman's, above all a poor Irishman's, reckless abandonment and naturalness, or compare it with the only fragment that has come down to us of Shakespeare's own conversation.'

GEORGE BERNARD SHAW, from the Epilogue to *Fanny's First Play*, 1911:

All Shaw's characters are himself: mere puppets stuck up to spout Shaw.

JEAN RACINE (1639–99), from the First Preface to *Andromache*, 1668:

However that may be, the public has been too indulgent to me for me to concern myself with the personal annoyance of two or three people who would like all the heroes of antiquity to be reformed and made into perfect heroes. I find very praiseworthy their desire that only flawless characters be shown on the stage. But I beg them to remember that it is not up to me to change the rules of the theatre. Horace charges us to depict Achilles as fierce, inexorable, violent, just as he was and just as his son is depicted. And Aristotle, far from demanding perfect heroes of us, on the contrary wants tragic characters (that is, those whose misfortune causes the catastrophe of the tragedy) to be neither completely good nor completely evil. He does not want them to be wholly good because the punishment of a good man excites in the spectator more indignation than pity; nor to be wholly evil because one has no pity for a villain. Therefore, they must be moderately good – that is, good but capable of weakness – and they should fall into misfortune through some error that makes us pity rather than hate them.

Molière, from *La Critique de l'Ecole des femmes*, 1663:

You people are funny with your rules, with which you embarrass the ignorant and deafen the rest of us every day . . . I've noticed one thing . . . that those who talk the most about the rules, and know them better than anyone else, write comedies that nobody considers good . . . if the plays that are according to the rules are not liked, and if those that are liked are not according to the rules, then the rules must necessarily have been badly made. So . . . let's consult nothing about a play but the effect it had on us. Let's allow ourselves to go wholeheartedly to the things that grip us by the entrails, and let's not seek our arguments to keep ourselves from having pleasure.

Thomas Babington Macaulay (1800–59) from *Dramatists of the Restoration*, 1841:

But morality is deeply interested in this – that what is immoral shall not be presented to the imagination of the young and susceptible in constant connection with what is attractive. For every person who has observed the operation of the law of association in his own mind and in the minds of others knows that whatever is constantly presented to the imagination in connection with what is attractive will itself become attractive. There is undoubtedly a great deal of indelicate writing in Fletcher and Massinger, and more than might be wished even in Ben Jonson and Shakespeare, who are comparatively pure. But it is impossible to trace in their plays any systematic attempt to associate vice with those things which men value most and desire most, and virtue with everything ridiculous and degrading. And such a systematic attempt we find in the whole dramatic literature of the generation which followed the return of Charles the Second.

HROSWITHA, playwright and abbess, fl. 10th century AD, quoted in Preface to *The Plays of Hroswitha, German religious and virgin of the Saxon Race* (ed. Winterfield, 1901):

I . . . have not hesitated to imitate in my writings the poet Terence, whose works are so widely read, my object being to glorify, within the limits of my poor talent, the laudable chastity of Christian virgins in that self-same form of composition which has been used to describe the shameless acts of licentious women. One thing has all the same embarrassed me and often brought a blush to my cheek. It is that I have been compelled through the nature of this work to apply my mind and pen to depicting the dreadful frenzy of those possessed by unlawful love, and the insidious sweetness of passion – things which should not even be named among us. Yet if from modesty I had refrained from treating these subjects I should not have been able to attain my object – to glorify the innocent to the best of my ability . . . In the humbler works of my salad days I gathered up my poor researches in heroic strophes, but here I have sifted them into a series of dramatic scenes

and avoided through omission the pernicious voluptuousness of pagan
writers.

BEN JONSON (1572–1637), from the Dedication to *Volpone*, 1607:

. . . If men will impartially, and not asquint, look toward the offices
and function of a poet, they will easily conclude to themselves the
impossibility of any man's being the good poet without first being a
good man.

NICHOLAS ROWE (1674–1718), playwright, poet and critic, from *Some Account
of the Life &c. of Mr William Shakespeare*, 1709:

His Aquaintance with *Ben Johnson* began with a remarkable piece of
Humanity and good Nature; Mr *Johnson*, who was at that Time
altogether unknown to the World, had offer'd one of his Plays to the
Players, in order to have it acted; and the Persons into whose Hands it
was put, after having turn'd it carelessly and superciliously over, were
just upon returning it to him with an ill-natur'd Answer, that it would
be of no service to their Company, when *Shakespear* luckily cast his
Eye upon it, and found something so well in it as to engage him first to
read it through, and afterwards to recommend Mr *Johnson* and his
Writings to the Publick. After this they were profess'd Friends; tho' I
don't know whether the other ever made him an equal return of
Gentleness and Sincerity.

ALAN AYCKBOURN (b. 1939), quoted in the *Daily Telegraph*, 1986:

Whatever else I am, I am a fairly good craftsman. If a chap is walking across the stage with the tea things, I tend to give him enough time to get to the other side.

GEORGE BERNARD SHAW, from *The Quintessence of Ibsenism*, 1891:

The highest type of play is completely homogeneous, often consisting of a single very complex incident; and not even the most exhaustive information as to the story enables a spectator to receive the full force of the impression aimed at in any given passage if he enters the theatre for that passage alone. The success of such plays depends upon the exercise by the audience of powers of memory, imagination, insight, reasoning, and sympathy, which only a small minority of the play-going public at present possesses. To the rest the higher drama is as disagreeably perplexing as the game of chess is to a man who has barely enough capacity to understand skittles.

MOSS HART (1904–61), playwright and director, from *Act One*, 1959:

With each new play the playwright is a Columbus sailing uncharted seas, with the unhappy knowledge that those unfriendly Indian tribes – the critics and the public – will be lining the shores at the end of the voyage waiting to scalp him, even if he survives the mutiny. Little wonder that he shivers and shakes and groans too loudly in the public prints and into the ears of his forbearing friends when he writes 'Act I' anew. For if he is a man who respects his craft and not merely a dealer in theatrical merchandise, he very well knows that no matter how skilful or successful he may be, each time he scribbles 'Act One' on a blank piece of paper he is starting afresh, and, if he will allow himself the full and bitter truth, he is writing a play for the first time. His years of experience and his past successes count for nothing. Each time, if he is honest, he must face his own inadequacy and come to terms with it, for he has learned almost nothing about his profession in the meantime.

GEORG BÜCHNER (1813–37), playwright, after completing *Danton's Death* in five weeks, 1835:

I feel as though I had been annihilated by the dreadful fatalism of history. I find a terrible uniformity in human nature, an inexorable force ... The individual: mere foam on the wave, greatness pure chance, the mastery of genius a puppet play, a ridiculous struggle against an iron law to acknowledge which is the highest good, to defeat the impossible. I'm no longer in the mood to bow my head to the dress uniforms and street-corner orators of history. I am accustoming my eyes to blood.

NoËL COWARD (1899–1973), from his autobiography *Future Indefinite*, 1954:

On Friday, May the 2nd, Joyce Carey and I caught a morning train from Paddington, bound for Port Meirion in North Wales. For some time past an idea for a light comedy had been rattling at the door of my mind, and I thought that the time had come to let it in and show it a little courtesy. Joyce was engaged in writing a play about Keats, so here we were, 'Hurrah for the holidays', without buckets and spades, but with typewriters, paper, carbons, bathing suits, sun-tan oil, and bezique cards. We arrived on a golden evening, sighed with pleasure at the mountains and the sea in the late sunlight, and settled ourselves into a pink guest-house. The next morning we sat on the beach with our backs against the sea-wall and discussed my idea exclusively for several hours. Keats, I regret to say, was not referred to. By lunchtime the title had emerged together with the names of the characters, and a rough – very rough – outline of the plot. At seven-thirty the next morning I sat, with the usual nervous palpitations, at my typewriter. Joyce was upstairs in her room wrestling with Fanny Brawne. There was a pile of virgin paper on my left and a box of carbons on my right. The table wobbled and I had to put a wedge under one of its legs. I smoked several cigarettes in rapid succession, staring gloomily out of the window at the tide running out. I fixed the paper into the machine and started: *Blithe Spirit: A Light Comedy in Three Acts.*

For six days I worked from eight to one each morning and from two to seven each afternoon. On Friday evening, May the 9th, the play was finished and, disdaining archness and false modesty, I will admit that I knew it was witty, I knew it was well constructed, and I also knew that it was going to be a success. My gift for comedy dialogue, which I feared might have atrophied from disuse, had obviously profited from its period of inactivity. Beyond a few typographical errors, I made no corrections, and only two lines of the original script were ultimately cut. I take pride in these assertions, but it is a detached pride, natural enough in the circumstances and not to be confused with boastfulness. I was not attempting to break any records, to prove how quickly I could write and how clever I was. I was fully prepared to revise and re-write the whole play had I thought it necessary, but I did not think it necessary. I knew from the first morning's work that I was on the right track and that it would be difficult, with that situation and those characters to go far wrong. I can see no particular virtue in writing quickly; on the contrary, I am well aware that too great a facility is often dangerous, and should be curbed when it shows signs of getting the bit too freely between its teeth. No reputable writer should permit his talent to bolt with him. I am also aware, from past experience, that when the right note is struck and the structure of a play is carefully built in advance, it is both wise and profitable to start at the beginning and write through to the end in as short a time as possible.

CARLOTTA MONTEREY, third wife of the American playwright Eugene O'Neill (1888–1953), describing the writing of *Long Day's Journey Into Night* (quoted in *Son and Artist* by Louis Sheagger, 1990):

When he started *Long Day's Journey* it was a most strange experience to watch the man being tortured every day by his own writing. He would come out of his study at the end of the day gaunt and sometimes weeping. His eyes would be all red, and he looked ten years older than when he went in in the morning . . . It nearly killed him to write this play. After his day's stint he would be physically and mentally exhausted. Night after night I had to hold him tight in my arms so he could relax and sleep. Thus the play was written.

HESKETH PEARSON (1887–1964), biographer, from *The Life of Oscar Wilde*, 1946:

In September he went with his family to Worthing, where, at The Haven, 5 Esplanade, he began and finished what he called his 'somewhat farcical comedy' [*The Importance of Being Earnest*] in three weeks, reporting to Alexander that it was an admirable play, 'the best I have written.' Having no money, he could not go up to town, so he sent it to Alexander, warning him that it ought really to be acted by Charles Wyndham or Hawtrey: 'Of course the play is not suitable to you at all. You are a romantic actor . . . you would be sorry if you altered the definite artistic line of progress you have always followed at the St James's.' He wrote it with such ease, scarcely blotting a line, that he had plenty of time for other things, and in a letter to William Rothenstein, asking him to give sittings, recommendations, and advice to an actress named Marion Grey who wanted to earn money as a model, he said: 'I am away by the seaside, bathing and sailing and amusing myself.'

AUGUST STRINDBERG, 1888:

I have avoided the mathematically symmetrical construction of French dialogue and let people's brains work irregularly as they do in actual life, where no topic of conversation is drained to the dregs but one brain receives haphazard from the other a cog to engage with. Consequently my dialogue too wanders about, providing itself in the earlier scenes with material which is afterwards worked up, admitted, repeated, developed, and built up, like the theme in a musical composition.

BEN JONSON, from the Induction to *Every Man out of His Humour*, 1600:

ASPER . . . Gracious, and kind spectators, you are welcome,
    Apollo and the Muses feast your eyes
    With graceful objects, and may our Minerva
    Answer your hopes, unto their largest strain!
    Yet here mistake me not, judicious friends.
    I do not this, to be your patience,
    Or servilely to fawn on your applause,
    Like some dry brain, despairing in his merit.
    Let me be censured by the austerest brow,
    Where I want art, or judgment; tax me freely:
    Let envious censors, with their broadest eyes,
    Look through, and through me, I pursue no favor.
    Only vouchsafe me your attentions,
    And I will give you music worth your ears,
    O, how I hate the monstrousness of time,
    Where every servile imitating spirit,
    Plagued with an itching leprosy of wit,
    In a mere halting fury, strives to fling
    His ulcerous body in the Thespian spring,
    And straight leaps forth a poet! but as lame
    As Vulcan, or the founder of Cripplegate.

MITIS In faith, this humour will come ill to some,
  You will be thought to be too peremptory.
ASPER 'This humour'? good! and why 'this humour,' Mitis?
  Nay, do not turn, but answer.
MITIS   Answer, what?
ASPER I will not stir your patience, pardon me,
  I urged it for some reasons, and the rather
  To give these ignorant, well-spoken days
  Some taste of their abuse of this word 'humour'.
CORDATUS O, do not let your purpose fall, good Asper,
  It cannot but arrive most acceptable,
  Chiefly to such, as have the happiness
  Daily to see how the poor innocent word
  Is racked and tortured.
MITIS   Ay, I pray you proceed.
ASPER Ha! what? what is't?
CORDATUS   For the abuse of humour.
ASPER O, I crave pardon, I had lost my thoughts.
  Why, humour, as 'tis *ens*, we thus define it.
  To be a quality of air, or water,
  And in itself holds these two properties,
  Moisture, and fluxure: as, for demonstration,
  Pour water on this floor, 'twill wet, and run:
  Likewise the air, forced through a horn, or trumpet,
  Flows instantly away, and leaves behind
  A kind of dew; and hence we do conclude,
  That whatso'ever hath fluxure, and humidity,
  As wanting power to contain itself,
  Is humour. So in every human body,
  The choler, melancholy, phlegm, and blood,
  By reason that they flow continually
  In some one part, and are not continent,
  Receive the name of Humours. Now thus far
  It may, by metaphor, apply itself
  Unto the general disposition:
  As when some one peculiar quality
  Doth so possess a man, that it doth draw

All his affects, his spirits, and his powers,
In their confluctions, all to run one way,
This may be truly said to be a humour.
But that a rook, by wearing a pied feather,
The cable hat-band, or the three-piled ruff,
A yard of shoe-tie, or the Switzer's knot
On his French garters, should affect a 'humour'!
O, it is more than most ridiculous.

CORDATUS He speaks pure truth, now, if an idiot
 Have but an apish, or fantastic strain,
 It is 'his humour.'

ASPER   Well, I will scourge those apes.
 And to these courteous eyes oppose a mirror,
 As large as is the stage whereon we act,
 Where they shall see the time's deformity
 Anatomized in every nerve, and sinew,
 With constant courage, and contempt of fear . . .

ASPER . . . Attentive auditors,
 Such as will join their profits with their pleasure,
 And come to feed their understanding parts:
 For these, I'll prodigally spend myself,
 And speak away my spirit into air;
 For these, I'll melt my brain into invention,
 Coin new conceits, and hang my richest words
 As polished jewels in their bounteous ears?
 But stay, I lose myself, and wrong their patience;
 If I dwell here, they'll not begin, I see.
 Friends, sit you still, and entertain this troop
 With some familiar, and by-conference,
 I'll haste them sound. [*To audience.*] Now, gentlemen, I go
 To turn an actor, and a humourist,
 Where, ere I do resume my present person,
 We hope to make the circles of your eyes
 Flow with distillèd laughter: if we fail,
 We must impute it to this only chance,
 Art hath an enemy called Ignorance.   [*Exit*]

CORDATUS How do you like his spirit, Mitis?

MITIS I should like it much better, if he were less confident.

CORDATUS Why, do you suspect his merit?

MITIS No, but I fear this will procure him much envy.

CORDATUS O, that sets the stronger seal on his desert; if he had no enemies, I should esteem his fortunes most wretched at this instant.

MITIS You have seen his play, Cordatus? pray you, how is't?

CORDATUS Faith sir, I must refrain to judge; only this I can say of it, 'tis strange, and of a particular kind by itself, somewhat like *Vetus Comoedia*; a work that hath bounteously pleased me; how it will answer the general expectation, I know not.

MITIS Does he observe all the laws of comedy in it?

CORDATUS What laws mean you?

MITIS Why, the equal division of it into acts, and scenes, according to the Terentian manner; his true number of actors; the furnishing of the scene with Grex, or Chorus, and that the whole argument fall within compass of a day's business.

CORDATUS O no, these are too nice observations.

MITIS They are such as must be received, by your favor, or it cannot be authentic.

CORDATUS Troth, I can discern no such necessity.

MITIS No?

CORDATUS No, I assure you signior. If those laws, you speak of, had been delivered us, *ab initio*, and in their present virtue and perfection, there had been some reason of obeying their powers: but 'tis extant, that that which we called *Comoedia*, was at first nothing but a simple and continued song, sung by one only person, till Susario invented a second; after him, Epicharmus a third; Phormus and Chionides devised to have four actors, with a prologue and chorus; to which Cratinus, long after, added a fifth, and sixth; Eupolis, more; Aristophanes, more than they; every man in the dignity of his spirit and judgment supplied something. And, though that in him this kind of poem appeared absolute, and fully perfected, yet how is the face of it changed since, in Menander, Philemon, Cecilius, Plautus, and the rest; who have utterly excluded the chorus, altered the property of the persons, their names, and natures, and augmented it with all liberty, according to the elegancy

27

and disposition of those times, wherein they wrote. I see not then, but we should enjoy the same licence of free power to illustrate and heighten our invention, as they did; and not be tied to those strict and regular forms, which the niceness of a few – who are nothing but form – would thrust upon us.

MITIS Well, we will not dispute of this now; but what's his scene?

CORDATUS Marry, *Insula Fortunata*, sir.

MITIS O, 'the Fortunate Island!' mass, he has bound himself to a strict law there.

CORDATUS Why so?

MITIS He cannot lightly alter the scene, without crossing the seas.

CORDATUS He needs not, having a whole island to run through, I think.

MITIS No? how comes it then, that in some one play we see so many seas, countries, and kingdoms, passed over with such admirable dexterity?

CORDATUS O, that but shows how well the authors can travel in their vocation, and outrun the apprehension of their auditory. But, leaving this, I would they begin once: this protraction is able to sour the best settled patience in the theatre.

ANTONIN ARTAUD (1896–1948), from *The Theatre and its Double*, 1938, published the year after he was committed to an insane asylum:

Instead of continuing to rely upon texts considered definitive and sacred, it is essential to put an end to the subjugation of the theatre to the text, and to recover the notion of unique language, halfway between gesture and thought . . . It is not a question of suppressing the spoken language, but of giving words approximately the importance they have in dreams.

Anonymous, fifth century AD (quoted in E. K. Chambers, *The Medieval Stage*, 1903):

What tumult! What satanic clamour! What diabolic dress! Here are to be seen naught but fornication, adultery, courtesan women, men pretending to be women and soft-limbed boys.

Anonymous, medieval cleric (quoted by E. K. Chambers, 1903):

Some transform and transfigure their bodies with obscene dance and gesture, now indecently unclothing themselves, now putting on horrible masks.

Shelley Winters (b. 1922), American actress:

Nudity on stage? I think it's disgusting. But if I were twenty-two with a great body, it would be artistic, tasteful, patriotic and a progressive religious experience.

George Henry Lewes (1817–78), philosopher, literary critic, playwright, actor, from the *Leader*, April 1853:

At Drury Lane we were threatened with a version of *La Dame aux Camellias*, but the Lord Chamberlain refused a licence to this unhealthy idealization of one of the worst evils of our social life. Paris may delight in such pictures, but London, thank God!, has still enough instinctive repulsion against pruriency not to tolerate them.

ANTON CHEKHOV, from a letter to Alexei Suvorin, editor of the St Petersburg *New Times*, 1 April 1890:

You reproach me for objectivity, calling it indifference to good and evil, an absence of ideals and principles, and so forth. When I describe horse thieves, you want me to say stealing horses is evil. But surely that's been known for a long time now without my having to say it. Let the members of the jury judge them, but my business is only to show what kind of people they are.

ALAN AYCKBOURN, quoted in the *New York Times*, 1979:

The characters have to be allowed to control their own destinies. I sometimes say to one of them, 'I wish you'd leave the stage, because that would give me a nice neat ending.' And he refuses to go, and the ending is bungled. But then you find you're left with something much more interesting.

ANTON CHEKHOV, from a letter to Alexei Suvorin, 21 October 1895:

. . . just imagine, I am writing a play [*The Seagull*] which I probably will not finish until the end of November. I am writing it with considerable pleasure, though I sin frightfully against the conventions of the stage. It is a comedy with three female parts, six male, four acts, a landscape (view of lake), lots of talk on literature, little action and tons of love.

From a letter to Elena Shavrova, writer and actress, 18 November 1895:

I have finished my play. It is called *The Seagull*. It's nothing to ooh and ah about. On the whole I would say I am an indifferent playwright.

To Mikhail Chekhov, the playwright's youngest brother, 18 October 1896:

The play [*The Seagull*] fell flat and flopped with a bang. The audience was bewildered. They behaved as if they were ashamed to be in the theatre. The performances were vile and stupid.

The moral of the story is: I shouldn't write plays. Nevertheless and just the same I am alive and well and my insides are in good spirits.

GEORGE BERNARD SHAW, from a letter to Arthur Clark, an aspiring playwright, 18 May 1895:

Dear Sir
At thirty-eight you should have written half a dozen plays if you intend to become a dramatist by profession. And you must not write them with a view to reforming your fortune, or with any other view than the production of a work of art that satisfies your own judgment and fulfils the purpose created by your instinct as a dramatist. You are mistaken in supposing that plays are not read. Not only managers, but actors who are waiting to become managers until they have a few good plays in hand, spend their days in drudging through manuscripts, 99% of which are hopelessly bad. But they naturally turn first to the plays with promising titles; and 'The Vegetarian' is quite impossible. I have no hesitation in saying that unless that title is a purposely misleading one, the play *must* be a bad one. The only advice I can give you is not to waste any thought or anxiety on the play you have finished, but go on and write another, & then another & so on until you have either learnt the business or discovered that you have not the necessary turn for it. Refusals mean nothing: a play may be a masterpiece and yet not suit this or that particular manager. Besides the actual managers, you may take it that almost every 'leading man' in London – Fred Terry, Yorke Stephens, Forbes Robertson, Arthur Bourchier, &c. &c. &c. would read anything

on the chance of picking up something good enough to start with. There is also a great demand for good one-act 'curtain raisers.'

yrs faithfully
G. BERNARD SHAW

NOËL COWARD, from *Present Laughter*, 1939 (the actor Garry Essendyne gives advice to the aspiring playwright, Roland Maule):

GARRY: I don't give a hoot about posterity. Why should I worry about what people think of me when I'm dead as a doornail, anyway? My worst defect is that I am apt to worry too much about what people think of me when I'm alive. But I'm not going to do that any more. I'm changing my methods and you're my first experiment. As a rule, when insufferable young beginners have the impertinence to criticise me, I dismiss the whole thing lightly because I'm embarrassed for them and consider it not quite fair game to puncture their inflated egos too sharply. But this time my high-brow young friend you're going to get it in the neck. To begin with, your play is not a play at all. It's a meaningless jumble of adolescent, pseudo intellectual poppycock. It bears no relation to the theatre or to life or to anything. And you yourself wouldn't be here at all if I hadn't been bloody fool enough to pick up the telephone when my secretary wasn't looking. Now that you are here, however, I would like to tell you this. If you wish to be a playwright you just leave the theatre of tomorrow to take care of itself. Go and get yourself a job as a butler in a repertory company if they'll have you. Learn from the ground up how plays are constructed and what is actable and what isn't. Then sit down and write at least twenty plays one after the other, and if you can manage to get the twenty-first produced for a Sunday night performance you'll be damned lucky!

GEORGE CRABBE (1754–1832), a writer of verse tales memorable for their realistic details of everyday life, from his epic *The Borough*, 1810:

Drawn by the annual call, we now behold
Our troop dramatic, heroes known of old,
And those, since last they march'd, inlisted and enroll'd:
Mounted on hacks or borne in waggons some,
The rest on foot (the humbler brethren) come.
Three favour'd places, an unequal time,
Join to support this company sublime:
Ours for the longer period – see how light
Yon parties move, their former friends in sight,
Whose claims are all allow'd, and friendship glads the night.
Now public rooms shall sound with words divine,
And private lodgings hear how heroes shine;
No talk of pay shall yet on pleasure steal,
But kindest welcome bless the friendly meal;
While o'er the social jug and decent cheer,
Shall be described the fortune of the year.

Peruse these bills, and see what each can do.
Behold! The prince, the slave, the monk, the Jew;
Change but the garment, and they'll all engage
To take each part, and act in every age:
Cull'd from all houses, what a house are they!
Swept from all barns, our borough-critics say;
But with some portion of a critic's ire,
We all endure them; there are some admire:
They might have praise, confined to farce alone;
Full well they grin, they should not try to groan;
But then our servants' and our seamen's wives
Love all that rant and rapture as their lives;
He who Squire Richard's part could well sustain,
Finds as King Richard he must roar amain –
'My horse! My horse!' Lo! Now to their abodes,
Come lords and lovers, empresses and gods.

The master-mover of these scenes has made
No trifling gain in this adventurous trade;
Trade we may term it, for he duly buys
Arms out of use and undirected eyes;
These he instructs, and guides them as he can,
And vends each night the manufactured man:
Long as our custom lasts, they gladly stay,
Then strike their tents, like Tartars, and away!
The place grows bare where they too long remain,
But grass will rise ere they return again.

Children of Thespis, welcome! Knights and queens!
Counts! Barons! Beauties! When before your scenes,
And mighty monarchs thund'ring from your throne;
Then step behind, and all your glory's gone:
Of crown and palace, throne and guards bereft,
The pomp is vanish'd, and the care is left.
Yet strong and lively is the joy they feel,
When the full house secures the plenteous meal;
Flatt'ring and flatter'd, each attempts to raise
A brother's merits for a brother's praise:

For never hero shows a prouder heart,
Then he who proudly acts a hero's part;
Nor without cause; the boards, we know, can yield
Place for fierce contest, like the tented field.

Graceful to tread the stage, to be in turn
The prince we honour, and the knave we spurn;
Bravely to bear the tumult of the crowd,
The hiss tremendous, and the censure loud:
These are their parts, – and he who these sustains
Deserves some praise and profit for his pains.
Heroes at least of gentler kind are they,
Against whose swords no weeping widows pray,
No blood their fury sheds, nor havoc marks their way.

Sad happy race! Soon raised and soon depress'd,
Your days all pass'd in jeopardy and jest;

34

Poor without prudence, with afflictions vain,
Not warn'd by misery, not enrich'd by gain;
Whom justice pitying, chides from place to place,
A wandering, careless, wretched, merry race,
Who cheerful looks assume, and play the parts
Of happy rovers with repining hearts;
Then cast off care, and in the mimic pain
Of tragic woe, feel spirits light and vain,
Distress and hope – the mind's, the body's wear,
The man's affliction, and the actor's tear:
Alternate times of fasting and excess
Are yours, ye smiling children of distress.

Slaves though ye be, your wandering freedom seems,
And with your varying views and restless schemes,
Your griefs are transient, as your joys are dreams.
Yet keen those griefs – ah! What avail thy charms,
Fair Juliet! What that infant in thine arms

What those heroic lines thy patience learns
What all the aid thy present Romeo earns,
Whilst thou art crowded in that lumbering wain,
With all thy plaintive sisters to complain?
Nor is there lack of labour: to rehearse,
Day after day, poor scraps of prose and verse
To bear each other's spirit, pride, and spite
To hide in rant the heart-ache of the night
To dress in gaudy patch-work, and to force
The mind to think on the appointed course –
This is laborious, and may be defined
The bootless labour of the thriftless mind.

TIMBERLAKE WERTENBAKER, playwright, from *Our Country's Good* (1988):

The theatre is an expression of civilization, we belong to a great country which has spawned great playwrights. Shakespeare, Marlowe, Jonson, and even in our own time, Sheridan. The convicts will be speaking a refined, a literate language and expressing sentiments of a delicacy they are not used to. The convicts watching this will not be overawed because the play is light, funny, and they will be seeing their fellows in crime doing something of a higher nature than usual. It will remind them that there is more to life than crime, punishment. And we, this colony of a few hundred, will be watching this together, for a few hours we will no longer be despised prisoners and hated gaolers. We will laugh, we may be moved, we may even think a little. Can you think of something else that will provide such an evening?

2

Places

The circumstances in which a play may first see the light of day have always been varied and numerous. Theatre folk are infinitely resourceful and can adapt themselves to venues ranging from excruciatingly small rooms, tents and cellars to the plush playhouses of large cities.

The theatre building itself reflects the society that built it. The Greek theatre was more or less democratic, with extraordinary acoustics that made it possible to hear a whisper at the furthest point from the stage; the disposition of the audience in Elizabethan playhouses reflected social rank, as did the theatres designed in the eighteenth and nineteenth centuries with their 'gods', upper circles, Royal circles, boxes, stalls and pits. These auditoria allowed the grandees to see and to be seen by other members of the audience rather than to look at what was happening on the stage.

Our own times have produced some very fine buildings and also, of course, some, like the National Theatre and the Barbican in London, that are anything but fine. Both the National and the Barbican, however, have splendid foyers, which no doubt says much about the society for which they were built.

MARGARETE BIEBER describes the early Classical Greek theatres in Athens in *The History of the Greek and Roman Theatre* (1939). These structures were made mostly of wood and none has survived. The great stone and marble theatres of the later Hellenistic period – the one in Epidaurus which seats 12,000 is an example – were much grander and more elaborate, an infallible sign of the theatre's decadence. The theatre, and the term includes buildings and production, has always been at its best and most influential when at its simplest.

The smooth surface and the circular shape of the Greek orchestra have recently been explained from the form of the threshing floor, which has remained the same in Greece since antiquity. It is possible that gay dances at religious festivals and particularly at harvest time were performed at the same place where the oxen had trodden out the grain or the grapes had been dried. The 'ox-driving dithyramb' (Pindar) may have received its name from this usage.

The oldest comedies were given in the Lenaion precinct, which Dörpfeld has located in the Dionysion in Limnais, the marshy hollow between the west slope of the Acropolis, the Areopagus, and the Pnyx. Most of the state performances of comedy after 487/6 during the fifth and the first half of the fourth centuries also took place in the Lenaion, thus the *Frogs* by Aristophanes. Here, beginning about 442 the contests of comic actors took place, and after about 432 tragedies were also occasionally performed; but no permanent theatre was ever built. After the completion of the theatre of Dionysus Eleuthereus on the southern slope of the Acropolis, the Lenaean plays were transferred to this sanctuary.

The sacred precinct on the south slope of the Acropolis was probably dedicated to Dionysus about the middle of the sixth century, when the little temple in soft poros stone was erected and decorated perhaps with a pediment relief representing a bacchic dance of satyrs and maenads, which, however, might have decorated a still earlier monument in the sanctuary. There certainly was also an altar and sacred grove, with an enclosing wall. As the oldest form of the Dionysiac service was the dancing and singing of a chorus, there must have been from the beginning a chorus (χορός) or an orchestra (from orcheisthai, ὀρχεῖσθαι, to dance), that is, a dancing place for the chorus, named after its purpose. We call an orchestra a body of people playing instruments, and we also apply the term to the ground floor of the modern theatre. These modern definitions are, however, derived from the term describing the nuclear center of the theatre building, the arena, where originally music was produced and dances performed.

PETER BROOK, from *The Empty Space*, 1968:

It has also been pointed out that the nature of the permanent structure of the Elizabethan playhouse, with its flat open arena and its large balcony and its second smaller gallery, was a diagram of the universe as seen by the sixteenth-century audience and playwright – the gods, the court and the people – three levels, separate and yet often intermingling – a stage that was a perfect philosopher's machine.

In WILLIAM SHAKESPEARE's (1564–1616) day the theatres were circular and made of wood. The actors played in their own clothes so that all plays were given what would now be called 'a modern-dress' production. The Elizabethan theatre was another example of simplicity of style. The play was the thing. It is no accident that in a theatre, any theatre, the patrons sit or stand in the auditorium – a place where one listens. In his opening chorus to *King Henry V*, Shakespeare seems to delight in both the limitations and the glories of the wooden O.

> O for a Muse of fire, that would ascend
> The brightest heaven of invention,
> A kingdom for a stage, princes to act,
> And monarchs to behold the swelling scene!
> Then should the warlike Harry, like himself,
> Assume the port of Mars; and at his heels,
> Leash'd in like hounds, should famine, sword, and fire,
> Crouch for employment. But pardon, gentles all,

The flat unraised spirits that hath dar'd
On this unworthy scaffold to bring forth
So great an object. Can this cockpit hold
The vasty fields of France? Or may we cram
Within this wooden O the very casques
That did affright the air at Agincourt?
O, pardon! since a crooked figure may
Attest in little place a million;
And let us, ciphers to this great accompt,
On your imaginary forces work.
Suppose within the girdle of these walls
Are now confin'd two mighty monarchies,
Whose high upreared and abutting fronts
The perilous narrow ocean parts asunder.
Piece out our imperfections with your thoughts:
Into a thousand parts divide one man,
And make imaginary puissance;
Think, when we talk of horses, that you see them
Printing their proud hoofs i' th' receiving earth;
For 'tis your thoughts that now must deck our kings,
Carry them here and there, jumping o'er times,
Turning th' accomplishment of many years
Into an hour-glass; for the which supply,
Admit me Chorus to this history;
Who, prologue-like, your humble patience pray
Gently to hear, kindly to judge, our play.

The Mystery and Miracle Plays were performed in the streets of cities such as
Chester and York. They endeavoured to display the entire history of the universe
from creation to the end of the world. Moveable stage wagons were used that were
pulled along the streets to stop at chosen places along the route where the
particular play would be given – *The Fall of Lucifer*, perhaps, or *The Ascension of
Jesus into Heaven*. ARCHDEACON ROGERS, writing in 1594, describes the style
of presentation in Chester:

The manner of these plays were, every company had his pageant ['pageant' comes from *pagina*, a board] . . . a high scaffold with two rooms, a higher and a lower, upon four wheels. In the lower they apparelled themselves, and in the higher room they played, being all open at the top, that all beholders might hear and see them. They began first at the abbey gates, and when the first pageant was played, it was wheeled to the high cross before the mayor, and so to every street. So every street had a pageant playing before it at one time, till all the pageants for the day appointed, were played. When one pageant was near ended, word was brought from street to street, that they might come in place thereof, exceedingly orderly, and all the streets have their pageants before them, all at one time playing together.

Simpler still might have been the performances reported by CAPTAIN KEELING in his journal of a voyage to the East Indies:

1607, Sept. 5. I sent the interpreter, according to his desier, abord the Hector whear he brooke fast, and after came abord mee, wher we gave the tragedie of Hamlett. 30. Captain Hawkins dined with me, wher my companions acted Kinge Richard the Second.

1608, Mar. 31. I envited Captain Hawkins to a ffishe dinner, and had Hamlet acted abord mee: which I permitt to keepe my people from idlenes and unlawful games, or sleepe.

PETER BROOK, from *The Empty Space*, 1968, perhaps the simplest of all:

I can take any empty space and call it a bare stage. A man walks across this empty space whilst someone else is watching him, and this is all that is needed for an act of theatre to be engaged. Yet when we talk about theatre this is not quite what we mean. Red curtains, spotlights, blank verse, laughter, darkness, these are all confusedly superimposed in a messy image covered by one all-purpose word. We talk of the cinema killing the theatre, and in that phrase we refer to the theatre as it was when the cinema was born, a theatre of box office, foyer, tip-up seats, footlights, scene changes, intervals, music, as though the theatre was by very definition these and little more.

I will try to split the word four ways and distinguish four different meanings – and so will talk about a Deadly Theatre, a Holy Theatre, a Rough Theatre and an Immediate Theatre. Sometimes these four theatres really exist, standing side by side, in the West End of London, or in New York off Times Square. Sometimes they are hundreds of miles apart, the Holy in Warsaw and the Rough in Prague, and sometimes they are metaphoric: two of them mixing together within one evening, within one act. Sometimes within one single moment, the four of them, Holy, Rough, Immediate and Deadly intertwine.

The Fortune Theatre was another Elizabethan playhouse. In 1611, the playwrights THOMAS DEKKER (1570–1640) and THOMAS MIDDLETON (?1570–1627) celebrated the most welcome of all theatrical events:

'Full House at the Fortune'
A VIEW FROM THE STAGE

> Nay, when you look into my galleries,
> How bravely they're trimm'd up, you all shall swear
> You're highly pleas'd to see what's set down there:
> Storeys of men and women, mix'd together,
> Fair ones with foul, like sunshine in wet weather;
> Within one square a thousand heads are laid,
> So close that all of heads the room seems made;
> As many faces there, fill'd with blithe looks
> Shew like the promising titles of new books
> Writ merrily, the readers being their own eyes,
> Which seem to move and to give plaudities;
> And here and there, whilst with obsequious ears
> Throng'd heaps do listen, a cut-purse thrusts and leers
> With hawk's eyes for his prey; I need not shew him;
> By a hanging, villainous look yourselves may know him,
> The face is drawn so rarely: then, sir, below,

> The very floor, as 't were, waves to and fro,
> And, like a floating island, seems to move
> Upon a sea bound in with shores above.

The Globe and the Fortune were two of several theatres sited on the south bank of the River Thames. WILLIAM BULL in 1612 names two of the others:

> The players on the Bankside
> The round Globe and the Swan,
> Will teach you idle tricks of love,
> But the Bull will play the man.

ANONYMOUS French writer, eighteenth century:

. . . an amphitheatre filled with Benches without backboards, adorn'd and cover'd with green cloth. Men of Quality, particularly the young sort, some Ladies of Reputation and Vertue, and an abundance of Damsels that hunt for Prey, sit all together in this place, higgledy, piggledy, chatter, toy, play, hear, hear not, and just opposite to the stage rises another Amphitheatre which is taken up by persons of the best Quality – among whom are generally very few men.

ANTONIN ARTAUD, in *The Theatre and its Double* (1938), advocated a radical approach that was to find favour in the years following his death:

THE STAGE – THE AUDITORIUM: We abolish the stage and the auditorium and replace them by a single site, without partition or barrier of any kind, which will become the theatre of the action. A direct communication will be re-established between the spectator and the spectacle, between the actor and the spectator, from the fact that the spectator, placed in the middle of the action, is engulfed and physically affected by it. This envelopment results, in part, from the very configuration of the room itself.

Until the arrival of Henrik Ibsen, the ninteenth century theatre, especially in England and America but also in Europe, was dominated by actors and actresses. Of these, Sir Henry Irving (1838–1905) was the most famous. He was the first actor to be knighted and he was the apostle of the theatre of good taste. He liked fine parts not fine plays and, as a result, neglected new playwrights. SIR MAX BEERBOHM (1872–1956), the most stylish of theatre critics, in *Around Theatres* (1905) suggests reasons:

That he [Irving], throughout his memorable tenancy of the Lyceum Theatre, did nothing to encourage the better sort of modern play-wright, is a fact for which not he himself should be blamed. It was the fault of the Lyceum Theatre. In that vast and yawning gulf the better sort of modern drama would (for that it consists in the realistic handling of a few characters in ordinary modern life) have been drowned and lost utterly. On a huge stage, facing a huge auditorium, there must be plenty of crowds, bustle, uproar. Drama that gives no scope for these things must be performed in reasonably small places.

He was the first man to give Shakespeare a setting contrived with archaic and aesthetic care – a setting that should match the pleasure of the eye with the pleasure of the ear. That was a noble conception. Many people object, quite honestly, that the pleasure of the ear is diminished by that of the eye – that spectacle is a foe to poetry. Of course, spectacle may be overdone. Irving may sometimes have overdone it; but he always overdid it beautifully.

In the seven years of the Commonwealth (1653–60) under Cromwell, the Puritans closed theatres and destroyed them. When Charles II was restored to the throne, the theatre quickly re-established itself and flourished. But where to present the plays? There were around London several empty 'real' or royal tennis courts, long narrow tunnels that were easily converted. Presently, custom-built playhouses were erected. SAMUEL PEPYS (1633–1703) visited such a one in 1666:

. . . I away before to White Hall and into the new play-house there, the first time I ever was there, . . . By and by the King and Queene, Duke and Duchesse, and all the great ladies of the Court; which, indeed, was a fine sight. But the play being *Love in a Tub*, a silly play, and though done by the Duke's people, yet having neither Betterton nor his wife, and the whole thing done ill, and being ill also, I had no manner of pleasure in the play. Besides, the House, though very fine, yet bad for the voice, for hearing . . .

JOHN DRYDEN (1631–1700) wrote a Prologue for the opening on 26 March 1674 of the new King's House in Drury Lane. The previous theatre on the site had been gutted by fire three years before. (The present Drury Lane theatre dates from 1812.)

'Sir Christopher Wren's Plain-Built House'

A plain-built house, after so long a stay,
Will send you half unsatisfied away;
When, fallen from your expected pomp, you find
A bare convenience only is designed.
You, who each day can theatre behold,
Like Nero's palace, shining all with gold,
Our mean ungilded stage will scorn, we fear,
And for the homely room disdain the cheer.
Yet now cheap druggets to a mode are grown,
And a plain suit, since we can make but one,
Is better than to be by tarnished gawdry known.
They, who are by your favours wealthy made,

With mighty sums may carry on the trade;
We, broken banquiers, half destroyed by fire,
With our small stock to humble roofs retire;
Pity our loss, while you their pomp admire.

For fame and honour we no longer strive;
We yield in both, and only beg to live;
Unable to support their vast expense,
Who build and treat with such magnificence,
That, like the ambitious monarchs of the age,
They give the law to our provincial stage . . .

'Twere folly now a stately pile to raise,
To build a playhouse, while you throw down plays;
Whilst scenes, machines, and empty operas reign,
And for the pencil you the pen disdain;
While troops of famished Frenchmen hither drive,
And laugh at those upon whose alms they live:
Old English authors vanish, and give place
To these new conquerors of the Norman race . . .

Well, please yourselves; but sure 'tis understood,
That French machines have ne'er done England good.
I would not prophesy our house's fate;
But while vain shows and scenes you overrate,
'Tis to be feared –
That, as a fire the former house o'erthrew,
Machines and tempests will destroy the new.

After a visit to London in 1618, an Italian, SIGNOR BUSONI, left a valuable recollection of the theatre in Whitehall:

A large hall is fitted up like a theatre, with well-secured boxes all round. The stage is at one end and his Majesty's chair in front under an ample canopy. Near him are stools for the foreign ambassadors . . .

47

Whilst waiting for the King we amused ourselves by admiring the decorations and the beauty of the house.

In 1962, KENNETH TYNAN, at that time the *Observer*'s drama critic, visited the newly built Festival Theatre in Chichester whose artistic director was Laurence Olivier. Tynan was not impressed (from *A View of the English Stage*, 1976):

And here begins my sad indictment of the peninsular Chichester stage. Shakespeare's actors performed on an out-thrust platform because they needed illumination from the sun's rays; the least desirable seats in the Globe Theatre – those occupied by the groundlings – were the ones nearest the stage. Proximity was a disadvantage. Nothing so quickly dispels one's sense of reality as a daubed and bedizened actor standing four feet from one's face and declaiming right over one's head. The picture-frame stage was invented in the seventeenth century to give all the spectators the same sightlines and the same viewpoint; but it encouraged expensive décor, and in the last fifty years we have been urged to revive the projecting stage, ostensibly for artistic reasons but actually because it cuts scenic costs to a minimum.

Chichester is a product of our gullibility: instead of letting the whole audience see the actors' faces (however distantly), we now prefer to bring them closer to the actors' backs. The Chichester stage is so vast that even the proximity argument falls down: an actor on the opposite side of the apron is farther away from one's front-row seat than he would be from the twelfth row of a proscenium theatre – where in any case he would not deliver a crucial speech with his rear turned towards one's face.

The more-or-less straight-edged stage (preferably stripped of its proscenium framing) remains the most cunning and intimate method yet devised for transmitting plays to playgoers: and it was on stages like this that you spent a quarter of a century polishing your technique. Alas, at Chichester your silky throwaway lines, flicked at the audience like leg-glances by Ranjitsinhji, are literally thrown away: they go for nothing and die unheard.

48

In a small theatre, where sound and sight present no problems, the promontory stage is perfectly viable. In a large theatre like Chichester's, it simply does not work, above all if the plays one is performing depend for their effect on verbal nuance. You might point out to the National Theatre Committee that, by recommending a stuck-out stage for the main playhouse and a proscenium for its junior partner, they have got things exactly the wrong way round.

3

Before
the First Performance

The moment a playwright finishes writing a play a great many people automatically become involved. In ideal circumstances the chain of events begins with a play agent, either good or bad. A good agent makes the playwright feel that he or she is the agent's only client – a bad agent does not.

The agent has the task of 'placing the play' – which means finding an impresario (also called a producer) who will put up the money and offer an appropriate venue in which performances can take place. After that, more or less everything is done, or should be done, in concert with the playwright. First, and most important, a director (formerly and confusingly called a producer) will be chosen. The director's job is to select a scenic designer who will create a visual expression for the piece; then the director must cast the actors and rehearse the play in the hope of giving it life. The director may also suggest ways of improving the text or the play's construction; this cannot be done without the playwright's consent.

The presenters of plays can range from one humble, obsessive individual or an impoverished group of actors to an affluent mainstream producer or, of course, the State. In Athens the city presented plays with the help of rich citizens; in Elizabethan England, the Lord Chamberlain and the Sovereign financed the players; in medieval England the cost was borne by trade guilds.

The director is a comparatively new breed in the theatrical menagerie. Stanislavsky may be said to have created the animal. Nowadays, the director seeks to impose a personal and unmistakable stamp on productions, especially on revivals of the classic repertoire. As the director Ronald Eyre (1929–92) once remarked, 'Most directors don't choose to do Hamlet. They choose to do Hamlet as differently as possible from the last production they saw.' For this reason, many directors flounder when it comes to new plays, for they have to learn to serve the text and not themselves.

The director also guides the scenic designer. Often, a spectacular production of a classic play owes more to its design than its direction. The contemporary phrase 'design concept' tells all.

The most important directorial task is casting. If a star is involved, there will be a great many preliminary discussions intended to make the star feel wanted and confident. When it comes to casting the supporting actors, the director will seek the assistance of actors' agents ('flesh agents'), who will suggest their clients whether or not they are right for the parts. If the director casts accurately he reduces his burden. The playwright has final control over this aspect, but his contract insists he will not withhold approval 'unreasonably'. Once the play is cast and rehearsals begin, the good director should simply create an atmosphere in which actors feel free to act. This is more difficult than it sounds, and few directors know what is required of them.

The play, then, has been written. Now others must give it context and life.

KITTY BLACK (b. 1914), dramatic author, and formerly secretary to H. M. (Harry) Tennent and Hugh (Binkie) Beaumont, the most successful West End producers from the mid-1930s to the mid-1950s, from *Upper Circle – a theatrical chronicle*, 1984:

Like cutting the pages of a French novel, the thrill of reading a new play for the first time is a unique experience – you don't yet know what faces the actors will give the characters, or how the director will shape the scenes. If the author has done his job properly, the characters move and speak with their own voices, and the play grabs your attention from first to last. As nobody ever reads at acting speed, a normal script will not take more than thirty to forty minutes to read, after which a totally new pleasure begins, trying to imagine the right actors in the parts and visualizing sets and costumes. If the play is less than perfect you embark on a new mental exercise – trying to trace where the development goes wrong, imagining how certain elements could be strengthened and training an instinct that can be developed over many years and productions. I don't know how far Binkie influenced his authors – once a cast and director had been engaged, he would attend the first reading and then never interfere until the first run-through, when he would always put a finger unerringly on whatever might be in need of fixing. His taste was considered impeccable, but in my opinion he learned it originally from Harry Tennent, with his university and intellectual background.

VLADIMIR NEMIROVICH-DANCHENKO, co-founder of the Moscow Art Theatre, from a letter to Anton Chekhov, 1898:

If you won't give me your play I am undone, for *The Seagull* is the only modern play that appeals to me strongly as a producer, and you are the only living writer to be of interest to a theatre with a modern repertoire.

SIMON GRAY, from *An Unnatural Pursuit and Other Pieces*, 1985:

Surely people understand that when one hands them a script, one expects them to read it within minutes, and comment on it both profoundly and favourably for weeks afterwards.

HESKETH PEARSON, from *The Life of Oscar Wilde*, 1946. Wilde sent *The Importance of Being Earnest* to the actor-manager Sir George Alexander at the St James's Theatre in September 1894. Alexander decided it was 'not in his line'; four months later, after the failure of *Guy Domville* by Henry James, he changed his mind.

Earnest was originally in four acts. Alexander said that it should be in three. Wilde did not like to scrap any of his lines, which, after all, however easily conceived, had been indited with some effort. In telling me that Wilde had fought for nearly an hour to retain a scene, Alexander could only remember the end of their bout:

'Do you realize, Alec, what you are asking me to sacrifice?'

'You will be able to use it in another play.'

'It may not fit into another play.'

'What does that matter? You are clever enough to think of a hundred things just as good.'

'Of course I am . . . a thousand if need be . . . but that is not the point. This scene that you feel is superfluous cost me terrible exhausting labour and heart-rending nerve-racking strain. You may not believe me, but I assure you on my honour that it must have taken fully five minutes to write.'

The scene in question was one in which Algernon Moncrieff is arrested for debt, and in the light of Wilde's future a remark made by the solicitor has an ominous if comical significance: 'Time presses, Mr Moncrieff. We must present ourselves at Holloway Gaol at four o'clock. After that it is difficult to obtain admission.'

GEORGE BERNARD SHAW, from *On Cutting Shakespear*, 1919:

The moment you admit that the producer's business is to improve Shakespear by cutting out everything that he himself would not have written, and everything that he thinks the audience will either not like or not understand, and everything that does not make prosaic sense, you are launched on a slope on which there is no stopping until you reach the abyss where Irving's Lear lies forgotten. The reason stares us in the face. The producer's disapprovals, and consequently his cuts, are the symptoms of the differences between Shakespear and himself; and his assumption that all these differences are differences of superiority on his part and inferiority on Shakespear's, must end in the cutting down or raising up of Shakespear to his level. Tree thought a third-rate ballet more interesting than the colloquy of Cassio with Iago on the subject of temperance. No doubt many people agreed with him. It was certainly more expensive. Irving, when he was producing *Cymbeline*, cut out of his own part the lines:

> 'Tis her breathing that
> Perfumes the chamber thus. The flame o' the taper
> Bows towards her, and would underpeep her lids
> To see the unclosed lights, now canopied
> Under those windows, white and azure, laced
> With blue of heaven's own tinct.

He was genuinely astonished when he was told that he must not do it, as the lines were the most famous for their beauty of all the purple patches in Shakespear. A glance at the passage will shew how very 'sensible' his cut was. Mr Archer wants to cut, 'O single-soled jest, solely singular for the singleness,' because it is 'absolutely meaningless.' But think of all the other lines that must go with it on the same ground! The gayer side of Shakespear's poetic ecstasy expressed itself in word-dances of jingling nonsense which are, from the point of view of the grave Scots commentator who demands a meaning and a moral from every text, mere delirium and echolalia. But what would Shakespear be without them? 'The spring time, the only merry ring time, when birds do sing hey dinga ding ding' is certainly not good sense nor even accurate ornithological observation! Who ever heard a bird sing 'hey ding a ding ding' or anything even remotely resembling it? Out with it, then; and away, too, with such absurdities as Beatrice's obviously untrue statement that a star danced at her birth, which must revolt all the obstetricians and astronomers in the audience. As to Othello's fustian about the Propontick and the Hellespont, is this senseless hullabaloo of sonorous vowels and precipitate consonants to be retained when people have trains to catch? Mr Archer is credulous in imagining that in these orchestral passages the wit has evaporated and the meaning become inscrutable. There never was any meaning or wit in them in his sense any more than there is wit or meaning in the crash of Wagner's cymbals or the gallop of his trombones in the Valkyries' ride. The producer who has a head for syllogisms cuts such passages out. The producer who has an ear for music, like Mr Granville-Barker, breaks his heart in trying to get them adequately executed . . .

. . . The people who really want Shakespear want all of him, and not merely Mr Archer's or anyone else's favorite bits; and this not in the least because they enjoy every word of it, but because they want to be sure of hearing the words they do enjoy, and because the effect of the judiciously selected passages, not to mention injudiciously selected passages, is not the same as that of the whole play, just as the effect of the currants picked out of a bun is not the same as that of the whole bun, indigestible as it may be to people who do not like buns.

There are plenty of modern instances to go upon. I have seen *Peer Gynt* most judiciously and practically cut by Lugné-Poë, and *The Wild Duck* cut to the bone by Mr Archer. I have seen Wagner at full length at Bayreuth and Munich, and cut most sensibly at Covent Garden. I have actually seen *Il Trovatore*, most swift and concise of operas, cut by Sir Thomas Beecham. My own plays, notoriously too long, have been cut with masterly skill by American managers. Mr Henry Arthur

Jones made a capital acting version of *A Doll's House*, entitled *Breaking a Butterfly*. I do not allege that the result has always been disastrous failure, though it has sometimes gone that far. A hash makes a better meal than an empty plate. But I do aver without qualification that the mutilation has always been an offence, and the effect different and worse both in degree and in kind from the effect of a remorselessly faithful performance. Wagner's remark when he heard Rossini's *Barber of Seville* performed for once in its integrity in Turin applies to all the works of the great masters. You get something from such a performance that the selections never give you. And I suggest that this is not wholly a mystery. It occurs only when the work is produced under the direction of a manager who understands its value and can find in every passage the charm or the function which induced the author to write it, and who can dictate or suggest the method of execution that brings out that charm or discharges that function. Without this sense and this skill the manager will cut, cut, cut, every time he comes to a difficulty; and he will put the interest of the refreshment bars and the saving of electric light and the observance of the conventional hours of beginning the performance before his duty to the author, maintaining all the time that the manager who cuts most is the author's best friend.

In short, there are a thousand more sensible reasons for cutting not only Shakespear's plays, but all plays, all symphonies, all operas, all epics, and all pictures which are too large for the dining-room. And there is absolutely no reason on earth for not cutting them except the design of the author, who was probably too conceited to be a good judge of his own work.

The sane conclusion is therefore that cutting must be dogmatically ruled out, because, as Lao-Tse said, 'of the making of reforms there is no end.' The simple thing to do with a Shakespear play is to perform it. The alternative is to let it alone. If Shakespear made a mess of it, it is not likely that Smith or Robinson will succeed where he failed.

ARTHUR MURPHY, actor and dramatist (1727–1805):

'Garrick Assesses Shakespeare'

His plays are out of joint – O cursed spite!
That ever I was born to set them right!

Shakespeare's plays, especially his tragedies, were always subject to revisions by hacks. Nahum Tate (1652–1715) was perhaps the most infamous. His version of *King Lear* ends with Cordelia marrying Edgar and the line, 'And Cordelia shall be Queen!'

In *Shakespeare Improved* (1927), HAZELTON SPENCER reports on changes to *Macbeth* by Sir William Davenant (1606–68), a dramatist and theatre manager who was reputed to be Shakespeare's illegitimate son:

Davenant's version of *Macbeth*, published in 1674, was an archetypal Restoration adaptation of Shakespeare . . . And now follows V, iii, but his Macbeth is not Shakespeare's. Vanished is that fierce contumely which reveals the extremity of his bewildered spirit: we get instead such insipidities as
Now friend, what means thy change of Countenance?
For:
The divell damne thee blacke, thou cream-fac'd Loon:
Where got'st thou that Goose-looke?

MIKHAIL BULGAKOV (1891–1940), playwright and novelist, author of *The Master and Margarita*. His heartbreaking struggle in Stalin's Soviet Union is recorded in *Manuscripts Don't Burn: Mikhail Bulgakov, A Life in Letters and Diaries* by J. A. E. Curtis, 1991. His relationship with Stanislavsky began well (see a letter he wrote to the director in 1931 later in this section) but, like Chekhov before him, he was not always filled with admiration for Stanislavsky's dictatorial manner, as the letter to his friend Pavel Popov on 14 March 1935 shows:

Now Stanislavsky has taken command. They ran through *Molière* for him (except for the last scene, which wasn't ready), and he, instead of giving his opinion of the production and the acting, started to give his opinion of the play.

In the presence of the actors (five years on!) he began to tell me all about the fact that Molière was a genius, and how this genius ought to be depicted in the play.

The actors licked their lips in glee and began to ask that their parts be made larger.

I was overcome with fury. For a heady moment I wanted to fling the notebook down and say to them all, 'You write about geniuses and ungeniuses if you like, but don't teach me how to do it, I won't be able to do it anyway. I'd be better off acting instead of you.'

But you can't, you can't do it. So I stifled it all and began to defend myself.

Three days later the same. He patted my hand and said that I needed to be rubbed up the right way, and then it was the whole business all over again.

In other words I've got to write in something about Molière's significance for the theatre, and somehow I've got to demonstrate that Molière was a genius, and so on.

This is all primitive, feeble and unnecessary. And now I'm sitting in front of my copy of the text, and I can't lift my hand to work on it. I can't not write it in: declaring war would mean wrecking all that work, stirring up a proper commotion, and harming the play itself; but writing green patches into the trousers of a black tail-coat! . . . The devil knows what I should do?!

What on earth is going on, dear citizens?

And by the way, could you tell me when *Molière* is finally going to go on? [. . .]

And to Stanislavsky himself, 22 April 1935:

Much esteemed Konstantin Sergeyevich!

Today I received an excerpt from the stenographic record of the rehearsal of *Molière* on 17 April 1935, which was sent to me from the Theatre.

Having familiarized myself with it, I find myself obliged to refuse categorically to make any more changes in my play *Molière*, since the alterations sketched out in the record relating to the cabal scene, as well as the alterations to the text sketched out previously in relation to other scenes, utterly destroy, as I have become convinced, my artistic conception, and point to the composition of some entirely new play, which I am incapable of writing, since I am essentially in disagreement with it.

If *Molière* does not suit the Arts Theatre in the form in which it exists at present, although the Theatre accepted it precisely in this form and has been rehearsing it for several years, I would request you to take *Molière* off and to return it to me.

EDWARD GORDON CRAIG (1872–1966), stage designer, from *On the Art of the Theatre*, 1911, an imaginary conversation between a playgoer and a director, then called the Stage-Director. The Stage-Director speaks:

And now that we have disposed of the error that the author's directions are of any use, we can continue to speak of the way the stage-manager sets to work to interpret faithfully the play of the dramatist. I have said that he swears to follow the text faithfully, and that his first work is to read the play through and get the great impression; and in reading, as I have said, begins to see the whole colour, rhythm, action of the thing. He then puts the play aside for some time, and in his mind's eye mixes his palette (to use a painter's expression) with the colours which the impression of the play has called up. Therefore, on sitting down a second time to read through the play, he is surrounded by an atmosphere which he proposes to test. At the end of the second reading he will find that his more definite impressions have received clear and unmistakable corroboration, and that some of his impressions which were less positive have disappeared. He will then make a note of these. It is possible that he will

even now commence to suggest, in line and colour, some of the scenes
and ideas which are filling his head.

CHARLES DICKENS (1812–70), from *Nicholas Nickleby*, 1838–39. Nicholas is
employed by Mr Vincent Crummles, a resourceful actor-manager:

'You can be useful to us in a hundred ways,' said Mr Crummles.
'Think what capital bills a man of your education could write for the
shop-windows.'

'Well, I think I could manage that department,' said Nicholas.

'To be sure you could,' replied Mr Crummles. ' "For further
particulars see small hand-bills" – we might have half a volume in
every one of 'em. Pieces too; why, you could write us a piece to bring
out the whole strength of the company, whenever we wanted one.'

'I am not quite so confident about that,' replied Nicholas. 'But I dare
say I could scribble something now and then that would suit you.'

'We'll have a new show-piece out directly,' said the manager. 'Let
me see – peculiar resources of this establishment – new and splendid
scenery – you must manage to introduce a real pump and two
washing-tubs.'

'Into the piece!' said Nicholas.

'Yes,' replied the manager. 'I bought 'em cheap, at a sale the other
day; and they'll come in admirably. That's the London plan. They look
up some dresses, and properties, and have a piece written to fit them.
Most of the theatres keep an author on purpose.'

'Indeed!' cried Nicholas.

'Oh yes,' said the manager; 'a common thing. It'll look very well in
the bills in separate lines – Real pump!' – Splendid tubs! – Great
attraction! You don't happen to be anything of an artist, do you?'

'That is not one of my accomplishments,' rejoined Nicholas.

'Ah! Then it can't be helped,' said the manager. 'If you had been, we
might have had a large woodcut of the last scene for the posters,

showing the whole depth of the stage, with the pump and tubs in the middle; but, however, if you're not, it can't be helped.'

Most impresarios believe that their purpose in life is to keep the cost of production under control. One of the main items of expenditure was, and still is, the size of the cast. The following economic disposition of actors – from the Globe Theatre Museum Records – was for *The Lamentable Tragedy, Mixed Full of Pleasant Mirth, containing the Life of Cambises, King of Persia* (c. 1560–70):

Councell Huff Praxaspes Murder FOR ONE MAN Lob The Third Lord	Cambises Epilogue FOR ONE MAN
Lord Ruf Common Cry Commons Complaint FOR ONE MAN Lord Smirdis Venus	Prologue Sisamnes Diligence Cruelties FOR ONE MAN Hob Preparation The I Lord
Knight Snuf Small Hability Proof FOR ONE MAN Execution Attendance Second Lord	Ambidexter Triall FOR ONE MAN Menatrix Shame Otian Mother FOR ONE MAN Lady Queen

Young child
Cupid   FOR ONE MAN

The Lord Chamberlain's Warrant in 1662 suggests greater generosity:

Neccssaryes for ye Comaedians at Court: These are to signifie unto you his Mat[ies]. pleasure that you forth-with prouide and deliuer or cause to bee prouided and deliuered unto George Iohnson keeper of his Ma[ties]: Cockpitt Playhouse at Whitehall these perticulers followeing for his Ma[ties]: Comaedians upon those nights they act at the Cockpitt Playhouse (vizt) Twelue Quarts of Sack twelue Quarts of Clarrett twenty foure Torches sizes three Bunches Eight Gallons of Beere foure Basketts of Coales six dishes of Meate twelue Loaues of white Bread [*blank*] Loaues of Browne Bread Tallow Candles foure pounds twelue white dishes to drink in, and two Bumbards to fetch Beere.

NOËL COWARD, 1967:

The Boy Actor

I can remember. I can remember,
The months of November and December
Were filled for me with peculiar joys
So different from those of other boys
For other boys would be counting the days
Until end of term and holiday times
But I was acting in Christmas plays
While they were taken to pantomimes.
I didn't envy their Eton suits,
Their children's dances and Christmas trees.
My life had wonderful substitutes
For such conventional treats as these.
I didn't envy their country larks,
Their organized games in panelled halls:
While they made snow-men in stately parks
I was counting the curtain calls.

I remember the auditions, the nerve-racking auditions:
Darkened auditorium and empty, dusty stage,
Little girls in ballet dresses practising 'positions',

Gentlemen with pince-nez asking you your age.
Hopefulness and nervousness struggling within you,
Dreading that familiar phrase, 'Thank you dear, no more'.
Straining every muscle, every tendon, every sinew
To do your dance much better than you'd ever done before.
Think of your performance. Never mind the others,
Never mind the pianist, talent must prevail.
Never mind the baleful eyes of other children's mothers
Glaring from the corners and willing you to fail.

I can remember. I can remember.
The months of November and December
Were more significant to me
Than other months could ever be
For they were the months of high romance
When destiny waited on tip-toe,
When every boy actor stood a chance
Of getting into a Christmas show,
Not for me the dubious heaven
Of being some prefect's protégé!
Not for me the Second Eleven.
For me, two performances a day.

Ah those first rehearsals! Only very few lines:
Rushing home to mother, learning them by heart,
'Enter Left through window! – Dots to mark the cue lines:
'Exit with the others' – Still it *was* a part.
Opening performance; legs a bit unsteady,
Dedicated tension, shivers down my spine,
Powder, grease and eye-black, sticks of make-up ready
Leichner number three and number five and number nine.
World of strange enchantment, magic for a small boy
Dreaming of the future, reaching for the crown,
Rigid in the dressing-room, listening for the call-boy
'Overture Beginners – Everybody Down!'

I can remember. I can remember.
The months of November and December,
Although climatically cold and damp,
Meant more to me than Aladdin's lamp.
I see myself, having got a job,
Walking on wings along the Strand,
Uncertain whether to laugh or sob
And clutching tightly my mother's hand,
I never cared who scored the goal
Or which side won the silver cup,
I never learned to bat or bowl
But I heard the curtain going up.

JOHN BARTON (b. 1928), director, from *Playing Shakespeare*, 1982:

I think we ought to talk a bit about design now, because, whatever the size of theatre we're in, the costumes and sets are one of the things that give a production its contemporary flavour. I don't necessarily mean modern dress. I am thinking of a fashion we have just now, which I approve of, of designing shows so that their period can't be pinned down precisely. We go for a mixture of modern elements and Renaissance, Elizabethan or Jacobean elements. The word we use to describe it is 'timeless'. It springs from the belief that to put actors into, say, Renaissance costumes is to put them into fancy dress and to diminish their humanity. They don't seem real and their social background is often left obscure. But we also believe that to put them in modern dress can all too easily distort Shakespeare. This 'timeless' style is of course a healthy reaction against finicky historical exactness. And Shakespeare's actors themselves performed in what in their terms, was modern dress.

ELIZABETH BOWEN (1899–1973), author and theatre critic, from a review in
Night and Day, 1937:

At the Queen's Theatre Mr Gielgud presents Mr Gielgud's production
of *Richard II*, with Mr Gielgud in the title-ròle. Critics enthuse,
dowagers are melted, high-brows seek in vain for foot-faults, and even
the poor little smarties will have to go if they get back to London in
time (the run ends on Oct. 30). The production deserves all the nice
things that have been said about it; I find myself writing more as a fan
than as a critic, and propose therefore to lodge the only available
complaint before it is trampled to death by wild superlatives. This
complaint is against Motley's scenery. The sets are very greatly helped
by excellent lighting (a department in which the London theatre is apt
to be either under- or over-inspired); but for all that the sets are bad,
being liable to violent attacks of arty-and-crafty castellation. The chief
symptom of these attacks is an embryo form of real estate, something
like a cuckoo-clock, which breaks out over fireplaces, on the canopies
of thrones, and elsewhere. There is also a windswept tree, very nice in
its own way but too ubiquitous. They really are not good sets, and they
don't help the actors.

Costumiers are different from costume designers. The latter design carefully made
and fitted clothes for the actors. The costumier, on the other hand, has a vast
supply of costumes from all periods and of all sizes. Nathan of London was one of
the great theatrical and film costumiers. Archie Nathan in *Costumes by Nathan*,
1960, reprints three testimonials from actor-knights, LAURENCE OLIVIER,
DONALD WOLFIT and JOHN GIELGUD.

The House of Nathan has given great service of a very special kind to
the Theatre and I am glad to have this opportunity to offer my
congratulations and thanks, both in my own name and also on behalf
of countless other actors and managers, past and present and,
doubtless, future.

This great establishment has assiduously pursued its duties for
nearly 170 years – since Garrick was but recently dead and Kean but

recently born – and I sent it my respects and my good wishes for the next couple of centuries.

LAURENCE OLIVIER

My dear Archie,
How splendid that you should do this. Memory teems with visits to you – *Drake of England* film, Roger Furse's *Antony and Cleopatra*, when I played *Antony*, countless productions at Stratford, including Komis's *King Lear* and Aubrey Hammond's *Much Ado* – and when I ventured into management you did two plays for me – *Shrew* and *Twelfth Night* on my *very first tour* in 1937 . . .

And the evening we spent getting ready for *Twelfth Night* in the Middle Temple Hall in 1951 for H.M. The Queen Mother – then Queen Elizabeth.

I should think in the last thirty years I have been a more frequent visitor to your place than any other actor (and you still haven't got a photo up of me) and you have two of my most treasured belongings – my Asses Head and my Falstaff padding and costume.

Love from us both,

Yours,
DONALD.

Dear Archie Nathan,
For a beginner in the theatre one of the greatest thrills must surely be the first visit to a great theatrical costumier. How well I remember, when I was first a student, visiting your top-floor department, where patient Mr Gillings, almost hidden by innumerable bales of tunics, hats, shoes, doublets, in seemingly indistinguishable disorder, listened to my demands for a costume for some end-of-term performance. As I almost tip-toed past the main sanctuary on the first floor, I had the luck to glimpse the back of a famous star vanishing into the fitting room to discuss his new production with the designer and yourself. While Gillings was away searching for another belt or pouch to complete one's outfit, I stealthily did the round of signed photographs, playbills and designs which hung upon the walls. Then, half an hour later, when order had emerged from chaos, I left your shop, proudly equipped from top to toe, and already, in fancy, englamorised into a real professional actor.

Now that I have the privilege of being ushered into that first floor fitting room myself, I can still feel something of that early thrill. May it never vanish altogether, for it is surely part of the 'stuff which dreams are made on', the very magic of our craft. Long may you and your fine band of helpers flourish in the service of the theatre and keep the enthusiasm which is the secret of your long success.

Yours sincerely,
JOHN GIELGUD.

A Guild's expenditure for the costume and properties of a Mystery cycle, fifteenth century:

a pair of new gloves for Saint Thomas [Canterbury]
a leather coat for Christ
5 prophets (one wanting) [Chelmsford, 1564]
3 skins for Noah's coat, making it and a rope to hang the ship in the kirk . . . 7 shillings
Thomas Sawyr to play God . . . 10d.
a new pair of mittens for Noah . . . 4d. [Hull, 1494]
a face and heare for y Father, A cote w hosen and tayle for ye serpents-steyned [Norwich, 1565]
linen cloths for the angels heads, and Jesus hoose
Painting of angels wings . . . 8d. [Leicester, 1504]
for Gabriel carrying a lily . . . 4d.
for playing God . . . 3 shillings
for a new coat and shoes for Gabriel . . . 35/4d.

ANTONIN ARTAUD, from *The Theatre and its Double*, 1938:

LIGHTS, LIGHTING: The lighting equipment now in use in theatres is no longer adequate. The particular action of light upon the mind, the effects of all kinds of luminous vibration must be investigated, along with new ways of spreading the light waves, in sheets, in fusillades of fiery arrows. The colour gamut of the equipment now in use is to be revised from beginning to end. In order to produce the qualities of particular musical tones, light must recover an element of thinness, density, and opaqueness, with a view to producing the sensations of heat, cold, anger, fear, etc.

COSTUMES: Where costumes are concerned, modern dress will be avoided as much as possible without at the same time assuming a uniform theatrical costuming that would be the same for every play – not from a fetishist and superstitious reverence for the past, but because it seems absolutely evident that certain age-old costumes, of ritual intent, though they existed at a given moment of time, preserve a beauty and a revelational appearance from their closeness to the traditions that gave them birth.

JOAN WOOD, *The Casting Couch, the uninhibited memoirs of a young actress,* 1975. From the chapter entitled 'I don't care if you are my mother, I still get ten per cent':

Agents are like menstrual cramps. You hate to have them, but they serve a purpose.

Theatrical agents are, in fact, employment agencies.

An agent is supposed to know where the jobs are, and send his clients to fill the jobs, for a fee, of course, usually amounting to ten per cent of the client's earnings. Ten per cent is a small price to pay for success. It's a very large amount, however, if you get most of the work for yourself and have to pay your agent for the privilege of saying you have one.

I've had a number of agents in my career, most of them bad.

Well, maybe that's too harsh. Some of my 'bad' agents have gotten me work, and there's little more you can expect from them. They have their problems, too, primarily because actors and actresses are the most insecure breed of people on earth. Actors and actresses need not

FABER BOOK OF THE THEATRE

only an agent who finds them work, they need a father, priest, confidant, occasional lover, booster, champion and all-around best friend. Maybe that's asking too much for ten per cent.

The real problem with agents has to do with the business itself. For the thousands of young girls who seek work in the theatre, there are only a handful of jobs. That's why agents so often become little more than conduits through which young and willing female flesh is peddled around from agent to producer to director and back to agents again. And that's exactly how the casting couch works.

I sat down one night with some fellow-actresses and we made up a list of the different types of *bad agents*. We had a lot of fun doing it. It was a great way to get rid of our agent-gripes in one sitting. The wine was good, too.

PIMP   He becomes an agent to meet young girls. He generally has another income and couldn't care less whether he finds you work or not. Young girls starting out usually end up with one of these types early in the game. Good, solid, legitimate agents aren't interested in new faces until they prove themselves capable of making money. The pimps, however, are always looking for new faces, and if you aren't careful, you end up with a very old face at the age of twenty-five.

KNOCKER   He knocks everything and everybody, including his clients. The way he figures it, if he criticizes everything he can never be faulted for having bad taste. I was very impressed with one of these types until I found out he was telling producers and directors, prospective employers, that I wasn't very good, but might improve. More than anything, a young actress needs an advocate, and if ten per cent doesn't buy one, the money is down the drain.

SCATTERBRAIN   He's usually a decent guy, but he can't remember anything, including his clients. It's bad enough he forgets who you are when a producer is looking for precisely your type, but it's even worse when he finds you a job but loses your paycheck.

NAMEDROPPER   All agents are namedroppers, but some don't do anything else but drop names. 'Joan, I'll be seeing David Merrick this week for dinner and I'll put in the word for you.' He doesn't really know anyone whose name he drops, but it keeps you on the string for a few months.

FATHER IMAGE   Some agents, like some doctors, have fantastic bedside manners. These agents are all those things I mentioned earlier: father, priest, confidant, occasional lover, booster, champion and all-around best friend. The only failing they have is that they can't find you a job.

PROTECTOR   These agents claim to be sensitive to your needs and demand that you allow them to decide which jobs are right for you. They tell you of all the offers they've had for your talents, but add that none of the work was worthy of you. You go into your local supermarket and tell the manager that you'll pay your bill as soon as a role worthy of you comes along, and he tells you to get your ass out of the store.

TYPE-CASTER   These agents have no imagination. Unless a role calls for someone of exactly your physical proportions, hair color, speech and background, this agent won't send you. Pretty soon you're sixty-five, but you still aren't sent on the audition because the writer described the role as a woman of about sixty-six.

LITTLE FISH, BIG POND   There are a number of very large agencies, handling thousands of talents. If you manage to be taken on by one of these super-agencies, you're assigned the kid from the mailroom who has just been made an account executive, which means he can wear a suit at the same salary. Then, you go out and hire another agent for ten per cent who tries to get the super-agency to pay attention to you. Big agencies are not for little people, with the exception of those who work in them.

NICE GUY   He loves being an agent because it gives him the chance to be friendly with big names in the theatre and motion pictures. He wouldn't do anything to offend his friends and cause them to avoid his calls, so he takes any terms they offer. Most of these types are gay, which avoids any casting couch hassles for you, but seldom results in much paying work.

TOUGH GUY   The opposite of NICE GUY. He hates everybody, and spends all his time arguing with them. Most of his phone calls are avoided by everybody, including you, after a few weeks.

ONE-SHOT   He went to high school with a big star or name producer, and his office is filled with eight-by-ten glossies of them together. You figure you've got it made until his friend is run over in Rome while filming a chariot race.

But there are good agents too. They're hard to interest unless you appear to be a good bet for solid income.

CHARLES CHURCHILL (1731–64), poet and satirist, from *The Apology*, 1761:

> The strolling tribe, a despicable race,
> Like wand'ring Arabs, shift from place to place . . .

> In shabby state they strut, and tatter'd robe,
> The scene a blanket, and a barn the globe.
> No high conceits their mod'rate wishes raise,
> Content with humble profit, humble praise.
> Let dowdies simper, and let bumpkins stare,
> The strolling pageant hero treads in air:
> Pleas'd for his hour he to mankind gives law,
> And snores the next out on a truss of straw.

SIR SEYMOUR HICKS (1871–1949), actor-manager, from *Me and My Missus*, 1939:

Sport in the country makes me think, too, of Sir Frank Benson. I suppose no actor who ever lived has been such an all-round athlete as this old 'Varsity Blue. It is said of him, that, if he were debating which of two actors to engage for a certain part, the slightly inferior artist, if he was a fine cricketer, would most certainly have obtained the coveted honour of employment under the Bensonian banner.

I have heard, though I cannot vouch for the story, that Sir Frank's contracts with his artists were always worded: 'To play the Ghost in *Hamlet* and keep wicket,' or 'To play Laertes and field cover-point';

and it was said that no Polonius need apply unless he happened to be a first-class wicket-keeper.

NICHOLAS ROWE, from *Some Account of the life, &c. of Mr William Shakespear*, 1709:

His Name is Printed, as the Custom was in those Times, amongst those of the other Players, before some old Plays, but without any particular Account of what sort of Parts he us'd to play; and tho' I have inquir'd, I could never meet with any further Account of him this way, than that the top of his Performance was the Ghost in his own *Hamlet*.

CHARLES DICKENS, from *Nicholas Nickleby*, 1838–9:

Nicholas was up betimes in the morning; but he had scarcely begun to dress, notwithstanding, when he heard footsteps ascending the stairs, and was presently saluted by the voices of Mr Folair, the pantomimist, and Mr Lenville, the tragedian.

'House, house, house!' cried Mr Folair.

'What, ho! within there!' said Mr Lenville, in a deep voice.

'Confound these fellows!' thought Nicholas; 'they have come to breakfast, I suppose. I'll open the door directly, if you'll wait an instant.'

The gentlemen entreated him not to hurry himself; and, to beguile the interval, had a fencing bout with their walking-sticks on the very small landing-place, to the unspeakable discomposure of all the other lodgers downstairs.

'Here, come in,' said Nicholas, when he had completed his toilet. 'In the name of all that's horrible, don't make that noise outside.'

'An uncommon snug little box this,' said Mr Lenville, stepping into the front room, and taking his hat off before he could get in at all. 'Pernicious snug.'

'For a man at all particular in such matters it might be a trifle too snug,' said Nicholas; 'for although it is, undoubtedly, a great convenience to be able to reach anything you want from the ceiling or the floor, or either side of the room, without having to move from your chair, still these advantages can only be had in an apartment of the most limited size.'

'It isn't a bit too confined for a single man,' returned Mr Lenville. 'That reminds me – my wife, Mr Johnson – I hope she'll have some good part in this piece of yours?'

'I glanced at the French copy last night,' said Nicholas. 'It looks very good, I think.'

'What do you mean to do for me, old fellow?' asked Mr Lenville, poking the struggling fire with his walking-stick, and afterwards wiping it on the skirt of his coat. 'Anything in the gruff and grumble way?'

'You turn your wife and child out of doors,' said Nicholas; 'and, in a fit of rage and jealousy, stab your eldest son in the library.'

'Do I though!' exclaimed Mr Lenville. 'That's very good business.'

'After which,' said Nicholas, 'you are troubled with remorse till the last act, and then you make up your mind to destroy yourself. But just as you are raising the pistol to your head, a clock strikes – ten.'

'I see,' cried Mr Lenville. 'Very good.'

'You pause,' said Nicholas; 'you recollect to have heard a clock strike ten in your infancy. The pistol falls from your hand – you are overcome – you burst into tears, and become a virtuous and exemplary character for ever afterwards.'

'Capital!' said Mr Lenville; 'that's a sure card, a sure card. Get the curtain down with a touch of nature like that, and it'll be a triumphant success.'

'Is there anything good for me?' inquired Mr Folair anxiously.

'Let me see,' said Nicholas. 'You play the faithful and attached servant; you are turned out of doors with the wife and child.'

'Always coupled with that infernal phenomenon,' sighed Mr Folair; 'and we go into poor lodgings, where I won't take any wages, and talk sentiment, I suppose?'

'Why – yes,' replied Nicholas; 'that is the course of the piece.'

'I must have a dance of some kind, you know,' said Mr Folair.

'You'll have to introduce one for the phenomenon, so you'd better make it a *pas de deux*, and save time.'

'There's nothing easier than that,' said Mr Lenville, observing the disturbed looks of the young dramatist.

'Upon my word I don't see how it's to be done,' rejoined Nicholas.

'Why, isn't it obvious?' reasoned Mr Lenville. 'Gadzooks! who can help seeing the way to do it? – you astonish me! You get the distressed lady, and the little child, and the attached servant, into the poor lodgings, don't you? Well, look here. The distressed lady sinks into a chair, and buries her face in her pocket-handkerchief. "What makes you weep, mamma?" says the child. "Don't weep, mamma, or you'll make me weep too!" "And me!" says the faithful servant, rubbing his eyes with his arm. "What can we do to raise your spirits, dear mamma?" says the little child. "Aye, what *can* we do?" says the faithful servant. "Oh, Pierre!" says the distressed lady; "would that I could shake off these painful thoughts." "Try ma'am, try," says the faithful servant; "rouse yourself, ma'am; be amused." "I will," says the lady – "I will learn to suffer with fortitude. Do you remember that dance, my honest friend, which in happier days you practised with this sweet angel? It never failed to calm my spirits then. Oh, let me see it once again before I die!" There it is – cue for the band, *before I die* – and off they go. That's the regular thing; isn't it, Tommy?'

'That's it,' replied Mr Folair. 'The distressed lady, overpowered by old recollections, faints at the end of the dance, and you close in with a picture.'

ANONYMOUS, *The Return from Parnassus*, Part II, *c.* 1601–3, an imaginary dialogue put into the mouths of Richard Burbage, Shakespeare's leading actor, and William Kempe, the clown:

BURBAGE: Master Studioso, I pray you, take some part in this book, and act it, that I may see what will fit you best. I think your voice would serve for Hieronimo; observe how I act it, and then imitate me.

KEMP: Now for you. Methinks you should belong to my tuition; and your face, methinks, would be good for a foolish mayor or a foolish justice of peace. Mark me: . . .

KEMP: Thou wilt do well in time, if thou wilt be ruled by thy betters, that is, by myself, and such grave aldermen of the playhouse as I am.

BURBAGE: I like your face, and the proportion of your body for Richard the Third. I pray, Master Philomusus, let me see you act a little of it.

WILLIAM SHAKESPEARE, from *Hamlet, Prince of Denmark*, Act III, Scene 2:

(*Enter* HAMLET *and three of the* PLAYERS.)

HAMLET: Speak the speech, I pray you, as I pronounc'd it to you, trippingly on the tongue; but if you mouth it as many of your players do, I had as lief the town-crier spoke my lines. Nor do not saw the air too much with your hand, thus, but use all gently; for in the very torrent, tempest, and, as I may say, whirlwind of your passion, you must acquire and beget a temperance that may give it smoothness. O, it offends me to the soul to hear a robustious periwig-pated fellow tear a passion to tatters, to very rags, to split the ears of the groundlings, who for the most part are capable of nothing but inexplicable dumb-shows and noise. I would have such a fellow whipped for o'erdoing Termagant; it out-herods Herod. Pray you avoid it.

FIRST PLAYER: I warrant your honour.

HAMLET: Be not too tame neither, but let your own discretion be your tutor. Suit the action to the word, the word to the action, with this special observance, that you o'erstep not the modesty of nature. For anything so o'erdone is from the purpose of playing, whose end, both at the first and now, was and is to hold as 'twere the mirror up to nature; to show virtue her feature, scorn her own image, and the very age and body of the time his form and pressure. Now this overdone or come tardy off, though it makes the unskilful laugh, cannot but make the judicious grieve; the censure of the which one must, in your allowance, o'erweigh a whole theatre of others. O, there be players that I have seen play – and heard others praise, and that highly – not to speak it profanely, that, neither having th' accent of Christians, nor the gait of Christian, pagan, nor man, have so strutted and bellowed that I have thought some of Nature's journeymen had made men, and not made them well, they imitated humanity so abominably.

FIRST PLAYER: I hope we have reform'd that indifferently with us, sir.

HAMLET: O reform it altogether. And let those that play your clowns speak no more than is set down for them – for there be of them that will themselves laugh, to set on some quantity of barren spectators to laugh too, though in the meantime some necessary question of the play be then to be considered. That's villainous, and shows a most pitiful ambition in the fool that uses it. Go, make you ready.

THEOPHILUS CIBBER (1703–58), actor and theatre manager, from *Dissertations on Theatrical Subjects*, 1756:

I have heard of an actor who humorously told his brother comedians that, whenever he had a part where the redundancy of the author ran into too great a length in the scenes, he had recourse to a whimsical expedient for the shortening of them. He had the whole part wrote out, and then gave it to his cat to play with. What Puss clawed off, the actor left out; yet he generally found enough remained to satisfy his audience.

W. MACQUEEN-POPE (1888–1960), theatre historian, from *The Curtain Rises*, 1961, on the actor-manager Sir Herbert Beerbohm-Tree who owned Her Majesty's Theatre in the Haymarket, London. Tree was famous for his lavish productions of Shakespeare; he could be described as the forerunner of the over-designed productions in today's subsidized theatres.

As a producer he had no equal. His sense of beauty, his sense of the stage, and his ability to make crowds of 'supers' come to life and behave like real actors has never been surpassed. There was nothing about the stage which he did not understand. Once they were rehearsing a thunderstorm. A real one blew up outside and after a crash of real thunder Tree said it would not do. They told him it was real thunder. 'Ah,' said Tree, 'that may satisfy the people outside but we must do better at Her Majesty's.'

P. G. WODEHOUSE (1881–1975), 1907:

Mr Beerbohm Tree

He is the very model of the actor (managerial):
He uses Shakespeare's lines to form a sort of ground-material.
The bard, in fact, provides the major portion of the letter-press:
But the scenery's his own idea. ('Superb! Could not be better!' – Press.)

And no maiden at a matinee without a thrill can see
The strange exotic beauty of our only Beerbohm Tree.

> Tree, Tree, Beautiful Tree,
> What a wonderful actor you are!
> You stand all the time,
> In the light of the lime:
> You're a bright and particular star.
> We'd come miles for a sight
> Of that picturesque bend in your knee.
> Our Waller – we love him,
> But rank you above him,
> Our one and our only Tree!

If I'm asked to tell the reasons of his well-earned popularity,
His acting's always funny, while avoiding all vulgarity:
As Hamlet, when he had his conversation with the phantom, I'm
Not certain that he didn't beat the leading lights of pantomime.

You will burst your waistcoat-buttons, though sewn tightly on they
  be,
If you chance to see the Hamlet of our only Beerbohm Tree.

> Tree, Tree, Beautiful Tree.
> May you go from success to success.
> May the crowds block the streets,
> When they're fighting for seats;
> May you never fall out with the Press.
> Though your Antony might
> Be different without vexing me
> Still, the actor who's funny
> Is the man for my money,
> So I'll stick to my Beerbohm Tree.

WILLIAM POEL (1852–1934), teacher and director, from *Monthly Letters*, 1929:

The London stage still needs a producer who will have the courage to give up setting Shakespeare's plays as if they were written on the plan of eighteenth-century Italian Opera, or in other words, who will dare to give up the scenery, the costumes, and the properties which disfigured the Opera stage in the time of Handel, and which are hopelessly out of place in any form of entertainment except Christmas pantomime.

ALAN AYCKBOURN, quoted in the *Daily Telegraph*, 1986:

I remember doing a season with Stephen Joseph with one wooden box as all the scenery for every play we did. In the end the cast asked me as stage manager to intercede. 'The lads feel they have had the box,' I told

Stephen. 'You had better paint it then,' he said. So I painted it red. 'Is that it?' they said. 'Yes,' I said.

ANTON CHEKHOV, a letter from Yalta to Stanislavsky, 30 October 1903, in which he discusses the casting of *The Cherry Orchard*:

Dear Konstantin Sergeyevich,
Thank you very much for the letter and for the telegram. Letters are always very precious to me because, one, I am here all alone, and two, I sent the play off three weeks ago and your letter came only yesterday; if it were not for my wife, I would have been entirely in the dark and would have imagined any old thing that might have crept into my head. When I worked on the part of Lopakhin, I thought it might be for you. If for some reason it doesn't appeal to you, take Gayev. Lopakhin, of course, is only a merchant, but he is a decent person in every sense, should conduct himself with complete decorum, like a cultivated man, without pettiness or trickery, and it did seem to me that you would be brilliant in this part, which is central for the play. (If you do decide to play Gayev, let Vishnevski play Lopakhin. He won't make an artistic Lopakhin but still he won't be a petty one. Lujski would be a cold-blooded foreigner in this part and Leonidov would play it like a little kulak. You mustn't lose sight of the fact that Varya, an earnest, devout young girl, is in love with Lopakhin; she wouldn't love a little kulak.)

SYBIL (1883–1976) and RUSSELL THORNDIKE (1885–1972), actors who were sister and brother, from *Lilian Baylis*, 1938. Lilian Baylis (1874–1937) was the founder of the Old Vic Company; Ben Greet was a Shakespearean actor-manager. Russell Thorndike recounts an incident that occurred during the First World War:

Miss Baylis was very exercised in her mind about a proposed production of *Henry V*. Ben Greet had told her it was just the play to draw all the soldiers in London . . . She said the only thing she knew about the play was The Prayer. She then asked me if I could kneel. Thinking she was about to ask me to play Henry, I told her that at present I couldn't kneel or walk, but that I hoped to get better soon . . . She then knelt down by the roll-top desk, with one hand resting upon the base of the telephone. The prayer which followed was exactly like a business talk over the 'phone. The 'Dear God' she addressed seemed to be on the other end of the line. She told Him who she was and what she was praying for, and hoped that in the presence of the soldier home from the front, He would listen. She asked Him if it was right to do *Henry V*. It was a long cast and would need more actors, and that meant spending more money. The last sentence of the prayer was that God should send her some good actors – and as an after-thought she added the word 'cheap'.

THEOPHRASTUS, (*c.* 370–*c.* 288 BC), peripatetic philosopher and pupil of Aristotle, from *Characters*, *c.* 372 BC. The work consists of thirty brief and vigorous sketches identifying moral types, an early guide to typecasting:

The lout is the type who, when he meets womenfolk, lifts up his clothes and displays his private parts; who claps in the theatre when everyone else has stopped and hisses at actors the rest of the audience are enjoying, and when you could hear a pin drop, he lifts up his head and belches to make people turn round. In company he calls complete strangers by name as if he were a life-long friend. If he sees people in a hurry somewhere he calls out 'Wait a moment!' When his mother comes back from consulting some fortune teller, he goes out of his way to use ill-omened words. If he wants to spit, he does it over the table at the slave who is serving wine.

Attributed to KATHERINE HEPBURN (b. 1909):

Acting is the most minor of gifts and not a very high-class way to earn a living. After all, Shirley Temple could do it at the age of four.

❧

ANTON CHEKHOV, a letter from Yalta to Vladimir Danchenko, 2 November 1903, in which he again discusses the casting of *The Cherry Orchard*:

My dear Vladimir Ivanovich,
Two letters from you in one day, thanks a lot! I don't drink beer, the last time I drank any was in July; and I cannot eat honey, as it gives me a stomach ache. Now as to the play.

1. Anya can be played by any actress you'd like, even an utter unknown, if only she is young and looks like a young girl, and talks in a young, resonant voice. This ròle is not one of the important ones.

2. Varya's part is more on the serious side, if only Maria Petrovna would take it. If she doesn't the part will turn out rather flat and coarse, and I would have to do it over and soften it. M. P. won't repeat herself because, firstly, she is a gifted actress, and secondly, because Varya does not resemble Sonya or Natasha; she is a figure in a black dress, a little nun-like creature, somewhat simple-minded, plaintive and so forth and so on.

3. Gayev and Lopakhin – have Stanislavski try these parts and make his choice. If he takes Lopakhin and feels at home in the part, the play is bound to be a success. Certainly if Lopakhin is a pallid figure, played by a pallid actor, both the part and the play will fail.

4. Pishchik – the part for Gribunin. God have mercy on you if you assign the part to Vishnevski.

5. Charlotta – a big part. It would of course be impossible to give the part to Pomyalova; Muratova might be good, perhaps, but not funny. This is the part for Mme. Knipper.

6. Epikhodov – if Moskvin wants the part let him have it. He'll be a superb Epikhodov . . .

7. Firs – the role for Artem.

8. Dunyasha – for Khalutina.

9. Yasha. If it is the Alexandrov you wrote about, the one that is assistant to your producer, let him have it. Moskvin would make a splendid Yasha. And I haven't anything against Leonidov for the part.

10. The passer-by – Gromov.

11. The stationmaster who reads 'The Sinner' in Act III should have a bass voice.

Charlotta speaks with a good accent, not broken Russian, except that once in a while she gives a soft sound to a consonant at the end of a word rather than the hard sound that is proper, and she mixes masculine and feminine adjectives. Pishchik is an old Russian fellow broken down with gout, old age and satiety, plump, dressed in a long Russian coat (à la Simov) and boots without heels. Lopakhin wears a white vest and tan shoes, flails his arms when he is in motion, takes long strides, is lost in thought when he moves about and walks in a straight line. He doesn't cut his hair short and so he frequently tosses his head back; in reflection he strokes his beard back and forth, i.e., from his neck to his lips. I think Trofimov is clearly sketched. Varya wears a black dress and wide belt.

I have been intending to write 'The Cherry Orchard' these past three years and for three years have been telling you to hire an actress who could play a part like Lubov Andreyevna. This long waiting game never pays.

I have got into the stupidest position: I am here alone and don't know why. But you are unjust in saying that despite your work it is 'Stanislavski's theatre.' You are the one that people speak about and write about while they do nothing but criticize Stanislavski for his performance of Brutus. If you leave the theatre, so will I.

KITTY BLACK was secretary to Binkie Beaumont and, on a part-time basis, to Sir John Gielgud. In *Upper Circle* she recounts an early stage in Gielgud's 1942 production of *Macbeth*:

For a long time John couldn't make up his mind about the Lady, and finally announced that he would hold auditions in order to find a suitable new star. Among the letters was one application for the part of 'Lady McBeth' enclosing a photograph with the pathetic p.s. 'I do take my glasses off often.' Eventually he settled for Gwen Ffrangçon-Davies who had been his exquisite partner in the romantic smash-hit, *Richard of Bordeaux* as well as in *Three Sisters* and *The Importance of being Earnest*.

CARL SANDBURG, (1878–1967), 1920:

They All Want to Play Hamlet

They all want to play Hamlet.
They have not exactly seen their fathers killed
Nor their mothers in a frame-up to kill,
Nor an Ophelia dying with a dust gagging the heart,
Not exactly the spinning circles of singing golden spiders,
Not exactly this have they got at nor the meaning of flowers –
    O flowers, flowers slung by a dancing girl – in the saddest
    play the inkfish, Shakespeare, ever wrote;
Yet they all want to play Hamlet because it is sad like all actors
    are sad and to stand by an open grave with a joker's skull in
    the hand and then to say over slow and say over slow wise,
    keen, beautiful words masking a heart that's breaking, breaking,
This is something that calls and calls to their blood.
They are acting when they talk about it and they know it is acting
    to be particular about it and yet: They all want to play Hamlet.

NIGEL PLANER (b. 1955), writing as Nicholas Craig, from *I, An Actor*, 1988:

The rehearsal room is no place for the faint-hearted. You need strength to keep going when the coffee's running out and the workmen are drilling outside. You need stamina to carry on after lunch when the crossword's only a quarter done and you're ready to drop. You need self-belief, you need guts, you need animal determination, and if you're playing the lead you need to make a cheesecake to show everyone that you're not starry or grand or anything, that you're just one of the cast, a worker.

WILLIAM SHAKESPEARE, *A Midsummer Night's Dream*, Act I, Scene 2:

Quince's house. Enter Quince the Carpenter, and Snug the Joiner, and Bottom the Weaver, and Flute the Bellows Mender, and Snout the Tinker, and Starveling the Tailor.

QUINCE: Is all our company here?

BOTTOM: You were best to call them generally, man by man, according to the scrip.

QUINCE: Here is the scroll of every man's name, which is thought fit, through all Athens, to play in our interlude before the Duke and the Duchess, on his wedding day at night.

BOTTOM: First, good Peter Quince, say what the play treats on; then read the names of the actors; and so grow to a point.

QUINCE: Marry, our play is, 'The most lamentable comedy, and most cruel death of Pyramus and Thisby.'

BOTTOM: A very good piece of work, I assure you, and a merry. Now, good Peter Quince, call forth your actors by the scroll. Masters, spread yourselves.

QUINCE: Answer as I call you, Nick Bottom, the weaver.

BOTTOM: Ready. Name what part I am for, and proceed.

QUINCE: You, Nick Bottom, are set down for Pyramus.

BOTTOM: What is Pyramus? A lover, or a tyrant?

QUINCE: A lover that kills himself, most gallant, for love.

BOTTOM: That will ask some tears in the true performing of it: if I do it, let the audience look to their eyes. I will move storms, I will condole in some measure. To the rest: yet my chief humour is for a tyrant. I could play Ercles rarely, or a part to tear a cat in, to make all split.

> The raging rocks
> And shivering shocks
> Shall break the locks
>   Of prison gates;
> And Phibbus' car
> Shall shine from far,
> And make and mar
>   The foolish Fates.

This was lofty! Now name the rest of the players. This is Ercles' vein, a tyrant's vein. A lover is more condoling.

QUINCE: Francis Flute, the bellows mender.

FLUTE: Here, Peter Quince.

QUINCE: Flute, you must take Thisby on you.

FLUTE: What is Thisby? A wand'ring knight?

QUINCE: It is the lady that Pyramus must love.

FLUTE: Nay, faith, let not me play a woman. I have a beard coming.

QUINCE: That's all one. You shall play it in a mask, and you may speak as small as you will.

BOTTOM: An I may hide my face, let me play Thisby too, I'll speak in a monstrous little voice, 'Thisne, Thisne!' 'Ah Pyramus, my lover dear! Thy Thisby dear, and lady dear!'

QUINCE: No, no; you must play Pyramus; and, Flute, you Thisby.

BOTTOM: Well, proceed.

QUINCE: Robin Starveling, the tailor.

STARVELING: Here, Peter Quince.

QUINCE: Robin Starveling, you must play Thisby's mother. Tom Snout, the tinker.

SNOUT: Here, Peter Quince.

QUINCE: You, Pyramus' father: myself, Thisby's father: Snug, the joiner; you, the lion's part. And, I hope, here is a play fitted.

SNUG: Have you the lion's part written? Pray you, if it be, give it me, for I am slow of study.

QUINCE: You may do it extempore, for it is nothing but roaring.

BOTTOM: Let me play the lion too. I will roar that I will do any man's heart good to hear me. I will roar, that I will make the Duke say, 'Let him roar again, let him roar again.'

QUINCE: An you should do it too terribly, you would fright the Duchess and the ladies, that they would shriek; and that were enough to hang us all.

ALL: That would hang us, every mother's son.

BOTTOM: I grant you, friends, if you should fright the ladies out of their wits, they would have no more discretion but to hang us: but I will aggravate my voice so that I will roar you as gently as any sucking dove; I will roar you an 'twere any nightingale.

QUINCE: You can play no part but Pyramus; for Pyramus is a sweet-faced man; a proper man as one shall see in a summer's day; a most lovely, gentlemanlike man: therefore you must needs play Pyramus.

BOTTOM: Well, I will undertake it. What beard were I best to play it in?

QUINCE: Why, what you will.

BOTTOM: I will discharge it in either your straw-colour beard, your orange-tawny beard, your purple-in-grain beard, or your French-crown-colour beard, your perfit yellow.

QUINCE: Some of your French crowns have no hair at all, and then you will play barefaced. But, masters, here are your parts; and I am to entreat you, request you, and desire you, to con them by to-morrow night; and meet me in the palace wood, a mile without the town, by moonlight. There will we rehearse, for if we meet in the city, we shall be dogged with company, and our devices known.

CHARLES DICKENS, *Nicholas Nickleby*, 1838–9:

A pretty general muster of the company had by this time taken place; for besides Mr Lenville and his friend Tommy, there were pesent a slim young gentleman with weak eyes, who played the low-spirited lovers and sang tenor songs, and who had come arm-in-arm with the comic countryman – a man with a turned-up nose, large mouth, broad face, and staring eyes. Making himself very amiable to the infant phenome-non, was an inebriated elderly gentleman, in the last depths of shabbiness, who played the calm and virtuous old men; and paying especial court to Mrs Crummles was another elderly gentleman, a shade more respectable, who played the irascible old men – those funny fellows who have nephews in the army, and perpetually run about with thick sticks to compel them to marry heiresses. Besides these, there was a roving-looking person in a rough greatcoat, who strode up and down in front of the lamps, flourishing a dress cane, and rattling away, in an undertone, with great vivacity, for the amusement of an ideal audience. He was not quite so young as he had been, and his figure was rather running to seed; but there was an air of exaggerated gentility about him, which bespoke the hero of swaggering comedy. There was, also, a little group of three or four young men, with lantern jaws and thick eyebrows, who were conversing in one corner; but they seemed to be of secondary importance, and laughed and talked together without attracting any attention.

The ladies were gathered in a little knot by themselves round the rickety table before mentioned. There was Miss Snevellicci – who could do anything, from a medley dance to Lady Macbeth, and always played some part in blue silk knee-smalls at her benefit – glancing, from the depths of her coal-scuttle straw bonnet, at Nicholas, and affecting to be absorbed in the recital of a diverting story to her friend Miss Ledrook, who had brought her work, and was making up a ruff in the most natural manner possible. There was Miss Belvawney – who seldom aspired to speaking parts, and usually went on as a page in white silk hose, to stand with one leg bent, and contemplate the audience, or to go in and out after Mr Crummles in stately tragedy – twisting up the ringlets of the beautiful Miss Bravassa, who had once had her likeness taken 'in character' by an engraver's apprentice, whereof impressions were hung up for sale in the pastry-cook's window, and the greengrocer's, and at the circulating library, and the box-office, whenever the announce bills came out for her annual night. There was Mrs Lenville, in a very limp bonnet and veil, decidedly in that way in which she would wish to be if she truly loved Mr Lenville; there was Miss Gazingi, with an imitation ermine boa tied on a loose knot round her neck, flogging Mr Crummles, junior, with both ends, in fun. Lastly, there was Mrs Grudden, in a brown cloth pelisse and a beaver bonnet, who assisted Mrs Crummles in her domestic affairs, and took money at the doors, and dressed the ladies, and swept the house, and held the prompt-book when everybody else was on for the last scene, and acted any kind of part on any emergency without ever learning it, and was put down in the bills under any name or names whatever that occurred to Mr Crummles as looking well in print.

EVTIKHI KARPOV (1859–1926), author and St Petersburg impressario, was the first producer of Chekhov's *The Seagull* at the old-fashioned Alexandrinksi Theatre in 1896. It turned out to be a disaster. (Two years later the newly-formed Moscow Art Theatre would give it a triumphant revival.) Karpov kept an account of Chekhov's reactions at rehearsals, reporting him saying, 'They act a lot, I wish there was not so much acting.'

Chekhov winced at every false note uttered by the actors and at their conventional intonations. In spite of his natural shyness, he would stop the rehearsal, interrupting a scene in the middle, and trying to explain to the players in an excited, confused fashion what he wanted to say by a certain sentence, adding invariably: 'The chief thing, my dear fellows, is to play it simply, without any theatricality: just very simply. Remember that they are all ordinary people.'

In *An Actor Prepares*, (1926) KONSTANTIN STANISLAVSKY observes:

Experience has taught me that an actor can hold the attention of an audience by himself in a highly dramatic scene for at most *seven minutes* (that is the absolute maximum!). In a quiet scene the maximum is *one minute* (this, too, is a lot!). After that the diversity of the actor's means of expression is not sufficient to hold the attention of the audience, and he is forced to repeat himself with the result that the attention of the audience slackens until the next climax, which requires new methods of presentation. But please, note that this is true only in the cases of geniuses!

GEORGE BURNS, (b. 1896):

Acting is all about honesty. If you can fake that, you've got it made.

SIMON GRAY, from *An Unnatural Pursuit and Other Pieces*, 1985:

A read-through is never mundane. For my part I find it almost impossible to listen consciously. Where ever I turn, however much I attempt to block my ears by thinking of pleasant matters like cricket and sex and the first glass of wine, or the later first Scotch of the day, every word somehow gets through. The actors get through, too.

VLADIMIR NEMIROVICH-DANCHENKO, co-founder with Stanislavsky of the Moscow Art Theatre, from *The Seagull produced by Stanislavsky*, 1925, exploring new ways to extend and school the art of acting:

Psychological development, various features of social environment, problems of morality, attempts to find ways of merging with the author, striving after simplicity and truthfulness, search for greater expressiveness of diction, mimicry, plastic pose, individual surprise, discoveries, fascination, infectiousness, daring, confidence – these were some of the hundreds of ingredients of an exciting classwork.

HESKETH PEARSON, from *The Life of Oscar Wilde*, 1946. Rehearsals for *The Importance of Being Earnest* took place in January 1895 with Sir George Alexander as producer; later Wilde gave an interview to his friend, Robert Ross, whom he had known since 1886.

Franklin Dyall, who played the part of Merriman, has given me several interesting particulars: 'I can remember very clearly the first reading of the play – Wilde's delicious enjoyment of it – delicious is the only word – the actors' conceit that only they would appreciate it – it wouldn't get over to the public . . . I don't remember that Wilde interfered at all at rehearsal – or, if he did, it was privately, as it should be done, with the producer (G. A.). His attitude towards Alexander was that of one to a friend – open – free – and creating a very nice happy atmosphere in the theatre.' That was how a member of the company saw it; but privately Wilde had a great deal to say to Alexander, who was agitated by the stream of suggestions and at length determined to put his foot down, telling Wilde that everything he wanted would be done, but preferably in his absence. 'If you don't leave us alone, we'll never be ready; so go away like a good fellow and come back again for the first performance.' Having recovered from this, Wilde said with prelatic solemnity: 'My dear Alec, I have still one more thing to say to you and to Aynesworth. So if you will both of you come and have supper with me at the Albemarle Club to-night, I shall not trouble you again.' Following a weary evening's rehearsal, Alexander, who was playing 'John Worthing', and Allan Aynesworth, who was playing 'Algernon Moncrieff', walked up St James's Street to the Albemarle, both of them feeling tired, depressed and apprehensive. Wilde, in full evening dress, met them in the hall of the Club. He laid one hand on Alexander's shoulder, saying 'My dear Alec', laid the other hand on Aynesworth's shoulder, saying 'My dear Tony', and after an impressive pause went on: 'I have only one thing to say to you. You are neither of you my favourite actor. We will now go in to supper.'

Anxious lest *Earnest* might convert the press to a favourable view of his work, he gave an interview to Robert Ross, which appeared in *The St James's Gazette* on January 18th:

'The old dramatic critics talk of having seen Macready', he said: 'that must be a very painful memory. The middle-aged boast that they can recall *Diplomacy*: hardly a pleasant reminiscence . . . They should be pensioned off and only allowed to write on politics, or theology, or bimetallism, or some subject easier than art.'

'How would you define ideal dramatic criticism?'

'As far as my work is concerned, unqualified appreciation.'

'Have you heard it said that all the characters in your play (*An Ideal Husband*) talk as you do?'

'Rumours of that kind have reached me from time to time . . . My works are dominated by myself.'

'Do you think the critics will understand your new play?' (*Earnest*.)

'I hope not.'

'What sort of play are we to expect?'

'It is exquisitely trivial, a delicate bubble of fancy, and it has its philosophy.'

'Its philosophy?'

'That we should treat all the trivial things of life seriously, and all the serious things of life with sincere and studied triviality.'

After admitting that he had no leanings towards realism, he continued: 'If a journalist is run over by a four-wheeler in the Strand, an incident I regret to say I have never witnessed, it suggests nothing to me from a dramatic point of view. Perhaps I am wrong; but the artist must have his limitations.'

'Well,' said Ross at the conclusion of the interview, 'I have enjoyed myself immensely.'

'I was sure you would. But tell me how you manage your interviews.'

'Oh, Pitman.'

'Is that your name? It's not a very *nice* name.'

Leaving the actors and critics to their own thoughts, he went off with a friend to Algiers, explaining his absence from London at such a moment to Ada Leverson: 'I begged my friend to let me stay to rehearse, but so beautiful is his nature that he declined at once.' Returning in time for the dress rehearsal on February 12th, at the close of which he went on to the stage and staggered the company by saying 'Well, Alec, I suppose we must start rehearsals for the play on Monday', he informed a press reporter, who asked him whether he thought the play would be a success 'My dear fellow, you have got it wrong. The play *is* a success. The only question is whether the first night's audience will be one.' It was.

SIMON GRAY, from *An Unnatural Pursuit and Other Pieces*, 1985:

Of course, post-coital depression is common to all read-throughs. The actors are convinced that the producer and director are already recasting; the playwright is convinced that as soon as the actors get home they'll be on the phone to their agents, demanding to be got out of this; the director is convinced that the playwright is blaming him for landing the play with a dud cast, while at the same time thinking that the actors are blaming him for landing them with a dud play.

KONSTANTIN STANISLAVSKY, from *My Life in Art*, 1924:

I hated all falsehood on the stage, especially theatrical falsehood. I began to hate the theatre in the theatre, and I was beginning to look for genuine life in it, not ordinary life, of course, but artistic life. Perhaps at the time I was not able to distinguish between the one and the other. Besides, I understood them only externally. But even external truth helped me to create truthful and interesting mise-en-scenes which set me on the road to truth; truth gave birth to feeling, and feeling aroused creative intuition.

KENNETH TYNAN in *A View of the English Stage*, 1976, on two distinguished English directors:

Having closely compared Peter Brook's production of *Titus Andronicus* with Peter Hall's production of *Cymbeline*, I am persuaded that

93

these two young directors should at once go into partnership. I have even worked out business cards for them:

Hall & Brook, Ltd, the Home of Lost Theatrical Causes. Collapsing plays shored up, unspeakable lines glossed over, unactable scenes made bearable. Wrecks salvaged, ruins refurbished: Unpopular plays at popular prices. Masterpieces dealt with only if neglected. Shakespearian juvenilia and senilia our speciality: if it can walk, we'll make it run. Bad last acts no obstacle: if it peters out, call Peter in. Don't be fobbed off with Glenvilles, Woods, or Zadeks: look for the trademark – Hall & Brook.

WILLIAM POEL, teacher and director, from *Monthly Letters*, 1929:

Not only can children be taught acting, but better results can sometimes be obtained from teaching them than are possible when the same time and trouble are devoted to 'grown-ups' . . . The preparation of *The Comedy of Errors*, for performance by Jewish children chosen from a mixed school of girls and boys, was a unique experience. The animated youngsters did not regard their task as class instruction. They refused to sit down, or to sit still, or to leave off talking, or to pay attention to what anyone else was saying or doing when they had nothing to do themselves.

CHARLES DICKENS, from a letter written from Devonshire Terrace, 28 February 1848, to the London theatrical costumiers Nathan's (established 1790):

Mr Charles Dickens begs to inform Mr Nathan that he and Mr Lemon will call on Mr Nathan on Wednesday morning punctually at 12 to see all the gentlemen's dresses and satisfy themselves that everything is complete. The polished leather shoes with red heels which were sent to

Mr Nathan with Mr Dickens's dress are for Mr Dickens's animal magnetism and with fine paste buckles.

Attributed to SIR PETER USTINOV (b. 1921), actor, playwright and raconteur:

The French theatre is a playwright's theatre; the English an actor's theatre; the American is a director's theatre.

HAROLD CLURMAN (1901–80), American director and critic, offers advice in his book *On Directing*, 1972:

What do you do about the resistant actor, the one who disagrees with your interpretation of a part?

Before answering the question point blank it is important to realize that refractoriness in an actor has diverse, not always immediately recognizable, psychological causes. Vanity may enter into it, or a too-great susceptibility to criticism, a fear of disapproval, a 'star' complex, unfamiliarity with the director's mode of procedure and other peculiarities.

Every director invents or improvises 'tricks' to deal with the individual actor's hang-ups. An actor in whose talent Stanislavsky believed lacked self-confidence. He was always breaking down with a sense of inadequacy after his finest flights. Stanislavsky instructed his company to prepare placards on which were inscribed something like 'Y is a superb artist.' Whenever Stanislavsky noticed that an attack of inferiority tremens was about to overpower the actor, he would call on the others to parade around the despondent man. This always produced the desired effect: the actor felt refreshed.

In directing Thomas Mitchell in the touring company of *Death of a Salesman* I found that no matter how brief a remark I made about some small point, he would elaborate with extended comments of his own to show me not only that he had understood what I had said, but that he understood more and better. After all, he was a veteran actor and director many years before I had begun my career. I realized that if I betrayed impatience or attempted to silence him he would resent it. On the other hand, if I let him continue to interpolate his disquisitions at every bit of direction I proposed, the rehearsals would deteriorate into hours of futile discourse.

I ceased offering him any direct guidance. I would turn instead to whomever he was playing a scene with and say something like this: 'You are annoyed because your father [Mitchell] has just reprimanded you,' or 'Willy [Mitchell] has begun to plead with you so touchingly that you answer in kind,' or 'You see in Willy's face the clouds of anger gather and you try to calm his impending fury.' In other words, I directed Mitchell through his partners in the scene. The stratagem worked.

But my principal maxim in cases of personal difficulty with an actor is: Never, never, never win an argument with him, never persuade him that he is 'wrong,' just get him to do what you want! The director who beats an actor down by the force of his own authority does so at his own cost. The director-martinet is an obsolete phenomenon today – and should be. A director who insists that he is always absolutely right is indulging his own ego. Much rehearsal time is wasted through such indulgence.

Still! When an actor tells me that he differs with me, I usually say, 'Don't talk, *show me*.' If his demonstration fails to convince me, I explain why what he has shown me doesn't fulfil the play's or the scene's demands. Or I choose two or three other possible directives, not previously proposed, which he may follow. The actor more often than not will then turn back to the directorial suggestions which he had initially rejected.

Though I am given to close analysis of all the interpretive problems which may arise at rehearsal, I am aware that too much cerebration of this sort tends to be redundant and obstructive.

In casting *The Time of the Cuckoo*, I had Katina Paxinou in mind for a certain part. Arthur Laurents, the author, had reservations on this score. We chose another actress: Lydia St Clair. But the Paxinou image persisted in my thinking. I directed Miss St Clair as if the Greek actress were playing the role. After the first major run-through Miss St

Clair said, 'I'm bad in this role. If you wanted it acted as you have directed it, you should have cast Katina Paxinou.' 'I never thought of such a thing,' I lied. 'Please show me how you would prefer to play the part.' She did, and was excellent. Thank heavens she 'won'!

The actor is seen on the stage, not the director. It is also important to realize that there is a moment – very late in the rehearsal or preview period – when the actor knows more about the part he is playing than the director. The director must be ever vigilant in seeing that the actor doesn't become sidetracked in his performance; he must be kept 'in line.' But the role is finally the actor's possession.

An actor, after due compensation of course, may be dismissed. I have very rarely had recourse to this method of improving the quality of a production.

It is rare that one actor's advice to another is recorded. The warning given by the Shakespearean actor Sir Donald Wolfit (1902–68) to his colleague Michael Redgrave, who was about to play King Lear, is well-known. 'Watch your Fool,' said Wolfit. The American actor EDWIN BOOTH (1833–93), however, had more detailed recommendations to offer a would-be Iago in 1855:

Do not smile, or sneer, or glower, – try to impress even *the audience* with your sincerity. 'Tis better, however, always to ignore the audience; if you can forget that you are a 'shew' you will be natural. The more sincere your manner, the more devilish your deceit. I think the 'light comedian' should play the villain's part, not the 'heavy man'; I mean the Shakespearian villains. Iago should appear to be what all but the audience believe he is. Even when alone, there is little need to remove the mask entirely. Shakespeare spares you that trouble.

Don't *act* the villain, don't *look* it or *speak* it (by scowling and growing, I mean), but *think* it all the time. Be genial, sometimes jovial, always gentlemanly. Quick in motion as in thought; lithe and sinuous as a snake. A certain bluffness (which my temperament does not afford) should be added to preserve the military flavour of the character; in this particular I fail utterly, my Iago lacks the soldierly quality.

Michael Billington (b. 1939), theatre critic, from *Peggy Ashcroft*, 1988:

Despite these initial uncertainties, Peggy had a very clear idea of the character she was playing. Indeed, not for the first time, her total immersion in a role made her almost proprietorial in her attitude towards it. 'Peggy herself,' Nunn recalls, 'had become obsessed with Katharine of Aragon to the point where she brought into rehearsals every day, a kind of defence of the character. She was on Katharine's side to the extent that she was against Shakespeare's. She would turn up with extra lines from the historical trial or from Katharine's letters and try and put them into the text. I had to argue that Shakespeare is not interested in that, so it doesn't matter if we are being historically inaccurate. Shakespeare is loading the dice and we have to help him. That is why Katharine is, to some extent, a tragic figure; she is much maligned in this version but the play goes on to other things. But, although we had minor disagreements, I don't think I ever argued Peggy out of her conviction that she was not playing Katharine but that she *was* Katharine.'

William Poel, from *Monthly Letters*, 1929:

The fault of English actors in Shakespeare is over-emphasis, which tends to rob a sentence of its meaning. Most actors, if they emphasize the right words will stress the wrong ones too, so that the thought which lies behind the speaker's words is not expressed.

KONSTANTIN STANISLAVSKY, from *My Life in Art*, 1924:

My 'system' is divided into two main parts: (1) the inner and the outer work of the actor on himself, and (2) the inner and outer work of the actor on his part. The inner work on the actor himself is based on a psychic technique which enables him to evoke a creative state of mind during which inspiration descends on him more easily. The actor's external work on himself consists of the preparation of his bodily mechanism for the embodiment of his part and the exact presentation of its inner life. The work on the part consists of the study of the spiritual essence of a dramatic work, the germ from which it has emerged and which defines its meaning as well as the meaning of all its parts.

MIKHAIL BULGAKOV, as recorded in *Manuscripts Don't Burn* by J. A. E. Curtis, 1991:

31 DECEMBER 1931. MOSCOW
To Konstantin Stanislavsky (joint director of the Moscow Arts Theatre)

I wanted to write this letter to you the day after the rehearsal of the party scene in *Dead Souls*. But in the first place I was shy, and secondly I wasn't in the Theatre (I had a cold).

The purpose of this informal letter is to express to you the delight that I have been carrying around with me during these past days. In the space of three hours before my very eyes you transformed the key scene, which had frozen and got stuck, into something alive.

Theatrical magic does exist!

It arouses the highest hopes in me and revives my spirits when I am feeling low. I find it difficult to say what delighted me the most. I don't know, truly. Perhaps your remark about Manilov: 'You mustn't say anything or ask him about anything, because he would instantly glue himself to you' – that was the high point. It's an astonishing definition, precisely in a theatrical sense, and as for your demonstration of how it should be done – that showed the most profound mastery!

I do not worry about Gogol when you are at the rehearsal. Through you he will come. He will come amid laughter in the first scenes of the performance, and in the last he will go off, covered in a shroud of profound meditations. He will come.

NOËL COWARD, from *The Noel Coward Diaries* (ed. Graham Payn and Sheridan Morley, 1982). Binkie is the impresario Hugh Beaumont; the first Gladys mentioned is Gladys Calthrop, Coward's scenic designer; Gladys Cooper (1888–1971), actress and great beauty; Judy Campbell (b. 1916), actress; Ivor Brown (1891–1974), drama critic of the *Observer* from 1928 to 1954. These entries are from 1951:

Thursday 7 June
Three hours with Binkie talking about *Relative Values* – everything he said was sensible and, I think, right. He wants it in three acts instead of two and strengthened here and there. Left him finally to go to a cocktail party at Annie Rothermere's for the Duke of Windsor – did not stay long. Then went to Gladys and told her, as I had discussed with Binkie, the news that I would be having a new set-up for *Relative Values*. She behaved superbly, as always, and I believe in her secret heart she is relieved. At all events she was very fine indeed.

Monday 10 September
Reading of the play at 2.30 – very satisfactory. Gladys Cooper obviously going to be wonderful, although slow at learning. Judy Campbell read brilliantly – everybody good.

Thursday 27 September
Disastrous rehearsal owing to Gladys knowing less and less. I am really getting worried. She faffs and stammers and we can never open on Monday fortnight as things are now.

Tuesday 9 October
Rehearsal good up to the middle of act two, then disaster.
Decided to go to evening word rehearsal – absolute agony but still kept my temper. Gladys really trying hard and I have to admit that,

angry as I am with her for not learning the play as I asked her to, she is so good an actress that I have to forgive her. Also I am fond of her. It is the greatest strain to hear her day after day, but at least she is being good about her clothes. She really cannot retain lines. She will be brilliant eventually but, oh, the poor company – and poor me!

Thursday 29 November
Well, well, what a surprise! Rave notices. Quite a lot of them irritating and ill-written but all, with the exception of the dear little *Daily Mirror*, enthusiastic and wonderful box-office. This should mean a smash hit – very nice too.

Sunday 2 December
All Sunday papers virtually rave notices except Ivor Brown, who was a bit pernickety and obviously had not listened to the play very carefully.

W. MACQUEEN-POPE, theatre historian on a production of *Macbeth* by the actor-manager Sir Herbert Beerbohm Tree, from *Carriages at Eleven: The Story of the Edwardian Theatre*, 1947:

At rehearsals of *Macbeth* he made some famous cracks. He had real Guardsmen for the armies in the battle scene. These men entered into the spirit of the fight with gusto and laid about them so heartily that their swords chopped pieces off the scenery and smacked against the backcloth. 'Soldiers, soldiers,' shouted Tree. 'Listen to me. Never hit a backcloth when it's down.' And later, when an over-zealous soldier had inflicted a slight flesh wound on his stage opponent, he declared: 'I make a ruling. Any one soldier found killing any other soldier will be fined.'

KITTY BLACK, writing in *Upper Circle*, reveals more about Sir John Gielgud's 1942 production of *Macbeth*:

From the first the disasters that seem to dog the Scottish play began to accumulate. First, William Walton disappeared. His agent had no idea where he was and as the music he had been commissioned to write had been conceived as an accompaniment to all the witches' scenes, which were to be spoken rhythmically against a recorded score, nobody could rehearse anything final until the composer had set down what had been agreed with the director. One day the office boy came into my room saying: 'There's a bloke outside who says he's supposed to be composing the music for *Macbeth*.'

'Mr Walton, Mr Walton,' I cried, hurrying out to meet him, 'where have you been? Where is the music?'

'I haven't written it yet,' he replied.

'Not written it!' I gasped. 'But we need it right away.'

'It won't take long,' he replied and proceeded to explain that composing the twenty-odd minutes of music required would barely take him a week, and he was as good as his word. He attended only one run-through of the play, made careful notes and when the score was delivered, every fanfare and musical bridge was correctly timed to the very last second. A piano version was made to enable the witches to rehearse their 'Double double' bits and eventually the whole thing was recorded by HMV on acetate one/sided 78s with thirty members of the LPO conducted by Ernest Irving. They over-ran the recording session by an incredible amount of overtime and poor John had to produce a personal cheque as nobody would leave the studio until every last penny had been paid. Came the day when there was a run-through of the play with the music, and in the empty theatre I felt like Ludwig of Bavaria listening to the final versions of *Tannhäuser* or *Lohengrin*.

John had put together a tremendously complicated effects score with wind howling at all the climaxes, bells ringing, doors being hammered on, etc. and the only way all this could be coordinated was for two operators – Mary and Viola – to manipulate the panatropes – gramophones with pick-up arms that could be spotted on to any given groove of the 78s – with the effects records on one machine and the Walton music on the other. John kept changing his mind and adding or subtracting effects with the result that finally there were one hundred and forty separate cues for effects, while the music was fed in to complement or underline the action. After the final matinée, John came to Viola and asked her to add another wind cue to the plot.

'But Mr Gielgud, there's only one more performance,' wailed the harassed stage manager.

'Yes, I know, but I *would* like to hear it just once,' said John, and who could resist him?

PETER BROOK, from *The Ages of Gielgud: An Actor at Eighty*, 1984:

Despite his great gifts as a director, as an actor, he needs to be directed. When he develops a part, he has too many ideas: they pile in so fast, hour after hour, day after day, that in the end the variation on top of variation, the detail added to details all overload and clog his original impulses. When we worked together, I found that the most important time was just before the first performance, when I had to help him ruthlessly to scrap ninety per cent of his over-rich material and remind him of what he had himself discovered at the start. Deeply self-critical, he would always cut and discard without regret. When we did *Measure for Measure* he was inspired by the name of Angelo and spent long, secret hours with the wigmaker, preparing an angelic wig of shoulder-length blond locks. At the dress rehearsal no one was allowed to see him, until he came on to the stage, delighted at his new disguise. To his surprise, we all howled our disapproval. 'Ah!' he sighed, 'Goodbye, my youth!' There were no regrets and the next day he made a triumph, appearing for the first time with a bald head.

ANTON CHEKHOV in a letter:

You tell me that people cry at my plays. I've heard others say the same. But that is not why I wrote them. It is Alexeyev [Stanislavsky] who made my characters into cry-babies. All I wanted was to say honestly to people: 'Have a look at yourselves and see how bad and dreary your lives are!' The important thing is that people should realize that, for when they do, they will certainly create another and better life for themselves. I will not live to see it, but I know that it will be quite different, quite unlike our present life. And so long as this different life does not exist, I shall go on saying to people again and again: 'Please, understand that your life is bad and dreary!' What is there in this to cry about?

And in conversation with a friend:

Take my *Cherry Orchard*. Is it my *Cherry Orchard*? With the exception of two or three parts nothing in it is mine. I am describing life, ordinary life, and not blank despondency. They either make me into a cry-baby or into a bore. They invent something about me out of their own heads, anything they like, something I never thought of or dreamed about. This is beginning to make me angry.

THOMAS DE CHABHAM of Salisbury, late thirteenth century:

There are three kinds of HISTRIONES [actors]. Some transform and transfigure their bodies in indecent dance and gesture, and without any decency unclothe themselves and wear grotesque masks. There are others who have no definite profession, but act as vagabonds, not having any permanent home; they frequent the Courts of the great and say scandalous and shameful things concerning those who are not present so as to delight the rest. There is also a third class of *Histriones* who play musical instruments for the delight of men, and of these there are two types. Some frequent drinking places and lewd gatherings, and sing their stanzas to move men to lasciviousness. There are others, who are called *Jongleurs*, who sing of the gestes [actions] of princes and the lives of the saints.

Konstantin Stanislavsky, from *An Actor Prepares*, 1926:

When the inner world of the man the actor is observing is revealed into his actions, thoughts, or impulses, the actor should devote all his attention to the study of those actions. He should ask himself, 'Why did this man act thus and not thus? What was he thinking of?' and draw his own conclusions, define his attitude to the observed object, and try to understand the character of the man. When after a prolonged and penetrating process of observation and investigation he is successful in this task, he will obtain valuable creative material for his work on the stage. It often happens, however, that the inner life of the man the actor is observing is not accessible to his reason, but only to his intuition. In that case, he should try to find a way into the innermost recesses of the man's mind and look there for the material of his creative work with the help of as it were, 'the antennae of his own feelings'. This process requires very delicate powers of observation of the actor's own subconscious mind; for his ordinary attention is not sufficiently penetrating for probing into the living human soul in search of his material. In this complex process of looking for the most delicate emotional creative material, which cannot be perceived by his consciousness, the actor must rely on his common sense, experience of life, sensibility and intuition. While waiting for science to discover the practical approaches towards an understanding of a man's soul, the actor must do his best to learn how to discern the logic and consistency of its feelings and workings. This may help him to discover the best methods of finding the subconscious creative material in the external as well as the internal life of man.

MIKHAIL BULGAKOV, 5 November 1938:

What an unpleasant book Stanislavsky's *An Actor Prepares* is. It's superfluous. Even if you were to learn it off by heart you still wouldn't become an actor. And it's deadly dull.

HAROLD CLURMAN on failure, from *On Directing*, 1972:

A sixteen-year-old student once asked me, '*What is the worst thing that happens to a director?*'

My answer was: 'You see from all I've told you how thoughtfully, how painstakingly, how sincerely and how knowledgeably I labor on a production. Yet for all that my efforts to bring about the hoped for result may be in vain. The magic doesn't happen. I fail.'

'What do you do then?' the candid youth asked.

'I forgive myself.'

4

Performances & Players

Once the curtain rises, the physical presence of author, director, designer, producer and most of the other contributors to a theatrical enterprise is no longer of any importance. Their work is done. The onus now is on actors and audience.

First nights are hell; yet close friends and allies of the participants insist on attending. Some playwrights are brave enough to sit in the audience; others stand at the back of the stalls; W. S. Gilbert used to pace the Thames embankment, timing his return to the theatre to coincide with the end of the performance. In our contemporary theatre, drama critics from the daily newspapers, magazines and periodicals occupy a great number of seats. To see them rushing for the exits at the fall of the final curtain, even before the applause has begun is, to put it mildly, disheartening. Second nights are purgatory but, thankfully, are rarely well attended.

Most first nights are rounded off with some sort of celebration – a party perhaps, drinks in the bar on the management (red or white wine, Cheddar cheese stabbed with a toothpick) or small dinners in restaurants and wine bars. Then home to wait for the reviews, which might mean waiting for anything up to three days.

What follows is really about actors, called in ancient days hypocrites, which can mean either 'interpreters of dreams and riddles' or 'answerers of questions'. There are also observations, descriptions and reconstructions of evenings in the theatre: first nights, actors in performance, the reaction of audiences, without whose presence the *whole enterprise becomes entirely pointless, the aftermath, the expectations of success or failure. Only those reviews that give a flavour of the performance witnessed have been included.*

T. S. ELIOT from *Old Possum's Book of Practical Cats*, 1939:

Gus: The Theatre Cat

Gus is the Cat at the Theatre Door.
His name, as I ought to have told you before,
Is really Asparagus. That's such a fuss
To pronounce, that we usually call him just Gus.
His coat's very shabby, he's thin as a rake,
And he suffers from palsy that makes his paw shake.
Yet he was, in his youth, quite the smartest of Cats –
But no longer a terror to mice and to rats.

For he isn't the Cat that he was in his prime;
Though his name was quite famous, he says, in its time.
And whenever he joins his friends at their club
(Which takes place at the back of the neighbouring pub)
He loves to regale them, if someone else pays,
With anecdotes drawn from his palmiest days.
For he once was a Star of the highest degree –
He has acted with Irving, he's acted with Tree.
And he likes to relate his success on the Halls,
Where the Gallery once gave him seven cat-calls.
But his grandest creation, as he loves to tell,
Was Firefrorefiddle, the Fiend of the Fell.

'I have played,' so he says, 'every possible part,
And I used to know seventy speeches by heart.
I'd extemporize back-chat, I knew how to gag,
And I knew how to let the cat out of the bag.
I knew how to act with my back and my tail;
With an hour of rehearsal, I never could fail.
I'd a voice that would soften the hardest of hearts,
Whether I took the lead, or in character parts.
I have sat by the bedside of poor Little Nell;
When the Curfew was rung, then I swung on the bell.
In the Pantomime season I never fell flat,

And I once understudied Dick Whittington's Cat.
But my grandest creation, as history will tell,
Was Firefrorefiddle, the Fiend of the Fell.'

Then, if someone will give him a toothful of gin,
He will tell how he once played a part in *East Lynne*.
At a Shakespeare performance he once walked on pat,
When some actor suggested the need for a cat.
He once played a Tiger – could do it again –
Which an Indian Colonel pursued down a drain.
And he thinks that he still can, much better than most,
Produce blood-curdling noises to bring on the Ghost.
And he once crossed the stage on a telegraph wire,
To rescue a child when a house was on fire.
And he says: 'Now, these kittens, they do not get trained
As we did in the days when Victoria reigned.
They never get drilled in a regular troupe,
And they think they are smart, just to jump through a hoop.'

And he'll say, as he scratches himself with his claws,
'Well, the Theatre's certainly not what it was.
These modern productions are all very well,
But there's nothing to equal, from what I hear tell,
      That moment of mystery
      When I made history
As Firefrorefiddle, the Fiend of the Fell.'

ANTONY ASTON, a wild Irish actor, whose precise dates of birth and death are unknown but who flourished in the first half of the eighteenth century, recorded a description of Thomas Betterton (?1635–1710), the greatest actor of the Restoration period:

Mr Betterton, although a superlative good actor, laboured under an ill figure, being clumsily made, having a great head, short, thick neck, stooped in the shoulders, and had fat short arms which he rarely lifted higher than his stomach . . . He had little eyes and a broad face, a little pock-bitten, a corpulent body, with thick legs and large feet. He was better to meet than to follow, for his aspect was serious, venerable and majestic – in his latter time a little paralytic. His voice was low and grumbling; yet he could time it by an artful climax which enforced universal attention even from the fops and orange-girls.

Yet SAMUEL PEPYS had this to say about Betterton on 28 May 1663:

And so the Duke's house; and there saw Hamlet done, giving us fresh reason never to think enough of Mr Betterton.

There seem to be more attempts to describe the performances of David Garrick (1717–79) than any other actor. Indeed, one Joshua Steele, in 1775, in *An Essay Towards Establishing The Melody & Measure Of Speech To Be Expressed And Perpetuated By Peculiar Symbols*, tried to record Garrick's inflections in soliloquy of Hamlet but, alas, the symbols are too peculiar to be intelligible. Others used more conventional means. HENRY FIELDING (1707–54), for example, in *Tom Jones*:

As soon as the play, which was *Hamlet, Prince of Denmark*, began, Partridge was all attention, nor did he break silence till the entrance of the ghost; upon which he asked Jones, 'What man that was in the strange dress; something,' said he, 'like what I have seen in a picture. Sure it is not armour, is it?' Jones answered, 'That is the ghost.' To which Partridge replied with a smile, 'Persuade me to that, sir, if you can. Though I can't say I ever actually saw a ghost in my life, yet I am certain I should know one, if I saw him, better than that comes to. No, no, sir, ghosts don't appear in such dresses as that, neither.' In this mistake, which caused much laughter in the neighbourhood of Partridge, he was suffered to continue, 'till the scene between the ghost and Hamlet, when Partridge gave that credit to Mr Garrick, which he had denied to Jones, and fell into so violent a trembling, that his knees knocked against each other, Jones asked him what was the matter, and whether he was afraid of the warrior upon the stage? 'O la! sir,' said he, 'I perceive now it is what you told me. I am not afraid of anything; for I know it is but a play: and if it was really a ghost, it could do no harm at such a distance, and in so much company; and yet if I was frightened, I am not the only person.' 'Why, who,' cries Jones, 'dost thou take to be such a coward here besides thyself?' 'Nay, you may call me coward if you will; but if that little man there upon the stage is not frightened, I never saw any man frightened in my life. Ay, ay; *go along with you*! Ay, to be sure! Who's fool then? Will you? Lud have mercy upon such fool-hardiness! – Whatever happens it is good enough for you. – *Follow you?* I'd follow the devil as soon. Nay, perhaps, it is the devil – for they say he can put on what likeness he pleases. – Oh! here he is again. – *No farther!* No, you have gone far enough already; farther than I'd have gone for all the King's dominions.' Jones offered to speak, but Partridge cried, 'Hush, hush, dear sir, don't you hear him!' And during the whole speech of the ghost, he sat with his eyes fixed partly on the ghost, and partly on Hamlet, and with his mouth open; the same passions which succeeded each other in Hamlet, succeeding likewise in him.

When the scene was over, Jones said, 'Why, Partridge, you exceed my expectations. You enjoy the play more than I conceived possible.' 'Nay, sir,' answered Partridge, 'if you are not afraid of the devil, I can't help it; but to be sure it is natural to be surprized at such things, though I know there is nothing in them: not that it was the ghost that surprized me neither; for I should have known that to have been only a man in a strange dress: but when I saw the little man so frightened himself, it was that which took hold of me.' 'And dost thou imagine then, Partridge,' cries Jones, 'that he was really frightened?' 'Nay, sir,' said Partridge, 'did not you yourself observe afterwards, when he found out it was his own father's spirit, and how he was murdered in the garden, how his fear forsook him by degrees, and he was struck dumb with sorrow, as it were, just as I should have been, had it been my own case. – But hush! O la! What noise is that? There he is again. – Well, to be certain, though I know there is nothing at all in it, I am glad I am not down yonder, where those men are.' Then turning his eyes again upon Hamlet, 'Ay, you may draw your sword; what signifies a sword against the power of the devil?'

During the second act, Partridge made very few remarks. He greatly admired the fineness of the dresses; nor could he help observing upon the king's countenance. 'Well,' said he, 'how people may be deceived by faces? *Nulla fides fronti* is, I find a true saying. Who would think, by looking in the king's face, that he had ever committed a murder?' He then enquired after the ghost; but Jones, who intended he should be surprised, gave him no other satisfaction, than 'that he might possibly see him again soon, and in a flash of fire.'

Partridge sat in fearful expectation of this; and now, when the ghost made his next appearance, Partridge cried out, 'There, sir, now; what say you now? Is he frightened now or no? As much frightened as you think me, and, to be sure, nobody can help some fears, I would not be in so bad a condition as what's his name, Squire Hamlet, is there, for all the world. Bless me! What's become of the spirit? As I am a living soul, I thought I saw him sink into the earth.' 'Indeed, you saw right,' answered Jones. 'Well, well,' cries Partridge, 'I know it is only a play; and besides, if there was anything in all this, Madame Miller would not laugh so: for as to you, sir, you would not be afraid, I believe, if the devil was here in person. – There, there – Ay, no wonder you are in such a passion; shake the vile wicked wretch to pieces. If she was my own mother I should serve her so. To be sure, all duty to a mother is forfeited by such wicked doings. – Ay, go about your business: I hate the sight of you.'

Our critic was now pretty silent till the play, which Hamlet introduces before the king. This he did not at first understand, 'till Jones explained it to him; but he no sooner entered into the spirit of it, than he began to bless himself that he had never committed murder. Then turning to Mrs Miller, he asked her, 'If she did not imagine the king looked as if he was touched; though he is,' said he, 'a good actor, and doth all he can to hide it. Well, I would not have so much to answer for, as that wicked man there hath, to sit upon a much higher chair than he sits upon. – No wonder he run away; for your sake I'll never trust an innocent face again.'

The grave-digging scene next engaged the attention of Partridge, who expressed much surprize at the number of skulls thrown upon the stage. To which Jones answered, 'That it was one of the most famous burial-places about town.' 'No wonder then,' cries Partridge, 'that the place is haunted. But I never saw in my life a worse grave-digger. I had a sexton, when I was clerk, that should have dug three graves while he is digging one. The fellow handles a spade as if it was the first time he had ever had one in his hand. Ay, ay, you may sing. You had rather sing than work, I believe.' – Upon Hamlet's taking up the skull, he cried out, 'Well, it is strange to see how fearless some men are: I never could bring myself to touch anything belonging to a dead man on any account. – He seemed frightened enough too at the ghost I thought. *Nemo omnibus horis sapit.*'

Little more worth remembering occurred during the play; at the end of which Jones asked him, 'which of the players he had liked best?' To this he answered, with some appearance of indignation at the question. 'The king without doubt.' 'Indeed, Mr Partridge,' says Mrs Miller, 'you are not of the same opinion with the town; for they are all agreed, that Hamlet is acted by the best player who was ever on the stage.' 'He the best player!' cries Partridge, with a contemptuous sneer, 'Why I could act as well as he myself. I am sure if I had seen a ghost, I should have looked in the very same manner, and done just as he did. And then, to be sure, in that scene, as you called it, between him and his mother, where you told me he acted so fine, why, Lord help me, any man, that is, any good man, that had had such a mother, would have done exactly the same. I know you are only joking with me; but, indeed, madam, though I was never at a play in London, yet I have seen acting before in the country; and the king for my money; he speaks all his words distinctly, half as loud again as the other. – Anybody may see he is an actor.'

While Mrs Miller was thus engaged in conversation with Partridge, a lady came up to Mr Jones, whom he immediately knew to be Mrs Fitzpatrick. She said, she had seen him from the other part of the gallery, and had taken that opportunity of speaking to him, as she had something to say, which might be of great service to himself. She then acquainted him with her lodgings, and made him an appointment the next day in the morning; which, upon recollection, she presently changed to the afternoons at which time Jones promised to attend her.

Thus ended the adventure at the playhouse; where Partridge had afforded great mirth, not only to Jones and Mrs Miller, but to all who sat within hearing, who were more attentive to what he said, than to anything that passed on the stage.

He durst not go to bed all that night, for fear of the ghost; and for many nights after, sweat two or three hours before he went to sleep, with the same apprehensions, and waked several times in great horrors, crying out, 'Lord have mercy upon us! there it is.'

From *Lichtenberg's Visits to England*, 1775:

At these words [Horatio's 'Look, my lord, it comes'] Garrick turns sharply and at the same moment staggers back two or three paces with his knees giving way under him; his hat falls to the ground and both his arms, especially the left, are stretched out nearly to their full length, with the hands as high as his head, the right arm more bent and the hand lower, and the fingers apart; his mouth is open: thus he stands rooted to the spot, with legs apart, but no loss of dignity, supported by his friends.

RICHARD CUMBERLAND, then in the sixth form at Westminster School, but later to become a prominent dramatist, wrote an account of David Garrick as the young Lothario in Nicholas Rowe's *The Fair Penintent*, 1746:

Little Garrick enters young and light and alive in every muscle and feature; heavens what a transition! It seemed as if a whole century had been stepped over in the transition of a single scene; old things were done away, and a new order at once brought forward, bright and luminous, and clearly destined to dispel the barbarisms and bigotry of a tasteless age, too long attached to the prejudices of custom, and superstitiously devoted to the illusions of imposing declamation.

LAURENCE STERNE (1713–68) in *Tristram Shandy*, 1761:

'And how did Garrick speak the soliloquy last night?' 'Oh against all rule, My Lord, Most ungrammatically! Betwixt the substantive and the adjective, which should agree together in number, case, and gender, he made a breech thus – stopping as if the point wanted settling; and betwixt the nominative case, which your Lordship knows must govern the verb, he suspended his voice in the Epilogue a dozen times, three seconds and three fifths by a stop-watch, my Lord, each time!' – 'Admirable grammarian! But in suspending his voice was the sense suspended likewise? Did no expression of attitude, or countenance fill up the chasm? Was the eye silent? Did you narrowly look?' 'I looked only at the stop-watch, My Lord.' – 'Excellent observer!'

DR J. DORAN (1807–78) reports on a comparison made between two actors, David Garrick and the handsome Irishman Spranger Barry (1719–77), in *Annals of the English Stage from Thomas Betterton to Edmund Kean*, 1888:

Perhaps, after all, the truest idea of the two Romeos may be gathered from the remark of a lady who did not pretend to be a critic, and who was guided by her feelings. 'Had I been Juliet,' she said, 'to Garrick's Romeo, – so ardent and impassioned was he, I should have expected that he would have *come up* to me in the balcony; but had I been Juliet to Barry's Romeo, so tender, so eloquent, and so seductive was he, I should certainly have *gone down* to him!'

In CHARLES DICKENS's *Great Expectations* (1862) Mr Wopsle, once the clerk of Pip's little village church, gives up his profession, goes on the stage and appears as Hamlet in the hope of 'reviving the drama'. Pip and his friend, Herbert Pocket, decide to see the performance:

On our arrival in Denmark, we found the king and queen of that country elevated in two arm-chairs on a kitchen-table, holding a Court. The whole of the Danish nobility were in attendance; consisting of a noble boy in the wash-leather boots of a gigantic ancestor, a venerable Peer with a dirty face, who seemed to have risen from the people late in life, and the Danish chivalry with a comb in its hair and a pair of white silk legs, and presenting on the whole a feminine appearance. My gifted townsman stood gloomily apart, with folded arms, and I could have wished that his curls and forehead had been more probable.

Several curious little circumstances transpired as the action proceeded. The late king of the country not only appeared to have been troubled with a cough at the time of his decease, but to have taken it with him to the tomb, and to have brought it back. The royal phantom also carried a ghostly manuscript round its truncheon, to which it had the appearance of occasionally referring, and that, too, with an air of anxiety and a tendency to lose the place of reference which were suggestive of a state of mortality. It was this, I conceive, which led to the Shade's being advised by the gallery to 'turn over!' – a recommendation which it took extremely ill. It was likewise to be noted of this majestic spirit that whereas it always appeared with an air of having been out a long time and walked an immense distance, it perceptibly came from a closely-contiguous wall. This occasioned its terrors to be received derisively. The Queen of Denmark, a very buxom lady, though no doubt historically brazen, was considered by the public to have too much brass about her; her chin being attached to her diadem by a broad band of that metal (as if she had a gorgeous toothache), her waist being encircled by another, and each of her arms by another, so that she was openly mentioned as 'the kettle-drum.' The noble boy in the ancestral boots, was inconsistent; representing himself, as it were in one breath, as an able seaman, a strolling actor, a gravedigger, a clergyman, and a person of the utmost importance at a Court fencing-match, on the authority of whose practised eye and nice discrimination the finest strokes were judged. This gradually led to a want of toleration for him, and even – on his being detected in holy orders, and declining to perform the funeral service – to the general indignation taking the form of nuts. Lastly, Ophelia was a prey to such slow musical madness, that when, in course of time, she had taken off her white muslin scarf, folded it up, and buried it, a sulky man who had been long cooling his impatient nose against an iron bar in the front row of the gallery, growled, 'Now the baby's put to bed, let's have supper!' Which, to say the least of it, was out of keeping.

Upon my unfortunate townsman all these incidents accumulated with playful effect. Whenever that undecided Prince had to ask a question or state a doubt, the public helped him out with it. As for example; on the question whether 'twas nobler in the mind to suffer, some roared yes, and some no, and some inclining to both opinions said 'toss up for it'; and quite a Debating Society arose. When he asked what should such fellows as he do crawling between earth and heaven, he was encouraged with loud cries of 'Hear, hear!' When he appeared with his stocking disordered (its disorder expressed, according to usage, by one very neat fold in the top, which I suppose to be always got up with a flat iron), a conversation took place in the gallery respecting the paleness of his leg, and whether it was occasioned by the turn the ghost had given him. On his taking the recorders – very like a little black flute that had just been played in the orchestra and handed out at the door – he was called upon unanimously for Rule Britannia. When he recommended the player not to saw the air thus, the sulky man said, 'And don't *you* do it, neither; you're a deal worse than *him!*' And I grieve to add that peals of laughter greeted Mr Wopsle on every one of these occasions.

But his greatest trials were in the churchyard: which had the appearance of a primeval forest, with a kind of small ecclesiastical washhouse on one side, and a turnpike gate on the other. Mr Wopsle, in a comprehensive black cloak, being descried entering at the turnpike, the gravedigger was admonished in a friendly way, 'Look out! Here's the undertaker a coming, to see how you're getting on with your work!' I believe it is well known in a constitutional country that Mr Wopsle could not possibly have returned the skull, after moralising over it, without dusting his fingers on a white napkin taken from his breast; but even that innocent and indispensable action did not pass without the comment 'Wai-ter!' The arrival of the body for interment (in an empty black box with the lid tumbling open), was the signal for a general joy which was much enhanced by the discovery, among the bearers, of an individual obnoxious to identification. The joy attended Mr Wopsle through his struggle with Laertes on the brink of the orchestra and the grave, and slackened no more until he had tumbled the king off the kitchen-table, and had died by inches from the ankles upward.

A bad night in the theatre. An anonymous theatre-goer, 1810:

'Maudlin Old Stagers'
FROM *THE PROMPTER*

What blind delusion or theatric rage,
Can keep that gang upon our fallen stage,
Of ragamuffins; who with scarcely brains
To stick the play-bills or to shift the scenes,
Persist to fret and strut their night along
In dull monotony and tame sing-song;
With rueful visage and a dismal whine,
Gravely burlesquing every classic line;
Maudlin old stagers, who beneath all praise,
Can no one feeling but compassion raise!

HAROLD PINTER (b. 1930) started life in the theatre as an actor. In the early 1950s he toured Ireland with Anew McMaster (1894–1962), a great actor most famous for his Othello. Pinter, in a tribute called *Mac* (1968), recalls:

Mac gave about half a dozen magnificent performances of Othello while I was with him. Even when, on the other occasions, he conserved his energies in the role, he always gave the patrons their moneysworth. At his best his was the finest Othello I have seen. His age was always a mystery, but I would think he was in his sixties at the time. Sometimes, late at night, after the show, he looked very old. But on stage in Othello he stood, well over six foot, naked to the waist, his gestures complete, final, nothing jagged, his movement of the utmost fluidity and yet of the utmost precision: stood there, dead in the centre of the role, and the great sweeping symphonic playing would begin, the rare tension and release within him, the arrest, the swoop, the savagery, the majesty and repose. His voice was unique: in my experience of an unequalled range. A bass of extraordinary echo, resonance and gut, and remarkable sweep up into tenor, when the note would hit the back of the gallery and come straight back, a brilliant, stunning sound. I remember his delivery of this line: 'Methinks (bass) it should be now a huge (bass) eclipse (tenor) of sun and moon (baritone) and that th'affrighted glove (bass) Should yawn (very deep, the abyss) at alteration.' We all watched him from the wings.

He was capable, of course, of many indifferent and offhand performances. On these occasions an edgy depression and fatigue hung over him. He would gabble his way through the part, his movement fussed, his voice acting outside him, the man himself detached from its acrobatics. At such times his eyes would fix upon the other actors, appraising them coldly, emanating a grim dissatisfaction with himself and his company. Afterwards, over a drink, he would confide: I was bad tonight, wasn't I, really awful, but the damn cast was even worse. What a lot.

Kenneth Tynan, from *He That Plays The King*, 1950:

To be present, to assist at the spinning out of events which will surely plume up and refurbish the tapestry of Western culture – is not this a pleasant thing? Had it not been fine to have snapped up and savoured the first copy of *The Rape of the Lock* as it came, cool and acid and fair, from the press? To have seen and shaken at the face of Swift as he penned the last cruel, grimy pages of *Gulliver*? To have sat by and quivered at the embarrassed wriggles of some poor questioner, swallowed up in the terrific finality of a Johnsonian 'No, sir'? My point, when at last it comes wheeling round to us, is that I have seen a public event of constellated magnitude and radiance. I have watched a transfusion of bubbling hot blood into the invalid frame of our drama. Some, I am told, boast of having seen the Chicago fire; others of having escaped the Quetta earthquake by the merest pebble's breadth; and I have known men swell as they recalled the tremendous and bloody exploits at Hiroshima. My vaunt is this: I have lived for three hours on the red brink of a volcano, and the crust of lava crumbles still from my feet. I have witnessed a performance of *Othello* in which Donald Wolfit played Iago, and Frederick Valk Othello. How hushed I was! How young and how chastened: so much so that for days afterwards, long after I had sent my final particular roar of 'Bravo' coursing and resounding about the theatre, I could speak of little but these twin giants, and the authentic ring of their titles to greatness. In the mind's middle distance, I think I perceive that other players flickered intermittently across that bare stage – that flat scene of astounding war; I can, if I screw up my memory, hear them now, grunting and twittering and shrilling. Who they were, I have not the slightest notion. They lie *perdu*: an irrelevant flurry of colour and dim noise in the midst of which gigantic things were going forward. They it was, as I think, who buzzed and rattled when the big gladiators fell fatigued. I should prefer to ignore them, thus dismissively.

Sir Henry Irving (1838–1905), actor-manager, dominated the London stage for the last thirty years of Queen Victoria's reign. In 1871 he joined the Bateman management at the Lyceum Theatre, which had been going through a bad time. Irving forced on his partners a melodrama called *The Bells* by Leopold Lewis. The actor's grandson, LAURENCE IRVING, in his biography, *Henry Irving: The Actor And His World* (1951), describes the first night:

On the night of Saturday, November 25th, the audience which assembled at the Lyceum to see the first performance of *The Bells* was neither numerous nor distinguished. When the lights went up after the preliminary farce, *My Turn Next*, the stalls contained a handful of regular patrons, the critics, and a number of gentlemen from the West End clubs who, having heard that the play contained some nonsense about a mesmerist and a murderer, had reluctantly left their dinners with the idea of having a laugh at the expense of the actors. Bateman, depressed by his failure to dress the house, hovered anxiously in the corridors. In the stage box sat Florence with the Hain Friswells; in the opposite box sat Leopold Lewis with Joseph Hatton, an American journalist, who was a friend of Irving. Lewis, who at best was an unbalanced creature, was beside himself with excitement; but for Hatton's calming influence and, at times, his physical restraint, Lewis might have communicated his nervousness to those on the stage. As the house lights were dimmed, only those in these boxes leaned forward eagerly; the rest of the house showed hardly a flicker of interest; the clubmen were prepared for boredom, the critics looked forward gloomily to belabouring half-heartedly the corpse of a play which they had already killed.

The curtain rises on the interior of an Alsatian inn. It is night. There is something unusual about the scene – a warm glow pervades the picture which is low in key and, with its carefully conceived accent of local colour, immediately establishes a certain atmosphere. Outside it is snowing; beyond the windows the white landscape stretches away into the night. An occasional gust of wind suggests an approaching storm. For fifteen minutes the burgomaster's wife, who sits by her spinning wheel near the tall stove, gossips with one or two villagers who are drinking at a table. This overture is well handled, for they are all competent actors; naturally and without undue stress, the elements of the plot are stated. The burgomaster is expected any minute to return from a visit to a nearby town; it is a wild night, the wildest since the night the Polish Jew was murdered fifteen years ago; the burgo-master's daughter and her fiancé, a Captain of Gendarmes, hear the story. At its climax there is a crash of breaking glass which proves to be a kitchen window blown open by the storm; the audience are pleasantly startled by this old, but effective, theatrical trick. This conversation continues until over it is heard the 'hurry' music which rises to a crescendo as the door at the back of the stage is burst open. There stands Mathias, a gaunt figure wearing a fur cap and heavy coat, his fur-gloved hand, which is raised in greeting, holding a heavy horsewhip. Everyone, authors and actors, has skilfully directed each word and gesture towards this moment. Mathias's shout of 'It is I!' catches the climax at its peak and marks the end of a dramatic period. In years to come, Irving's appearance at this point will be greeted by such a storm of sustained applause that at the first sign of its dying he will be forced to break it off with a decisive gesture. On this night, the first of many hundred performances which he would give as Mathias, only a ragged little volley from the two boxes greeted his appearance. He sensed at once that the house was cold and hostile. He accepted the challenge. Mathias is welcomed by his family. They have taken his heavy coat and cap and he sits down in a chair downstage centre and begins to take off his gaiters. Easily and naturally the subordinate characters drop out of focus. Though they are talking to him, the audience is forced to concentrate on his every movement. While he is putting on his shoes, he describes the mesmerist whom he has seen at Ribeauville. As he stoops to adjust the buckles, one of the villagers mentions that the mesmerist can send a man to sleep and make him disclose what weighs upon his conscience. The effect on Mathias of this word 'conscience' is best described by Gordon Craig, who watched the scene many times and has made a penetrating analysis of this all-important moment in the play, for it is now or never that Irving must gain the mastery over his audience:

'Irving was buckling his second shoe, seated, and leaning over it with his two long hands stretched down over the buckles. We suddenly saw these fingers stop their work; the crown of the head suddenly seemed to glitter and become frozen – and then, at the pace of the slowest and most terrified snail, the two hands, still motionless and dead, were seen to be coming up the side of the leg . . . the whole torso of the man, also seeming frozen, was gradually and by an almost imperceptible movement, seen to be drawing up and back, as it would straighten a little and to lean against the back of the chair on which he was seated.'

'Exactly!' Mathias whispers, in such a way that the audience are allowed to share his half-formulated fears.

Mathias recovers himself and tells his daughter there is a present for her in his coat pocket. The scene proceeds. Food and drink is brought in and set out for him on the table. He invites the old villager to join him in a glass of wine. He pours it out, but as he is raising the glass to his lips, one of the company remarks that before he came in they had been talking of the Polish Jew's winter. At the mention of the Jew his movement is interrupted and then, to hide his reaction and to steady himself, very deliberately and delicately he takes an imaginary piece of cork out of his wine. As the villagers prattle on about the Polish Jew, he puts down his glass. The throbbing jingle of sleigh bells is heard but by Mathias and the audience alone, distant at first but becoming louder as the haunted man, bending his terrified gaze upon the audience, communicates to them the horror of his hallucination. Then:

'He moves his head slowly from us – the eyes still somehow with us – and moves it to the right – taking as long as a journey to discover a truth takes. He looks to the faces on the right – nothing. Slowly the head revolves back again, down, and along the tunnels of thought and sorrow and at the end the face and eyes are bent upon those to the left of him . . . utter stillness . . . nothing there either – everyone is concerned with his or her little doings – smoking or knitting or unravelling wool or scraping a plate slowly and silently. A long pause – endless, breaking our hearts, comes down over everything, and on and on go the bells. Puzzled, motionless . . . he glides up to a standing position; never has anyone seen another rising figure which slid slowly up like that. With one arm slightly raised, with sensitive hand speaking of far-off apprehended sounds, he asks, in the voice of some woman who is frightened yet does not wish to frighten those with her:

"Don't you . . . don't you hear the sound of sledgebells on the road?"

"Sledgebells?" grumbles the smoking man; "Sledgebells?" pipes his companion; "Sledgebells?" says the wife – all of them seemingly too sleepy and comfortable to apprehend anything . . . see anything . . . or understand . . . and, as they grumble a negative suddenly he staggers and shivers from his toes to his neck, his jaws begin to chatter; the hair on his forehead, falling over a little, writhes as though it were a nest of little snakes. Everyone is on his feet at once to help:

"Caught a chill" . . . "Let's get him to bed".'

The villagers leave the inn; the family go into the kitchen to prepare some mulled wine for him. Left alone, he listens in terror to the continual jangling of the bells. He rushes to the window and, tearing aside the curtains, stares into the empty night. The stage darkens as he staggers to a chair, muttering of giddiness . . . calling on his courage. The bells cease as suddenly as they began. At this relief he turns, only to see towering over him the vision of his act of murder. As the ghostly Jew standing in his sleigh turns his grey eyes upon his murderer, Mathias gives a cry of terror and falls senseless. The curtain falls.

The perfect illusion of the vision and the actor's coup de théâtre evoke a shout of applause. But it is not sustained. The audience is puzzled. The actor is not called before the curtain. Lewis leaps from his seat and makes for the pass-door to the stage. Throughout the act he had suffered agonies of apprehension. As each cue came for the sound of bells he tugged at his luxuriant red moustache and muttered in hoarse whispers: 'The Bells! Where are they? what the devil are they about?' The sound which terrified the burgomaster brought comfort to the author, who would sink back into his chair with an audible sigh of relief. In his dressing-room, Irving is composed and coldly determined. He knows that success still hangs in the balance but that he had the audience with him for the last five minutes of the act.

The second act is concerned with the festivities on the eve of his daughter's wedding. Now that the guilty secret is out, the audience is able to appreciate keenly the actor's brilliant handling of the burgomaster's appalling mental conflict. 'He is at once,' wrote Oxenford of this passage, 'in two worlds between which there is no link – an outer world which is ever smiling, an inner world which is purgatory. Hence the dreaminess in his manner which accurately represents his frequent transitions from a display of domestic affections to the fearful work of self-communion.'

Here Irving had taken the text and forced it to serve the mood of a man being destroyed by his remorse rather than of a cunning rogue in fear of detection. The audience is moved by his infinite tenderness towards his daughter. When, alone, he counts the gold set aside for his daughter's dowry and finds a coin which came from the Jew's girdle, he picks it out and puts it on one side, murmuring: 'No, no . . . not for them, for me,' as though it was an intolerably heavy burden that he must bear alone. Involuntarily he wipes his fingers, as though wet with blood, upon his coat. When his son-in-law, the gendarme, expounding his theories about the murder of the Jew, comes perilously near the truth, Mathias's kindly indulgence and gentle raillery conceals a pounding heart and a fevered mind from all but the audience.

The frantic Lewis, when he darted behind the scenes after the second act, was able to assure Irving that the audience was with him. Irving, of course, knew that as well as a mesmerist knows when his subject passes into a controlled trance. He felt the calm assurance of a general who, having heard that his troops have turned the enemy's flank, sets in motion the frontal attack which will turn their defeat into a rout. The last act would be entirely in his hands; for twenty minutes, he, whom they knew only as an accomplished comedian, had to hold their attention with a ghastly pantomime. If for a moment his hold weakened, the drama would totter and fall into bathos from which nothing could retrieve it.

The curtain rises on a shallow scene – a small bedroom with a door on the right and opposite to it on the extreme left a curtained alcove containing a bed. Mathias is escorted to his room by his family and friends, all a little exalted by the festivities, the sound of which can still be heard below. After interminable goodnights – which strain the burgomaster's nerves to breaking point, so much is he longing for rest and solitude – they leave him. Taking off his coat, he retires into the alcove; a hand comes through the curtain and puts out the candle. The sound of revelling fades away as, at first an uncertain nebula of lights and shadows, the dim shape of a vast court of justice is revealed as the wall of the bedroom melts away. Three judges in black crêpe and red robes, the only touch of colour in a grim grisaille, sit upon the bench, flanked by advocates and officials of the court. Before them, in the well of the court, is a table upon which lie the ragged blood-stained coat and cap of the murdered Jew. As the scene resolves itself, attention is focused on a figure huddled upon a stool in front of the table. It is Mathias. He is wearing a hooded, full-skirted blouse and gaiters – the clothes he wore on the night of the crime. He is on trial for his life. The president of the court begins his examination. His deadly questioning is parried by Mathias's denials, at first truculent but becoming increasingly hysterical and defiant. The president, unable to shake the prisoner's contradictions, summons the mesmerist and, in spite of Mathias's craven protests and appeals to common justice, hands the prisoner over to him. Mathias's staring eyes are fixed upon the audience. They are the symbols of his resistance, but they droop and close as he passes into a trance. The examination proceeds, but now the prisoner is his own accuser. Step by step, at the bidding of the mesmerist, he re-enacts his crime. In a low, hollow voice, he recalls every detail of the night's horror which is graven deeply on his tortured mind. The Jew has left the inn. Mathias rises from his stool. Now, like a sleepwalker, the wretch begins to mime the pursuit and murder of the Jew – his words recording the conflicting thoughts which pass through his mind. He is crossing the snow-covered field. 'How the dogs howl on Daniel's farm!' The word 'Howl' echoes through the court and with shuddering conviction the audience identify themselves with the loneliness of the night and of the slayer. For a moment Mathias, when he reaches the place where he has planned to make his attack, believes that the Jew has already passed. He thanks God fervently for his delivery from evil – but the prayer is still on his lips as the sound of bells announces the Jew's approach. He springs upon the sleigh and strikes down his victim with a hatchet. The body tumbles to the road. A flurry of bells suggests the panic flight of the horse. He fumbles with the body – ah – the girdle – full of gold, quite full. Bending down, he lifts the cumbrous corpse onto his back and staggers with it to the lime kiln. As the Jew is consumed in the flames his eyes linger accusingly on his murderer. Mathias screams and covers his face with his hands. Exhausted, he sinks onto the stool and is huddled once more in sleep. At the president's direction the mesmerist awakens him. Mathias is shown the transcript of his deposition. In cornered rage and dismay he tears it to pieces. His appeals for justice and mercy are drowned in the president's solemn pronouncement of the death sentence. The court dissolves into uncertain shadows which harden into the severe simplicities of the burgomaster's bedroom. It is morning – his daughter's wedding day. They are knocking at the door to wake him. Behind the curtained alcove there is no sign of movement. The voices outside and the knocking on the door become more urgent. Blows are struck upon the door which is burst open. As those who have come to wake him run towards the alcove, Mathias staggers through the curtain. His face is livid with terror – no make-believe pallor but waxen features drained of blood. His hands claw at his throat. A thin, strangled voice forces its way through invisible constrictions. 'Take the rope from my neck . . . take the rope from my neck!' A strong man is in his death agony. His unseeing eyes seek pitifully to recognize the delusions of a dream. The pupils of the eyes roll upwards. The ghastly mask is petrified and tinted with the greyness of death. The limbs grow cold. As he falls, his wife catches him in her arms.

The curtain fell. For several moments the audience sat in shocked silence, which was broken by the whispering flurry of attendants as they removed a lady who had fainted in the stalls. They had witnessed the violent egress of a soul from a body – hardly able to accept it as an illusion, such was the appalling physical and spiritual intensity of the acting. Suddenly the tension was relieved – the mesmerist had broken his spell. A tumult of cheers and round upon round of applause brought up the curtain once more. There was Irving, bowing in modest acceptance of their acclaim; there was Lewis, in an ecstasy, wringing the actor's hand. Another burst of shouting and applause, and there was old Bateman, leading Irving back onto the stage, beaming all over his handsome face and patting his friend on the back. The incredible had happened. Irving's intuition had proved faultless – the fortunes of the Bateman's were saved.

At length the applause died away. The excited chatter which drowned the orchestra during the interval subsided as the curtain rose on *Pickwick*. This piece served only to impress upon those who stayed to see it the contrast between the tragedian who had appalled them as Mathias and the comedian who now diverted them with his antics as Jingle. At its conclusion, Irving received another ovation and the curtain fell for the last time.

In the foyer, the critics jostled each other impatiently as they hurried to record their impressions of that extraordinary evening. Clement Scott, who had recently been appointed to the *Daily Telegraph*, bumped into Dutton Cook of the *Pall Mall Gazette*. The old critic, who was not much given to eulogy, was full of enthusiasm and praise for everything he had seen and heard – Irving's performance, the production and the *mise en scène*. Lord Lytton was loudly voicing his envy of authors who would be lucky enough to have their plays interpreted by such an actor. Scott hurried off to write the notice which he had to submit to J. M. Levy, the founder and proprietor of the *Daily Telegraph*, at his home in Gower Street. In the early days of the paper, Levy, who was an enthusiastic playgoer, had been his own dramatic critic. He still liked to edit the theatre notices. When first nights, which he himself usually attended, fell on a Saturday when the office was closed, he insisted on the critic coming to his house and discussing what was to be said about the play. That night Levy had seen *The Bells*; when Scott came to see him after the performance he greeted him by saying: 'Tonight I have seen a great actor at the Lyceum – a great actor. There was a poor house. Write about him so that everyone shall know he is great.'

P. G. WODEHOUSE wrote a letter to his step-daughter, Leonora, whom he called Snorky, about the first night of *The Cabaret Girl*, book by George Grossmith and Wodehouse, lyrics by Wodehouse and music by Jerome Kern. The musical opened at the Winter Garden Theatre on 19 September 1922 and ran for 462 performances. The letter is dated 20 September:

Darling angel Snorky,

Well, Bill, maybe we didn't do a thing to the customers last p.m. Wake me up in the night and ask me! Honestly old egg, you never saw such a first night. The audience were enthusiastic all through the first and second acts, and they never stopped applauding during the cabaret scene in act three – you know, the scene with no dialogue but all music and spectacle. I knew that scene would go big, because the same thing happened at the dress rehearsal.

I take it from your wire this morning that you have seen the notices. They are all very good, but I'm a bit sick that they don't even refer to the lyrics! I haven't seen the evening papers yet. I hope they will continue the good work.

Leslie Henson was up in the gallery through the show!!! It must have been rotten for him, for Griffin made a tremendous hit and there wasn't a moment when the show dropped because of him. Grossmith was immense, so was Heather Thatcher. As for Dorothy Dickson, she came right out and knocked 'em cold.

This morning Mummie and I are not our usual bright selves, as we didn't get to bed till six and woke up at nine! William Boosey gave a party at the Metropole and we didn't leave till 5.30. It was rather funny — we had the Oppenheims, Justine and Walter, and Beith with us at the show, so they the Opps gave us supper at Ciro's, then went on to the Metropole at one o'clock and sat right down to another supper. Even I began to feel as if I had tasted food recently when they brought on oysters and grouse just after I had surrounded a mess of lobster and lamb (with veg.) . . . There isn't any doubt that we've got an enormous hit. The libraries have taken a lot of seats for three months, the same number they took for *Sally*, and everybody was magnificent. Every number went wonderfully, especially 'Dancing Time'.

All the leading actors of the mid-twentieth century owed much to JAMES AGATE (1877–1947), drama critic of the *Sunday Times*. On 22 October 1944 he wrote a glowing tribute to Sir John Gielgud's performance as Hamlet at the Theatre Royal, Haymarket:

Hamlet is not a young man's part. Consider how ill it becomes a stripling to hold forth on the life after death, the propriety of suicide, the nature of man, the exuberance or restraint of matrons, the actor's art, the Creator's 'large discourse.' But Mr Gielgud could not be of a better age; he is at the height of his powers; the conjunction is marvellously happy. When, fourteen years ago at the Old Vic, the curtain went up on the new Hamlet there was perhaps not very much there except infinite grace. Four years later, after the production at the New Theatre, I find that I wrote, 'The impression gathered is that of a Hamlet who can fly into the most shattering of pets.' Five years later (Lyceum), 'One's impression of this brilliant performance does not outlast the moment of its brilliance. It is cometary. That was Hamlet, that was! and the sky is empty again.' It gives me the greatest pleasure to say that now at last Mr Gielgud has stopped all the gaps.

The too-young Hamlet takes one's thoughts off this play in the way the concert-hall's infant prodigy takes them off the music; one fritters away attention wondering how all those runs and trills have been managed. Mr Gielgud is now completely and authoritatively master of this tremendous part. He is, we feel, this generation's rightful tenant of this 'monstrous Gothic castle of a poem.' He has acquired an almost Irvingesque quality of pathos, and in the passages after the play scene an incisiveness, a raillery, a mordancy worthy of the Old Man. He imposes on us this play's questing feverishness. The middle act gives us ninety minutes of high excitement and assured virtuosity; Forbes-Robertson was not more bedazzling in the 'O, what a rogue and peasant slave' soliloquy. In short, I hold that this is, and is likely to remain, the best Hamlet of our time, and that is why I urge Mr Gielgud to stick to the mantle of tragedy and leave lesser garments to others. For this actor, like John Philip Kemble, is not really a comedian. John Philip had the notion that by taking thought an actor can qualify himself for the lighter as for the more serious side of his art. This is not so. All the trying in the world would not have turned, say, Matthew Arnold into a dinner-table wit. It is the same with acting. Again, in Mr Gielgud's case, the old couplet comes to mind:

> Whene'er he tries the airy and the gay,
> Judgment, not genius, marks the cold essay.

As a comedian our First Player has no warmth, whereas as a tragedian he is all fire. He lives up to G. H. Lewes's dictum: the greatest artist is he who is greatest in the highest reaches of his art. And that is why I conjure him to stick to those róles which entitle his critics to stand up and say to all the world: This is a great actor.

PERCY FITZGERALD, from *A New History of the English Stage*, 1882:

In 1858, Harley, while playing Bottom, was seized by paralysis and died in a few hours, his last strange words being from his part, 'I have an exposition of sleep come upon me.'

MASTER BETTY (William Henry West Betty, 1791–1874) was a boy actor who was taken up by the fashionable world. He played Romeo and Hamlet at the age of twelve, and also Richard III. Leigh Hunt campaigned against him and wrote in the *News*, 1804–5:

The charm of novelty is at length broken . . . and the town is just now somewhat in the position of a husband who, after passing the honeymoon with a beautiful but childish woman, finds his reason once more returning and is content to sit down and ask why he has been pleased.

LORD BYRON (1788–1824) reports on seeing Betty in 1812, when the actor was twenty-one. From letters to Lord Holland and Lady Melbourne:

. . . when I last saw him I was in raptures with his performances, but then I was sixteen – an age to which all London then condescended to subside . . . Betty is performing here, I fear, very ill, his figure is that of a hippopotamus, his face like the Bull and *mouth* on the pannels of a heavy coach, his arms are fins fattened out of shape, his voice the gargling of an Alderman with the quinsey, and his acting altogether ought to be natural, for it certainly is like nothing that *Art* has ever yet exhibited on the stage.

GEOFFREY KENDAL (b. 1969), actor-manager, whose Shakespearean company toured India; from his book written with Clare Colvin, *The Shakespeare Wallah*, 1986:

I remember telling Anwar, who was new to the company, to 'reduce the bulbs', as I wanted the footlights cut down for the final scenes of *Othello*. He obeyed all too readily. Iago was surprised to see, in mid-soliloquy, Anwar crawling round the side of the stage to the footlight, where he proceeded to remove bulb after bulb. Bowing to exigency, we played the murder scene solely by the light of the candle in Othello's hand. I am told it was strangely effective.

Anwar's appearance on-stage was not as unusual in India as it would have been in England. In the East the stage is not seen as being the preserve only of actors. With Chinese operas, for instance, when the heroine kneels down, one stage-hand will bring on a cushion for her and another will smooth out her train. There is no pretence that they are part of the play. An early example in our productions had been the canteen bearer with the bottle of lemonade, and there were a number of others. Once, in the middle of a tense scene between Othello and Iago, the dhobi, a pile of freshly laundered clothing on his head and an iron in his hand, came up to me on-stage and said, 'Dhobi finished now, sahib.'

T. C. KEMP and J. C. TREWIN from *The Stratford Festival: A History of the Shakespeare Memorial Theatre*, 1953:

Stratford enjoyed *The Winter's Tale* more than the Bensonians did . . . This revival [1903] seems to be remembered principally because Benson, who had a long wait as Leontes, left the theatre during the revels in Bohemia, slipped a coat and trousers over his costume, and went for a row on the Avon. Miscalculating, he arrived back just as his cue was spoken on the stage. There was no time to think. Still in grey flannel trousers he rushed on, realized his mistake – helped by the frenzied whispering of the stage manager – rushed off, and returned with some dignity, as the King of Sicilia, to enter on the appropriate phrase, 'I am ashamed.'

ARTHUR HORNBLOW in *A History of the Theatre in America* (1919) on Edwin Forrest (1806–72), one of the finest American tragedians of the nineteenth century:

In 1836 he was seen for the first time as Lear, which many critics considered his finest part. Forrest was of the same opinion himself. His magnificent physique, rugged exterior, tempestuous style of acting, all lent verisimilitude to the kingly role. A friend once remarked to him: 'Mr Forrest, I never saw you play Lear as well as you did last night.' Whereupon the actor drew himself up to his full height, and replied indignantly: '*Play* Lear! What do you mean, sir? I do not *play* Lear! I *play* Hamlet, Richard, Shylock, Virginius, but by God, sir, I *am* Lear!'

WILLIAM WINTER (1836–1917), American dramatic critic, on the actor Samuel Reddish (1735–85), from *Shakespeare on the Stage*, 1916:

On one occasion, at Covent Garden, when he was performing as *Hamlet*, the player (Whitfield) of *Laertes*, in the Fencing Scene, made an awkward lunge with his rapier, which removed the *Prince's* wig, showing him to be bald. The mortification of Reddish at this occurrence was so afflicting that, according to his friend John Taylor, it eventually caused mental derangement.

In 1708, *Roscius Anglicanus*, or *An Historical View of the Stage* was published. It included a moment from Mrs Holden's late-seventeenth-century portrayal of Lady Capulet:

There being a fight and scuffle in this play between the House of Capulet and the House of Paris, Mrs Holden acting his wife entered in a hurry crying 'Oh my dear Count.' She inadvertently left out the 'o' in the pronunciation of the word 'count', giving it a vehement accent, put the house into such a laughter that London Bridge at low tide was silence to it.

In 1660 a male actor introduced Margaret Hughes, the first woman to appear on the London stage, in the role of Desdemona. From THOMAS JORDAN's *A Royal Arbour of Loyal Poesie*, 1660:

> I come unknown to any of the rest
> To tell you news, I saw the lady drest,
> The Woman playes today, mistake me not,
> No Man in Gown, or Page in Petty-Coat . . .
> And how d'ye like her, come what is't ye drive at?
> Ahe's the thing in public as in private;
> As far from being what you call a Whore,
> As *Desdemona* innur'd by the Moor?

SAMUEL PEPYS assesses the actress Nell Gwynn who became the mistress of King Charles II. Although Pepys considered her dreadful in serious or tragic roles, he was bowled over by her performance in lighter vein on 2 March 1667:

After dinner with my wife to the King's house to see *The Maiden Queen*, a new play of Dryden's . . . and the truth is there is a comical part done by Nell which is Florimel, that I never can hope ever to see the like done again, by man or woman . . . But so great a performance of a comical part was never, I believe in the world before as Nell do this, both as a mad girl, then most and best of all when she comes in like a young gallant; and hath the motions and carriage of a spark the most that ever I saw any man have. It makes me, I confess, admire her.

SIR HENRY WOTTON (1568–1639), poet, diplomat and art connoisseur, from a letter to Sir Edmond Bacon, 2 July 1613:

. . . I will entertain you at the present with what has happened this week at the Bank's side. The King's players had a new play, called *All is True*, representing some principal pieces of the reign of Henry VIII, which was set forth with many extraordinary circumstances of pomp and majesty, even to the matting of the stage; the Knights of the Order with their Georges and garters, the Guards with their embroidered coats, and the like: sufficient in truth within a while to make greatness very familiar, if not ridiculous. Now, King Henry making a masque at the Cardinal Wolsey's house, and certain chambers being shot off at his entry, some of the paper, or other stuff, wherewith one of them was stopped, did light on the thatch, where being thought at first but an idle smoke, and their eyes more attentive to the show, it kindled inwardly, and ran around like a train, consuming within less than an hour the whole house to the very grounds. This was the fatal period of that virtuous fabric, wherein yet nothing did perish but wood and straw, and a few forsaken cloaks; only one man had his breeches set on fire, that would perhaps have broiled him, if he had not by the benefit of a provident wit put it out with bottle ale.

SAMUEL PEPYS, 2 July 1661:

To the Duke's Theatre to see Sir William Davenant's opera, *The Siege of Rhodes*, this being the fourth day that it hath begun, and the first that I have seen it. Today was acted the second part, which Sir William wrote for the opening of his theatre. We stayed a very great while for the King and Queen of Bohemia; and by the breaking of a board above our heads, a great deal of dust fell into the ladies' necks and the men's hair, which made good sport. The King being come, the scene opened; which indeed is very fine and magnificent and well acted, all but the Eunuch, who was so much out that he was hissed off the stage.

LEIGH HUNT (1784–1859), poet, essayist and critic, was one of the pioneers of modern dramatic criticism. In *Dramatic Essays*, 1807, he made this observation about the actor Alexander Pope:

136

There is . . . an infallible method of obtaining a clap from the galleries, and there is an art known at the theatre by the name of *clap-trapping*, which Mr Pope has shown great wisdom in studying. It consists of nothing more than in gradually raising the voice as the speech draws to a conclusion, making an alarming outcry on the last four or five lines, or suddenly dropping them into a tremulous but energetic undertone, and with a vigorous jerk of the right arm rushing off the stage. All this astonishes the galleries; they are persuaded it must be something very fine, because it is so important and so unintelligible, and they clap for the sake of their own reputation.

ANONYMOUS, from *The Thespiad*, 1809:

> The Poet tells us that in ancient days
> Our ancestors in carts performed their plays.
> Methinks the custom we might now renew,
> And cart the gang of modern actors too.
> Immortal Garrick, in an happier age,
> Taught Sense to tread with Nature on the stage;
> What poets wrote, mimetic play'rs displayed.
> But now such narrow notions we condemn;
> Bards study actors and not actors them.
> To suit the play'r the drama is designed,
> And Reynolds copies Munden, not mankind.

In 1794 SAMUEL TAYLOR COLERIDGE (1772–1834) and CHARLES LAMB (1775–1834) collaborated to celebrate the great English actress Sarah Siddons (1775–1831):

> As when a child on some long winter's night,
> Affrighted, clinging to its grandame's knees,
> With eager wondering and perturb'd delight

Listens strange tales of fearful dark decrees
Mutter'd to wretch by necromantic spell;
Or of those hags, who, at the watching time
Of murky midnight, ride the air sublime,
And mingle foul embrace with fiends of hell,
Cold horror drinks its blood! Anon the tear
More gentle starts, to hear the beldame tell
Of pretty babes that lov'd each other dear,
Murder'd by cruel Uncle's mandate fell.
Ev'n such the shiv'ring joys thy tones impart,
Ev'n so thou, Siddons, meltest my sad heart.

The following celebration of Edmund Kean, dated *c.* 1851, is attributed to George Gordon, LORD BYRON:

Thou art the sun's bright child!
The genius that irradiates thy mind,
Caught all its purity and light from heaven!
Thine is the task, with majesty most perfect,
To bind the passions captive in thy train;
Each crystal tear, that slumbers in the depth
Of feeling's fountain, doth obey thy call.
There's not a joy or sorrow mortals prove,
Or passion to humanity allied,
But tribute of allegiance owes to thee.
The shrine thou worshipest is nature's self,
The only altar genius deigns to seek.
Thine offering – a bold and burning mind,
Whose impulse guides thee to the realms of fame,
Where, crowned with well-earned laurels – all thine own –
I herald thee to immortality.

NOËL COWARD's *Cavalcade* opened at the Theatre Royal, Drury Lane, on 13 October 1931. Cockie is C. B. Cochrane, the impresario. This is from Coward's autobiography, *Present Indicative* (1937):

The first night of *Cavalcade* will remain for ever in my memory as the most agonising three hours I have ever spent in a theatre. This, I am sure, will appear to be an over-statement to any reader who happened to be present at it. But nobody in that audience, excepting Cockie and a few who had been concerned with the production, had the remotest idea how near we came to bringing the curtain down after the third scene and sending the public home.

The evening started triumphantly. The atmosphere in the auditorium while the orchestra was tuning-up was tense with excitement. Many people had been waiting for the gallery and pit for three days and nights. Gradually the stalls and dress-circle filled; Reginald Burston, the musical director, took his place. I came into my box with Mother, Jack, Gladys and Jeffery, and received a big ovation. The overture started and we settled ourselves to wait, while the house-lights slowly faded. The first scene went smoothly. Mary was nervous, but played with experienced poise. The troop-ship, with our military band and real guardsmen, brought forth a burst of cheering. The third scene – inside the house again – went without a hitch. Half the strength of the orchestra crept out during this to take their place on the lower hydraulic lift, on which they played for the theatre scene.

It was a very complicated change. The second two lifts had to rise so many feet to make the stage. The first lift had to sink and rise again with the orchestra in place on it. The preceding interior had to be taken up into the flies, and the furniture taken off at the sides. Two enormous built side-wings, with two tiers of boxes filled with people, had to slide into place on rollers, when the first lift had risen to its mark. All this was timed to take place in just over thirty seconds, and had gone perfectly smoothly at the dress rehearsals.

We sat in the box on the first night with our eyes glued on to the conductor's desk, waiting for the little blue warning light to show us that the scene was set. We waited in vain. The conductor played the waltz through again – then again – people began to look up at us from the stalls; the gallery became restless and started to clap. Neither

Gladys nor I dared to move, there were too many eyes on us, and we didn't want to betray, more than we could help, that anything was wrong. I hissed at Jack out of the corner of my mouth, and he slipped out of the box and went down on to the stage. In a few moments he returned and said, in a dead voice: 'The downstage lift has stuck, and they think it will take two hours to fix it.'

Gladys and I talked without looking at each other, our eyes still set on where the blue light should appear. She said, very quietly: 'I think you'll have to make an announcement,' and I said: 'I'll give it another two minutes.' Still the orchestra continued to grind out the 'Mirabelle' waltz, there seemed to be a note of frenzy creeping into it. I longed passionately for it to play something else – anything else in the world. The audience became more restless, until suddenly, just as I was about to leave the box and walk on to the stage, the blue light came on, the black curtain rose and the scene started.

From then onwards there wasn't a moment's peace for us. The effect of the hitch on Dan O'Neil and the stage staff had obviously been shattering. The company caught panic too, and the performance for the rest of the evening lost its grip. I don't think this was noticed by the audience, but we knew it all right. That unfortunate accident took the fine edge off the play, and although the applause at the end was tremendous, we were heart-broken. I appeared at the end against my will, but in response to frantic signals from Cockie in the box opposite. It was one of the few occasions of my life that I have ever walked on to a stage not knowing what I was going to say. However, standing there, blinded by my own automatic lights, and nerve-stricken by the torment I had endured in course of the evening, I managed to make a rather incoherent little speech which finished with the phrase: 'I hope that this play has made you feel that, in spite of the troublous times we are living in, it is still pretty exciting to be English.' This brought a violent outburst of cheering, and the orchestra, frantic with indecision as to whether to play my waltz or 'God Save the King,' effected an unhappy compromise by playing them both at once. The curtain fell, missing my head by a fraction, and that was that.

J. C. TREWIN, drama critic (1908–91?), in *Five and Eighty Hamlets* (1987), on Tyrone Guthrie's production at Elsinore starring Laurence Olivier and Vivien Leigh in 1937:

The morning of June 2 was depressing. Several times, during a six-hour rehearsal until early in the afternoon, squalls whipped across the Sound: players (permitted now to use the courtyard) were soaked in their overcoats and mackintoshes, and a frigid north wind did nothing to help. Still, the company and the military cadets Guthrie was rehearsing as supers, a towering six-foot-five in his wet mackintosh, remained moderately hopeful. Only moderately. When, holding an umbrella, John Abbott – who had succeeded Sullivan as Claudius – put intense feeling into the line, 'Is there not rain enough in the sweet heavens?' the small and privileged audience, sheltered by an archway, could not forbear to cheer. George Bishop quoted the right line when a sparrow settled, it seemed permanently, on the shoulder of the Ghost (Torin Thatcher): 'There is special providence in the fall of a sparrow.'

Providence was not available that afternoon. A cloudburst saturated the stage and the courtyard benches which should have held 2,500 people; next, a full gale stormed the Sound. An open air production (it would have been Guthrie's first) was clearly impossible, even though it was supposed to be a gala occasion, with royalty present and the diplomatic corps. About an hour before the play should have begun at eight o'clock, I found myself, not knowing why, standing by Lilian Baylis at the door of the Marienlyst Hotel, half a mile from Kronborg. Huddled into a thick black coat, Miss Baylis was staring at the sky so angrily that I felt she might be shaking her fist at it. Realizing that someone was by her, she turned autocratically – and I saw then what an autocrat she was – pointed out to the streaming rain, and said: 'Look, this must stop!' I agreed, but felt, for an awful moment, that I might have been responsible for the whole affair, not forgetting the special trains that by then would have been leaving Copenhagen. While I tried to frame a suitable apology, Tyrone Guthrie came out into the hall, rubbing his hands, and (as he was inclined to do in an emergency) looking surprisingly pleased. 'Going to do it *here*' he said.

'*Here?*' Miss Baylis exclaimed in the kind of italics that Edith Evans would use for Lady Bracknell's 'A *handbag!*'

'Yes,' Guthrie repeated calmly. 'Here.' As he turned, she looked after him in utter bewilderment before pursuing him into the hotel depths.

Guthrie's intended theatre was the hotel ballroom, large, flamboyant, quite unsuitable, but, as George Bishop put it, with no other booking. Beyond its range of windows mist was so dense, obscuring the line of the Swedish coast, that we might have been poised on an unmapped height. The ballroom had only a tiny cabaret stage approached by a short stair and holding a potted palm which Guthrie loved though I have no idea whether it remained. The room had stacks of what Guthrie remembered as basket-chairs but that I think of now as small and not too well-balanced gilt ones. The plan was to present the play more or less in what before long would be called 'the round', a term unknown at that period, with the audience, members, as it were, of the Court, on three sides of the cabaret stage. Promptly Guthrie enlisted the press party which had swollen to include correspondents from several parts of Europe. 'Done nothing yet!' he said; and for the next twenty minutes we did something, organized by Guthrie and his stage manager, to set the chairs in a wide arc and to turn the place into a vague semblance of a theatre. I was paired with a Danish writer, who regarded the whole business as peculiar and at heart, I believe, suspected the storm to be a British stage effect.

Outside, waves were riding high in the narrow water between Denmark and Sweden, and it was plain that the storm had set in for the night, with a noise like the ride of the Valkyries. All the costumes and properties had been brought over from Kronborg; hotel bedrooms became dressing rooms; and not so long after eight o'clock the ballroom, with Danish royalty (Prince Knud and Princess Caroline Mathilde) in the front row, was filled for what, in effect, would be an improvisation. It had been left to the players, directed by Laurence Olivier whom Guthrie had put, wisely, in command, to get the night together with only the sketchiest of ideas of ways and means. We learned afterwards that one door, tightly closed, could not be used because a bird was nesting above it and must by no means be disturbed. Guthrie came forward to apologise briefly for 'the strangest performance of *Hamlet* on any stage', and presently Francisco and Barnardo were on 'the platform before the castle', Horatio and

Marcellus were on their way up through the audience, and some-where, within a few moments, a bell was beating one.

The company rallied with astonishing ease (heroes all of them, Olivier said), as if a group of strolling players had materialized from nowhere, resolved to let fly. Through much of the night those of us who had seen the play at the Vic wondered what might go wrong during the next minutes. Nothing that mattered did. Olivier, denied his athletics, had not been a surer Hamlet in grace and sympathy; we saw that the new young actress, Vivien Leigh, who had joined the cast as Ophelia, was acting with unflurried spirit. I recall, too, how expertly Torin Thatcher controlled the Ghost during a sustained gale that, battering against the windows, accompanied most of his speech until the glow-worm showed the matin to be near. Lilian Baylis, in cap and gown and with a benevolent gleam in her eye, at first stood at the back. Not for long. She moved to her proper place in the front row, and at the end was seen to be standing, as everybody was, to applaud her company.

Thomas Hardy (1840–1928), 1867:

To an Actress

I read your name when you were strange to me,
Where it stood blazoned bold with many more;
I passed it vacantly, and did not see
Any great glory in the shape it wore.

O cruelty, the insight barred me then!
Why did I not possess me with its sound,
And in its cadence catch and catch again
Your nature's essence floating thereround?

Could *that* man be this I, unknowing you,
When now the knowing you is all of me,
And the old world of then is now a new,
And purpose no more what it used to be —

A thing of formal journeywork, but due
To springs that then were sealed up utterly?

ARTHUR COLBY SPRAGUE in *Shakespearean Players and Performances*, 1953:

In 1785, tradition in the theatre was still a matter of consequence. When Mrs Siddons was preparing to go on, as Lady Macbeth, Sheridan came to her dressing-room and insisted upon being admitted. He had heard, he said, that she was planning to put down her candle, in the Sleepwalking Scene, thus leaving her hands free for the washing out of the imagined blood. Mrs Pritchard had carried her candle throughout the scene. 'It would be thought a presumptuous innovation' for Mrs Siddons to change the business. She, in turn, told him that it was too late, that she was too much agitated at this moment, to follow his advice. She had her way, and, when the curtain fell, Sheridan generously admitted that she was right. But the putting down of the candle was not to escape censure. It was called a palpable trick, 'an error, which would be inexcuseable in the youngest performer.' Her costume in this scene was also criticized. She wore, not the shroudlike garments so impressive in her later performances, but white satin. All mad heroines, according to Mr Puff, wore white satin; it was a rule. But since 'Lady *Macbeth* is supposed to be *asleep* and not *mad*,' custom did not warrant its adoption here.

JAMES SHERIDAN KNOWLES (1784–1862) was asked by the American actor Edwin Forrest about Mrs Siddons's playing of the Sleepwalking Scene in *Macbeth*:

'I have read all the high-flown descriptions of the critics, and they fall short. I want you to tell me in plain blunt phrase just what impression

she produced on you.' Knowles replied, with a sort of shudder . . .
'Well, sir, I smelt blood! I swear that I smelt blood!'

LEIGH HUNT, in *Dramatic Essays* (1894), on Edmund Kean's Othello, 1818:

His repeated fare-wells, with the division of the syllables strongly
marked, –

> Fare-well the tranquil mind! fare-well content!
> Fare-well the plumed troop, &c.

were spoken in long, lingering tones, like the sound of a parting knell.
The whole passage would have formed an admirable study for a young
actor, in showing him the beauty of sacrificing verbal painting to a
pervading sentiment . . . Mr Kean gave no vulgar importance to 'the
plumed troop' and the 'big wars', as commonplace actors do; because
the melancholy overcomes all: it merges the particular images into one
mass of regret.

SAMUEL PEPYS, 2 November 1607:

Up, and to the office, where busy all the morning; at noon home, and
after dinner my wife and Willett and I to the King's playhouse and
there saw *Henry the Fourth*; and contrary to expectations, was pleased
in nothing more than in Cartwright's speaking of Falstaffe's speech
about 'What is honour?' The house being full of Parliament-men, it
being holiday with them. And it was observable how a gentleman of
good habit, sitting just before us, eating of some fruit in the midst of
the play, did drop down as dead, being choked; but with much ado,

145

Orange Moll did thrust her finger down his throat, and brought him to life again.

Sir Johnston Forbes-Robertson (1853–1937), actor-manager, had a long and varied career. An astonishingly handsome man with a beautiful voice, he was the most famous Hamlet of his generation. The following is an unidentified description of his performance on 11 September 1897 (quoted by James Agate in *Those Were the Nights*, 1946):

Forbes-Robertson brings to his task all the admirable and invaluable equipments of the actor. His noble voice, capable of every tone and modulation, is priceless. It can be alternately deep and tender. It reminds one of the moan and wail of the 'cello.' He does not attempt to make himself fanciful or pretty. He wears his own hair, which so well suits his clear-cut and intellectual countenance, and he does not bedizen himself all over with stars and decorations and coloured orders. In fact, it would not be wrong to say that the Hamlet looked a little 'dowdy' in his suit of rusty black, unadorned and unrelieved. But it only emphasized the more the striking force of the face, on which every passion, every doubt, and each anxiety were deeply registered. What then – apart from new readings, or old readings, or omissions from the text, or what not – were the salient features of the newest of all the new Hamlets? We should say two things. First, his consummate good breeding, united with frankness of nature and lovableness of disposition. Secondly, a mind deeply sensitive to religious impression. We can conceive such a Hamlet to have been idolized by his fellow-students – to have been their 'chum' and their model of a downright 'good fellow.' It is with difficulty that he throws away this boyish impetuosity when confronted with the horror of the situation in which he is involved. Over and over again it bubbles up and bursts the bounds of will-power to subdue it – this keen sense of humour, this desperate, natural, impulsive *joie de vivre*. We have never before seen a Hamlet who has in him such a subtle element of fun, or such an appreciation of the whimsical. Where other Hamlets scowl or snarl,

Forbes-Robertson only smiles; not a cynical, cruel, or sarcastic smile, but a smile that lights up his mobile face and seems to say to Rosencrantz and Guildenstern, 'My dear fellows, you are both humbugs and fawning toadies, but I am too well-bred, too much of the Prince to snap at you'; or to Polonius, 'I should uncommonly like you to know that you are boring me to tears; but still, you are an officer of the Court, a far older man than I am, so I must show my contempt for you with a smile instead of a sneer.' There are frequent evidences of this buoyancy of nature united to a supreme courtesy of manner. In the scene where Polonius asks him what he is reading, and in the delivery of the well-known interpolated sentence in the scene with Polonius:

> It shall to the barber's with your beard.
> Prythee say on – he's for a jig, or a tale of bawdry,
>   or – he sleeps!

in the memorable sentences about the camel and the weasel and 'very like a whale' the new Hamlet does not show the slightest sign of irritability or contempt. His nature is too sweet to offend anyone, however much a toady or a bore, and he is too well-mannered to condescend to snappishness with his inferiors. This is why the new Hamlet was so beloved at the University, and so adored by the players. This vein of cheerfulness and humour, contrasting so admirably as it does with the serious and introspective side of Hamlet, is carried so far as the opening scene in the churchyard with the gravediggers who, we may remark in passing, are about the dullest and least humorous of delvers who ever joked in a grave. Most Hamlets approach this scene like mutes, and preach out their sentiment as if they were in a pulpit. Not so Forbes-Robertson. His banter with the first gravedigger is in the very lightest vein, and without a doubt these constant waves of brightness and sunshine are of extreme value to the spectator. For ourselves, we never remember to have sat out the play of *Hamlet* with less effort, or, on the whole, more mental enjoyment. Many present, to judge by their enthusiasm and their rapt attention, could have sat it out from end to end all over again. Of how few Hamlets can such a thing be said?

We now come to the second salient feature of the new Hamlet, and that is the religious fervour that evidently underlies the half-distracted mind. We do not say that Hamlet poses as a sanctimonious prig or anything of that sort, but it is impossible to believe that he has not thought, and thought very deeply, of the 'life to come,' that he has not pondered in his own heart of 'the dread of something after death,' the 'undiscovered country from whose bourn no traveller returns.' On these solemn things, according to Forbes-Robertson, Hamlet has thought very deeply, very earnestly, but with no suspicion of hypocritical cant. The mere touch with the supernatural accentuates these feelings, the communication with a spirit from the dead plays upon this sensitive nature as the wild wind on an Æolian harp, and it adds beauty and significance to the grand soliloquy on suicide and to countless passages that bring before Hamlet's mind the mysteries of the 'unknown land.' But if we wanted a pregnant example of Hamlet's philosophical pondering on the inevitable, and of Forbes-Robertson's exquisite appreciation of it, we have it in one passage which the actor does not preach or grunt at Horatio, but delivers to him earnestly and confidentially and with that winning smile and the pure mind 'half-way to heaven already,' as much as to say, 'Oh, dear friend, we all ought to think of these things.' These are the words so beautifully spoken which convey what we call the religious undergrowth in the perplexed mind of Hamlet. They constitute, as we have ever thought, the loveliest passage in the play.

'Not a whit! We defy augury. There is a special Providence in the fall of a sparrow. If it be now, 'tis not to come; if it be not to come, it will be now; if it be not now, yet it will come; the readiness is all. Since no man has aught of what he leaves, what is't to leave betimes? Let be!'

And Forbes-Robertson follows up this religious idea to the climax in the singularly beautiful death. Hamlet is wounded mortally, and totters feebly to the empty throne. We do not pause to inquire how the actor acquires that death pallor, but it is singularly effective. The finely chiselled face becomes rapt and inspired with a vision of the higher mystery. It is from the throne that Hamlet, weak, pale, and gazing on the golden gates of eternity, says:

> I cannot live to hear the news from England,
> But I do prophesy the election lights
> On Fortinbras; he has my dying voice;

So tell him, with the occurrents, more and less,
Which have solicited!

And then Hamlet, groping in vain for some 'dear head' with feeble fingers, 'the uncertain hand blindly searching for the dear head, and then finally closing on it with a sort of final adieu,' and finding no sweet companion for his lonely journey, whispers, still gazing on some unseen seraphic vision, 'The rest is silence,' and then passes out alone into the unknown! But this is not all! The prince is dead upon the throne he never filled. Horatio places the empty crown on his dead companion's knees, and Fortinbras enters with his men, and all that is left of the dreamer and philosopher is 'lifted on high by the shouldering crowd, on the battered boss of a shield.' The contrast between death and life is admirable. The stage is no longer left as a slaughterhouse of corpses, but as Shakespeare intended, with the majesty of death asserting itself against a background of martial splendour. 'Take up the bodies! Go, bid the soldiers shoot!'

We have spoken of the courtliness and grace of the new Hamlet, and alluded very strongly to the fact that the actor avoids all semblance of an irritability and petulance that might destroy his distinction and good breeding. But, at the same time, we are not blind to the fact that this consistently even tone on the part of Hamlet robs several scenes of their vigour and intensity. The pregnant passages with Ophelia and with the Queen mother, which were the strongest with Henry Irving, are the weakest with Forbes-Robertson. We are not inclined to lay the blame, as some have already done, on the unpoetical influence of the Ophelia or the inexperience of the Gertrude. We ascribe it to the horror on the part of the actor, to the expression of that very irritability which is the first sign of worry and a bewildered brain. He thinks it undignified. But, if we are not allowed to see the King peeping from behind the arras where he is concealed, a crafty face instantly seen by Hamlet, but not seen at all by Ophelia, how can we account for the wild and whirling words of Hamlet, or for his change from a lover into a fury, now loving, now storming, now gentle, now furious? We maintain that Hamlet must be irritable, and even rude at times, to account for his 'antic disposition.' Why should he be so rash and explosive with Ophelia if he did not know, or were not convinced, that he was being tricked by the King and Polonius, and that Ophelia was a willing decoy duck? And if Hamlet's brain were not overstrained by the play scene, how could he possibly be so curt, direct, downright, and unfilial to his mother? No actor can get out of that. There are moments when Hamlet's beautiful nature is warring against itself, and those moments are strongly expressed in the scenes with Ophelia and Gertrude, and elsewhere. It will not do to stretch the point of courtesy so far as to suggest that Hamlet was not really in love with Ophelia, or angry with his mother, and that, on the whole, he loved Laertes better than Horatio. These thoughts certainly do occur to the mind in following the new Hamlet with all its variety, beauty, and charm.

With such a student-Hamlet, some of the omissions and suggestions are extraordinary. Forbes-Robertson reverts to the old business of the two pictures embroidered on the arras or painted on the walls to explain, 'Look here upon this picture, and on this,' instead of the mental pictures which one would have thought would have commended themselves to such a scholar. But, strangest of all, he gives us the King's agonized prayer, 'Oh, my offence is rank, it smells to Heaven,' and omits that wonderful instance of Hamlet's irresolution, the sense of duty conquered by a kind heart, where he proposes to kill the King on his knees. 'Now I might do it pat; now he is praying, and now I'll do't!' Few Hamlets would omit that speech, and there is no reason for it, save a scenic change, which could be easily managed. The idea that Ophelia's mad scene occurs in a garden is pretty, but nothing comes of it. She does not gather the flowers and herbs from the flower-beds, but brings them in her lap, as of old, bound up with black net or crape. Neither the Ophelia nor the Gertrude are striking performances, but they will serve. Mrs Patrick Campbell substitutes weariness for innocence, and indifference for love. The chord of youth is never struck. Her madness is very realistic, but it strikes the note of pain, not pity. Ophelia does not make us weep, but shudder. Her heart is not broken, she is cross, and too palpably forced upon Hamlet for a State purpose or a Court intrigue. We do not feel one beat of Ophelia's heart. Parting from the Prince, or crooning her wild snatches of song over the flowers, she does not draw one tear from the most sympathetic of natures. Claudius and Gertrude are too obviously dressed up.

The one looks like the beautiful representative king of hearts on a pack of cards, and the other like Semiramide, or a new Cleopatra. They are both, as represented by H. Cooper Cliffe and Miss Granville, better by far than the Kings and Queens of old, but we are not convinced that the new idea of youth in sensualist and matron is of much advantage to the play as a whole. It was Wilson Barrett who introduced the conception with Mr Willard and Miss Margaret Leighton, but the dire necessity for the alteration has never been clearly pointed out. The Horatio of Mr Harrison Hunter was incomprehensible. What is the value to any Hamlet of an Horatio who is a prig, and a kind of overgrown Osric, an inanimate creature with no trace of sympathy or affection in his composition? Some Hamlets purposely select colourless Horatios because a good Horatio is too similar to Hamlet in temperament, and consequently detracts from the success of the Prince of Denmark. But Forbes-Robertson is not an actor of that pattern, and knows that the better Horatio is played the better it is for Hamlet. But to counteract this we had an excellent Laertes in that sound and accomplished artist Bernard Gould, and the result was that the scene between Hamlet and Laertes at the grave was one of the best acted and most vigorous moments of the play. Here Hamlet awoke from the dreamer into the man of action, and the torrent of 'rant,' which was not rant after all, but the natural relief to an imprisoned nature, brought down the house. An excellent Polonius was found in Mr J. H. Barnes, who was no senile dodderer, but a man who had been in early years a bit of a scholar and student himself, but who had the habitual tendency of old men to bore their juniors with reminiscences and old-world sentiments. Vanity, the root of most madness, had worked its will with the brain of Polonius. The Ghost of Ian Robertson was distinguished for its evenness of elocution and for its grim mystery of tone and idea. The Osric of Martin Harvey was just what it should be – perky, affected, and inoffensive; and it is seldom that the words of the player Queen are better spoken than by Miss Sidney Crowe, a clever and promising daughter of an accomplished mother.

D. H. LAWRENCE (1885–1930), from *Twilight in Italy*, 1913:

I had always felt an aversion from Hamlet: a creeping, unclean thing he seems, on the stage, whether he is Forbes-Robertson or anybody else. His nasty poking and sniffing at his mother, his setting traps for the King, his conceited perversion with Ophelia make him always intolerable. The character is repulsive in its conception, based on self-dislike and a spirit of disintegration.

There is, I think, this strain of cold dislike, or self-dislike, through much of the Renaissance art, and through all the later Shakespeare. In Shakespeare it is a kind of corruption in the flesh and a conscious revolt from this. A sense of corruption in the flesh makes Hamlet frenzied, for he will never admit that it is his own flesh. Leonardo da Vinci is the same, but Leonardo loves the corruption maliciously. Michael Angelo rejects any feeling of corruption, he stands by the flesh, the flesh only. It is the corresponding reaction, but in the opposite direction. But that is all four hundred years ago.

CLAIRE TOMALIN (b. 1933) describes the requirements for an actress in the nineteenth century in *The Invisible Woman: The story of Nelly Ternan and Charles Dickens*, 1990:

The truth is that, to succeed as an actress, you needed to be a woman of exceptional courage, intelligence and self-reliance. You had to be prepared to work yourself to the bone, to ignore sickness, pregnancy and childbirth as well as bereavement and any other personal distress. You had to be tough enough to endure the harsh opinion of the world as well as homelessness and discomfort. You had to know how to be a queen or a model of ladylike composure on stage just after emerging from a dressing room with the rain pouring through the ceiling. Being an actress meant, more than anything, that you were prepared for a life of risk. Freedom – of a kind – and real work that was not domestic work, these set you apart from the general condition of women.

Sarah Bernhardt (1845–1923) was the ultimate definition of a star. '*Le théâtre c'est moi!*' was her motto. Apart from her extraordinary histrionic gifts, she was beautiful, glamorous, mysterious and courageous. She led a scandalous private life. However, her début, in 1862, when she was aged eighteen, at the Comédie-Française did not bode well. The critic FRANCISQUE SARCEY (1827–99), had this to say:

Mlle Bernhardt is a tall, pretty girl with a slender figure and a very pleasing expression. The upper part of her face is remarkably beautiful. She holds herself well, and her enunciation is perfectly clear. That is all that can be said for her at present.

Her courage and theatrical impudence prompted her to play Hamlet in a production she brought to London in 1899. MAURICE BARING (1874–1945), man of letters, discusses the performance:

I believe that the secret of her art was that of all great art: that she was guided by an infallible instinct, and that whatever she did she could not go wrong. When what she did was done, it seemed simple, inevitable, and easy; and so swiftly accomplished, that you had no time to think of the *how*; nor was your sense sharp enough, however carefully you watched, to detect the divine conjury. It was the same whether she spoke lines of La Fontaine and Racine, or whether she asked, as she poured out a cup of coffee, as she did in one play: '*Du sucre, deux morceaux?*' She was artistically inerrant. It is this gift which was probably the secret of the great actors of the past: Garrick, Siddons, Talma, and Salvini. It is certainly to be seen in the work of the great singer of the present, Chaliapine, whether he is portraying Satan holding his court on the Brocken, or a foolish, good-natured Chinovnik, half-fuddled with drink after a night out. When such a gift is at work, the greater the material it is interpreting, the greater, of course, the effect.

The greater the play Sarah Bernhardt appeared in, the greater the demand on her instinct, which *was* her genius; the swifter and the fuller the response. As the occasion expanded, so did her genius rise to it.

Her Hamlet was and is still hotly discussed, and quite lately several eminent English writers have expressed opinions that are completely at variance with one another on the subject. But every critic when he reads *Hamlet* creates a Hamlet in his own image, and when he sees it acted, the more vivid the impersonation, the more likely it is to be at variance with his own conception. One critic finds her Hamlet an unpardonable Gallic liberty to take with Shakespeare; another, that she electrified Hamlet with the vigour of her personality. I remember a cultivated philosopher, who was a citizen of the world, telling me that he thought her Hamlet the only intelligible rendering he had seen of the part, just because it rendered the youthful inconsequence of the moods of the moody Dane. But whether you thought it justifiable or unjustifiable, true or untrue to Shakespeare, in witnessing it you were aware of the genius of the interpreter answering the genius of the dramatic poet. Deep was calling to deep.

When Hamlet looked into the guilty King's face at the end of the play within the play, or thought for one second that the King and not Polonius had blundered into death behind the arras; when Hamlet concealed his forebodings from Horatio, and when Hamlet looked at Laertes during the duel and let him know that he knew the swords had been exchanged and that one of them had been poisoned, all thought of the part – the rendering, tradition, the language, the authorship went to the winds: you knew only that something which had been invented by one great genius was being interpreted by another great genius, and that the situation had found an expression which was on its own level.

Another view of Sarah Bernhardt as Hamlet by an anonymous critic, 4 April 1905 (quoted by JAMES AGATE in *Those Were the Nights*, 1946):

The appearance at the Adelphi of Mdme Bernhardt as Hamlet has been, so far at least as fashionable London is concerned, the theatrical event of the season. In Paris the performance was received with unequivocal raptures, and there are many who hold it to be the greatest triumph in a career made up of triumphs. In London the interest is that chiefly of curiosity and admiration for the actress. In this aspect, even, some deduction has to be made. By appearing a couple of years ago as Lorenzaccio Mdme Bernhardt showed us what we were to expect in Hamlet, and the conclusions deduced from that performance prove in almost every respect to be accurate. Not very ready were we in early days to accept a French Hamlet, though the success of Fechter, to mention none other, removed some illusions. There are, indeed, still living some who hold Fechter's Hamlet the most interesting the world has seen. If we accept Hamlet as the typical *jeune premier*, earnest, impassioned, amorous, gallant and pictures-que, it satisfied most requirements. Female Hamlets, meanwhile whether the exponent be named Cushman, Marriott, or what not, are, and always will be, a delusion and a snare. For a Frenchwoman to play Hamlet before an English public is an experiment daring and unique. Mdme Bernhardt is not the first female Hamlet that has been seen in France, Mdme Judith, a relative of Rachel, having taken the role in an adaptation of the play by her husband, Bernard-Dérosne. This, however, did not appeal to English suffrages. It may at once be said that the Hamlet now exhibited will win no acceptance from English scholars. Society will, no doubt, rave about it, and there is much about which to rave. If Hamlet were other than he is we might praise the beauty, grave, and finesse of the rendering. Hamlet is, however, something other than a brisk, picturesque, vivacious, and amorous stripling, who dismisses sorrow with a gibe, and overflows with animal spirits.

It is, perhaps, no longer expedient to dwell in a newspaper report upon what Hamlet is. It may, however, and must be said that he is all Mdme Bernhardt is not. In appearance, Mdme Bernhardt is graceful. No question arises concerning Hamlet being fat or scant of breath. With her fair hair clustering round her head, a short tunic, apparently of black silk trimmed with sable, black hose, and a long and flowing silk cloak, she is the ideal of a young prince, whose sorrows, even if fantastical, are at least vivaciously and effectively expressed. The 'antic' disposition Hamlet elects to exhibit accounts for some imperti-nences of conduct, such as thrusting into the face of the King the torch which has been seized during the play scene. There is much of this class in the performance that is ingenious and little that is indefensible. What we miss is the burden which Hamlet strives to bear, and under which he sinks. Occasionally, as in the scene in which he climbs almost on to the raised throne of the King, when the monarch is 'frighted with false fire,' Hamlet is too demonstrative. As a rule his gestures are few and significant, and there is a wholly to be commended absence of all strain after effect. The version in which Mdme Bernhardt appears is a genuine rendering and is, it may be assumed, the most faithful ever put upon the French stage. All the things against which Voltaire and the Academy protested, and which, in the height of the movement of romanticism, Dumas dared not retain, are preserved, and there are moments when English freedom, apt to be a little shamefaced, is surpassed.

All the wonders of the original are accomplished, the naïve and not too decent songs of Ophelia, banished from the version in which Mdme Bernhardt previously appeared, herself playing Ophelia, are restored; and the utterances of the gravediggers are stripped of none of their grotesqueness, and prove in French hands sufficiently diverting. All the liberty that has been taken consists of omissions and abbreviations pardonable enough in any case, and indispensable in that of a play so long as *Hamlet*. When many scenes had been abridged, and some entirely excised, the play lasted over four hours, a time too long for a London public. In justice to the management it should be said that the waits, though numerous, were in no case long, and that the business was rattled through in a style not common on similar occasions. The scene of most importance that entirely disappeared was that in which Laertes takes his farewell of his father and sister, and he and Polonius both lecture Ophelia on the manner in which she should treat the advances of Hamlet. Many of the scenes were well managed; the ghost effects were effective, and the manner in which in the chamber scene the apparition of the murdered King walked, so to speak, out of his portrait on the wall, was to be commended. Less good was the disposition of the play scene, the King and Queen being too far removed from Hamlet. The address to the players was spoken by Hamlet while a valet was lighting the footlights of the mimic representation, and a small orchestra with flutes and recorders was seated in front of the false stage. During the play scene the manner of

Hamlet to Ophelia was caressing and amorous. He all but sat as he proposes on her lap, and he pressed endearingly with his hand her fair head.

On these things there is no temptation to dwell. Every point that can be made in the rendering of *Hamlet* has been tried, and every accessory that can simplify action has been adopted. We are, indeed, a little wearied of forced points and impossible readings. Mdme Bernhardt affords us no revelation or illumination. No woman has done this, and none ever will. The more inspired and divine a woman is, the less fitted is she to play Hamlet. There is, however, no need to treat the new Hamlet with ungracious coldness or discouragement. Mdme Bernhardt gives us conspicuous proof of courage and capacity, and does all that can be done to achieve the impossible. Her Hamlet is more than inoffensive. It is always bright and attractive, often impressive, and sometimes suggestive. Mdme Bernhardt was received with rapture, the calls of the audience were too numerous to be counted, and the entertainment, so far as society is concerned, is a prodigious success. All the afternoon and evening representations that can be given are too few to meet the exigencies of the British public, and some at least of those most anxious to see the performance will be unable to do so. The general cast was moderate, but not specially striking. The Ophelia was the typical French *ingénue*. The gravediggers were really diverting.

SIR MAX BEERBOHM (1872–1956), caricaturist, writer, dandy, wit and theatre critic had this to say on Bernhardt's Hamlet in the *Saturday Review*:

I cannot, on my heart, take Sarah's Hamlet seriously. I cannot even imagine any one capable of more than a hollow pretence at taking it seriously. However, the truly great are apt, in matters concerning themselves, to lose that sense of fitness which is usually called sense of humour, and I did not notice that Sarah was once hindered in her performance by any irresistible desire to burst out laughing. Her solemnity was politely fostered by the Adelphi audience. From first to last no one smiled. If any one had so far relaxed himself as to smile, he would have been bound to laugh. One laugh in that dangerous atmosphere, and the whole structure of polite solemnity would have toppled down, burying beneath its ruins the national reputation for good manners. I, therefore, like every one else, kept an iron control upon the corners of my lips. It was not until I was half-way home and well out of earshot of the Adelphi, that I unsealed the accumulations of my merriment.

T. S. ELIOT, from 'Hamlet and His Problems', 1919:

So far from being Shakespeare's masterpiece, the play is most certainly an artistic failure . . . *Hamlet*, like the sonnets, is full of some stuff that the writer could not drag to light, contemplate or manipulate into art. And when we search for this feeling, we find it, as in the sonnets, very difficult to localize . . . We must simply admit that here Shakespeare tackled a problem which proved too much for him. Why he attempted it at all is an insoluble problem; under compulsion of what experience he attempted to express the inexpressibly horrible, we cannot ever know.

Edmund Kean (1787–1833), was one of those great actors who was dogged by scandal and mystery, and so captured the imagination of his own and succeeding generations. Dimunitive and savage, he was especially famed for his interpretation of villains. He made his astonishing London début at Drury Lane on 26 January 1814. In *The Examiner*, on 13 February, LEIGH HUNT described Kean's performance:

If we were inclined to be very cautious, we should forbear at present to give our opinion on the acting of Mr Kean, especially as we have only seen him in one character; but as such prudence might be thought selfish and even cowardly, we will at once venture to commit ourselves, though perhaps we may hereafter be compelled to retract some of our sentence. We will not hesitate therefore to say, that the performance of *Shylock* by this Gentleman has impressed us with an idea that he will rise to the very summit of his profession, and that he already belongs to the first class of his art. This is sufficiently panegyrical; but our praise will be of little value unless we endeavour to explain a little the causes of our approbation. Though the accession of this new actor was announced with much pomp, and divers hints were thrown out that a second Garrick was to appear, yet our expectations were not at all excited. We were well aware of the old managerial artifice of preceding every first appearance with a flourish of trumpets, and could not but acknowledge that poor Drury, with its deserted benches, stood in great need of the customary fraud; nor had we forgot that even Mr Brunton was some years ago introduced to the public as a fac-simile of Garrick. Under these impressions we went to the Theatre, as it may be supposed, with as little disposition to wonder as Pythagoras or Lord Bolingbroke themselves. Our state of indifference was not at all shaken by the entrance of Mr Kean: his small person, which seems considerably under the middle height, and from its slightness is almost insignificant, was not adapted to bias our judgment; nor was his voice vastly prepossessing, for it was thick and hoarse, somewhat between an apoplexy and a cold. If such a person could delight us, it was evident that with such personal drawbacks he could not seduce us into fondness: it must be by the display of sheer excellence exposed to the calculating test of the understanding. We waited a few minutes, and saw as we think that he was a man who would pass triumphantly even through the rigid severity of this ordeal. There was an animating soul distinguishable in all he said and did, which at once gave a high interest to his performance, and excited those emotions which are always felt at the presence of genius – that is, at the union of great powers with a fine sensibility. It was this that gave fire to his eye, energy to his bones, and such a variety and expressiveness to all his gestures, that one might almost say 'his body thought.' We cannot name the actor who uses his hands and arms with such skill and propriety: we do not know whether he is ambi-dexter, but his left and right arm seem equally serviceable, and move with equal effect. We are aware that *Shylock* is an easy character: its traits are so broad and prominent as to be obvious to a child. One simple passion alone is to be expressed, for even the avarice of the usurer is swallowed up in the revenge of the insulted Jew. Of the various persons who have undertaken to represent this hateful being, we do not recollect one who failed; nay, who did not acquit himself respectably. No doubt they exhibited different degrees of merit; and between the impassioned energy of the late Mr Cooke, and the tame judiciousness of Mr Stephen Kemble, there was as immeasurable a distance as if the same song were to pass through these very different media, the voices of Madame Catalani and Madame Bianchi. Though the *Shylock* of Mr Kean had not the vehement force of the *Shylock* of Mr Cooke, yet as a whole it was little inferior, and in one or two passages, the *débutant* struck out beauties which were equally impressive and original. Everybody knows that the trial-scene is that in which the actor is most called upon to shew his powers; and all who have seen Mr Cooke must recollect the terrible strength with which he pourtrayed the most terrible of the passions – Revenge. Mr Kean had not the same dash and boldness of sketch, but he gave some touches that declared the master-artist. The 'learned doctor,' it will be remembered, explains the law in a way which the Jew considers entirely in his favour: his heart warms towards the friendly interpreter, and he calls him 'a very Daniel'. The pretended Judge then asks to look at the bond: the Jew, feeling assured that all is technically right, gives it with great readiness. And here we could not but admire the delighted eagerness with which Mr Kean perused the face of the supposed lawyer while the instrument was run over. His eye fairly reeled with joy. The legal counterfeit makes no objection to the bond, but advises *Shylock* to accept the offer of *thrice* the money. It is then the Jew utters that cruel and insolent impiety –

> An oath, an oath, I have an oath in heaven:
> Shall I lay perjury upon my soul?

This speech is usually given with a solemn severity of manner: Mr Kean's conception was new and excellent. He delivered the passage in a tone of humour almost bordering on the ludicrous: it was the bitter, ironical joke of a man sure of his darling purpose, and as he thought just about to triumph in his iniquity. The next touch was somewhat of the same kind and even better – *Portia* tells *Shylock* to procure a surgeon for *Antonio*: *Shylock* asks if it is so expressed in the bond.

Portia allows that it is not, but advises him to do it for charity. *Shylock* looks at the bond and answers –

> I cannot find it; 'tis not in the bond.

Mr Cooke, who was imitated by most of the other performers of this part, uttered this always with a savage sneer: Mr Kean gave it with a transported chuckle: his inmost heart seemed to laugh that no obstacle now remained to the completion of his murderous purpose. This was a fine touch of nature. The most ferocious and deadly passions will relapse into an almost idiot paroxysm of joy when they have their poor victim in their power: as the poet has made death grin horribly a ghastly smile on the prospect of an abundant food for his savage appetite.

We have been more than usually minute in our criticism, to shew that our admiration of Mr Kean has at least arisen from a careful observation, and is not a mere indiscriminate enthusiasm. We have given some reasons for our praise: if on examination they shall prove to be ill-founded, our eulogy will of course go for nothing. At the same time we have so much faith in our judgment, that we shall not easily be removed from it; and shall feel much surprise if the future acting of Mr Kean shall not be distinguished for that excellence which we now venture to pronounce that it unequivocally promises.

A letter to the *Examiner*, 15 May 1814:

Will you allow me, Sir, to make a few observations on Mr Kean's performance of *Othello*? I do not offer them as a criticism; but in the absence of *that*, they may perhaps be acceptable as expressions of the individual feelings of one who visits the Theatre, not as a critic, to discover beauties, or to detect faults, but as a passive recipient of the impressions, of whatever kind, that may be offered to him; and after all, perhaps this is the criticism upon which the merits of any production of the Fine Arts (for I do not hesitate to rank such acting as Mr Kean's among the Fine Arts) must be decided. But first let me endeavour to remove the prejudice, as it appears to me, which exists as to the personal qualifications required in a representative of *Othello*. To the 'imaginations' of those enlightened persons, the critics of the daily papers, from the time of Garrick to the present, the very name of *Othello* has conjured up a being, endowed with every thing that is noble in feature, every thing that is graceful in demeanour, every thing that is grand and dignified in person; in short, bating his colour, 'he looks an angel, and he moves a god.' But who told their 'imaginations' to invest him with any such exterior? Not Shakespear, I'm sure. What triumph would he have achieved for his favourite passion, in making his *Desdemona* love *such* a being? Why any of our boarding-school misses might fall in love, as they call it, with the outside of such an *Othello* as CONWAY. – Shakespear, I venture to conjecture, had a loftier object in view. He delighted to honour the female character; and was it ever, before or since, so highly honoured as in his own *Desdemona*? Did fiction, – even the fiction of Shakespear himself, – ever embody a more perfect character? The perfection however of Nature, not of Art. The *Venus* and the *Helen* are models of personal beauty; but it is the beauty of Art. The *Clarissa* is a model, and a sublime one, of mental perfection: but it is the perfection of Art. Did any of us ever hope for, – nay, should we even *desire*, such wives as *Clarissa*? But *Desdemona*, – 'the gentle lady married to the Moor,' – we can mingle in *her* joys, – we can luxuriate over *her* sorrows, with the most kindred, the most home-like feelings, – we can fancy ourselves, – some of us, I hope, can *feel* ourselves, – in the possession of *such* a wife or a sister, though there is not a part of her character that we could wish changed or away, yet we constantly feel that she is *only* a woman: it is precisely in this 'only' that her perfection consists. Shakespear, I say, delighted to honour the female character; and how exquisitely has he done so, in making this being love the Moor in spite of his personal defects! – He was a 'rough soldier,' 'black,' 'rude of speech,' without those 'soft parts of conversation that chamberers have,' and, above all, 'sunk into the vale of years.' But *she* saw his beauty in his goodness – *she* 'saw *Othello's* visage in his mind,' and *therefore* she loved him – loved him with a simplicity, a quietness, and yet a sublimity of self-devotion, that fiction itself has no where else depicted. On her death-bed – while the life-blood is flowing from the wound which he himself has inflicted on her, – she consigns her soul, as she believes, – for she is a Christian – to everlasting damnation, by pouring forth her last breath in a deliberate lie, to save him from temporary disgrace and punishment.

I had forgotten Mr Kean, but it was Shakespear who made me forget him. I am convinced, then, that the small, yet well-formed person of Mr Kean, and his deficiency of dignity, resulting, as I apprehend, entirely from that smallness, do not, in the slightest degree, disqualify him as a representative of Shakespear's *Othello*. I will first mention what struck me as faults in his performance of that character, that I may afterward dwell with unmingled delight upon its beauties. In the first act, in his speech to the Senate, where he relates his 'whole course of wooing,' in the centre of the 3rd or 4th row of the pit, and with the most anxious attention, I could distinguish scarcely three lines. I admire the mild and quiet tone of conscious rectitude with which he delivered the speech; such a contrast to the mock-heroic air with which it has usually been given, and in a moderate sized theatre it would have been distinctly heard; but Mr K. must remember that he is acting in a theatre, in point of size, admirably calculated for a Spanish bull-fight, but not at all adapted to the exhibition of those delicate shades of feeling which are depicted by a glance of the eye, a turn of the lip, or an under-tone of the voice. Another fault was, that in part of his reproaches to *Desdemona*, he assumed a cutting and sarcastic manner, which the words themselves did not warrant, and which was, besides, totally out of keeping with the rest of his conception of the character.

In the 1st and 2nd acts there was nothing striking, for there is no necessity to make *Othello* 'a hero to his valet-de-chambre.' Except from this, however, the words, 'If it were now to die, 'twere now to be most happy,' &c. Mingled with the most heartfelt happiness, there was a beautiful expression of pathos, which seemed almost to forbode the misery that awaited him. The 3rd act was the ordeal which was to try his powers as a great tragic actor, and most triumphantly he passed through it. Never were the workings of the human heart more successfully laid open than in the scene following that in which *Iago* first excites his jealousy. In every tone of the voice, in every movement of the face and body, it might be seen labouring under the accumulated agonies of unbounded love, struggling with and at length yielding to

163

doubt. The depth of expression thrown into the words, 'I found not *Cassio's kisses* on her lips,' has never been surpassed; then came the utter heart-sinking and helplessness which inevitably succeeds to the protracted operation of powerful passion. The speech beginning, 'Oh now for ever, farewell,' &c. was given in a tone of quiet despair, which evinced the most exquisite delicacy of conception, embodied in expression absolutely perfect. To this calm succeeded a storm of contending passions – rage, hatred, intervening doubts, – until at length the whole of his already excited energies were yielded up to revenge; the look and action accompanying the words, 'Oh blood! Iago, blood!' cast a chill over one's whole frame. There was a quietness about the last scenes of Mr K.'s performance, beautifully consistent with his manner of giving the speech I have alluded to, 'Oh now for ever,' &c. All is the dead calm of a midnight sea; passion seems to have 'raved itself to rest'; even when he learns, too late, that his wife was guiltless, it scarcely moves him; we feel sure that he had before determined not to live, and that the only change wrought by this certainty of her innocence is, that, whereas, before it, he would have sought death as a refuge from utter despair; *now* ''tis happiness to die'; for, amid the surrounding gloom, there is one bright spot to which he can turn, – she *did* love him, and all his devoted fondness was not cast away. There is a delicacy about the taste and feelings of this extraordinary young actor which must be instinctive. His genius, in this, as in some other of its characteristics, appears to me to bear a striking resemblance to that of Shakespear himself. Their schools have been alike, a green-room of a Theatre; their book of study alike, their own hearts. The blind adorers of Shakespear, the praisers of him by rote, will be greatly scandalized at this bringing their idol in contact with any thing human, – still more, with an everyday-looking person living and moving among ourselves: – not so would Shakespear himself have felt, had they lived in the same day; he would have stretched out his human hand to him, and have welcomed him with delight, as at least a kindred spirit. I was desirous of saying something on the exquisite acting that is lost by unnecessarily suppressing the whole of the 1st scene of the 4th act; but I fear I have already extended these desultory remarks to an inadmissible length. I am, sir,

Your obedient servant,

P.G.P.

JAMES WINSTON (1773–1843), the manager of Drury Lane Theatre, kept a journal and recorded several instances of Edmund Kean's appetites:

5 June 1820
On Kean being asked by Russell whether he would require to wait long between the acts [of *Richard III*], he said, 'No, not now, his *bubo* was broke' – same night a woman waiting.

17 January 1820
Kean requested the rehearsal might not be till twelve as he should get drunk that night – said he had frequently three women to stroke during performances and that two waited while the other was served. Penley said he had [formerly] seen Storace waiting for her turn. This night he had one woman (Smith) though he was much infected.

16 March 1825
Kean, about three o'clock in the morning, ordered a hackney coach to his door, took a lighted candle, got in, and rode off. He was not heard of till the Thursday noon when they found him in his room at the theatre fast asleep wrapt up in a large white greatcoat. He then sent off for a potence, some ginger, etc., and said, 'Send me Lewis or the other woman. I must have a fuck, and then I shall do.' He had it. They let him sleep till about six, when they awoke him, dressed him, and he acted but was not very sober. After the play [we] got him to supper at Sigel's lodgings and got him to a bedroom and locked him up till the morning.

Kean's agreement was signed in my room by Elliston on Thursday morning and by Kean in the evening just after he had finished playing Hamlet.

William Charles Macready (1793–1873) is accounted one of the greatest English actors of his own or any other time. He made his London début at Covent Garden on 25 September 1816. The following report from the *News* is thought to be by LEIGH HUNT:

A candidate for Theatrical honours – new to the London boards – made his appearance here on Monday last. Mr Macready has flourished so long in every Provincial Theatre and Newspaper – and appeared so often, and in so many characters in every exhibition of paintings at Somerset House – that we were long ago inclined to consider him as one of those assiduous Gentlemen of the profession who supply the place of genius by indefatigable exertion – and who, by the aid of puffing, sometimes wriggle themselves into a situation in which their bare merits never would exalt them. Little prepossessed therefore in his favour – but not at all prejudiced against him – we went to witness his first appearance in the Metropolis. He chose for his début – and as yet we cannot say whether judiciously or not – the part of Orestes, in Phillips' Tragedy of *The Distressed Mother*. This is, perhaps, the heaviest and coldest tragedy that has existed for any length of time upon the English stage. Hermione is a character beyond our comprehension. The author of it, perhaps, intended to show a few of the dreadful effects that love will cause in some constitutions, but we humbly conceive that his Hermione could never have been under the influence of the 'divine passion.' Hurried about by some unaccountable spell – she loves Pyrrhus and Orestes alternatively – devises the death of the former, and then falls by her own hand, for the mere purpose, one would suppose, of driving the latter to desperation, and so completing the butchery. Andromache is almost as inexplicable. She marries a man whom she cannot love, in the hope to 'secure a father to her child' – being pre-resolved 'with her pointed dagger and determined hand' to 'save her virtue and conclude her woes.' Well may Cephisa exclaim,

> But, Madam, what will be the rage of Pyrrhus
> Defrauded of his promised happiness?

But she appears to estimate 'Troy's vanquisher and great Achilles' son' very properly – for she shuffles off this question, and says,

> That will require *thy* utmost skill.
> Use every artifice to keep him stedfast –
> – let him *think* I loved him – &c.

and truly he is the weakest of all intemperate men. Agamemnon's son is a degree better; but heroes are like other mortals when in love.

Mr Macready is one of the plainest and most awkwardly made men that ever trod the stage. His voice is even coarser than his person. And yet – notwithstanding these apparently insurmountable defects, he is undoubtedly an actor – and we will add – (what would be considered a very high compliment from those who have not given publicity to their opinions of actors so frequently as we have) – he is an actor in many points superior to Mr Kean. They both labour under great imperfections of voice and figure – enormous drawbacks indeed to an actor – but Mr Macready strikes us as having a better conception of his Author's meaning. He trusts more to plain delivery and proper emphasis – and consequently has less occasion for starting – pointing – and slapping his forehead. His action is naturally not very good – and we think it is rather redundant. We cannot give great praise to his last scene. It was one continued bustling, incoherent rave – and we could only here and there catch a word. A madman on the stage must be a little systematic – and perhaps this anomaly increases our antipathy to such characters. We are satisfied they should not be represented – for the most perfect of them never fails to create in the audience a thorough feeling of disgust. We hope very soon to have an opportunity of seeing Mr Macready in some other character.

In Pyrrhus, Chas. Kemble appeared to feel the importance of his kingly character – but he entirely failed to give us an idea of Majesty – and really he seemed to forget that a King should talk common sense –

for point, emphasis, and the whole tribe of such inferior considerations were swept away in the impetuous stream of his declamation.

Of Mrs Glover, in Andromache, and Mrs Egerton, in Hermione,
charity forbids us to speak.

An anonymous playgoer's comments scrawled across a programme, 1819:

Macready was the first actor who went before the curtain at the
conclusion of a piece to take what is termed in theatrical parlance 'The
call;' – he done it after the last act of Richard the third at Covent
Garden Theatre on the 25th of October 1819, from that evening the
custom was adopted.

JULIE LUMSDEN:

Walk Ons

Into another public room
With the usual dingy set
And noisy cast. The plot,
Predictable. The dialogue
Far from rich (though
Colourful). Bit Players, all.
Hags and Gravediggers. Did they get
Phone calls and availability checks?
Were contracts signed?
Enter on cue: three pretty students.
And always that
Defeated couple in the corner –
Non Speaking Artistes
With no love scenes later.

I play
Demented woman in pub,
But quietly.
Underplaying was always my style.

Laurence Olivier (1907–89) was one of the half dozen great actors of the twentieth century. He was knighted in 1947 and created a Life Peer in 1970. In a famous Old Vic season at the New Theatre (now the Albery) in 1944 he played Shakespeare's Richard III for the first time. He himself felt that with the performance that he had come of age as a leading actor. On 17 September 1944, JAMES AGATE wrote in the *Sunday Times*:

Any critic sitting at Shakespeare's most rampageous melodrama must realize that he has three Richards to contend with. The first is the 'actual' Richard, and perhaps he need not bother very much about this largely conjectural figure. The second is the much more 'real' figure created by Shakespeare. The third is the Richard put forward by the actor. An eminent colleague has written of Mr Olivier in this role that he is 'wisely careful not to play it in the old way.' But is he sure that Mr Olivier possesses the physical means to play it in the old way? My colleague goes on, 'It is no part of his plan to return to full-blooded stage tradition and to carry conviction by storm.' But I submit that Mr Olivier carries almost complete conviction by a great deal of storm. It is the quality of the storm that has changed – the difference between the tropic cyclone and the polar blast. All stage storms must be vocal, and Mr Olivier cannot thunder. His high, shimmering tenor has not the oak-cleaving quality; it is a wind which gets between your ribs.

Let us look at what the other characters say of Richard. Seven times in this play he is alluded to as a 'boar.' Now Shakespeare was not in the habit of using words loosely; when he said 'boar' he meant 'boar.' 'The chafed boar, the mountain lioness, The ocean swells not so'; 'Who, like a boar too savage, doth root up His country's peace.' 'Have I not in my time heard lions roar? Have I not heard the sea puff'd up with winds Rage like an angry boar chafed with sweat?' Even more clinchingly, take Prince Hal's 'Where sups he? doth the old boar feed in the old frank?' Always in Shakespeare 'boar' stands for something powerful, massive, and even clumsy. (Oberon couples boar and bear.) Now let it be said that there is nothing of the boar about Mr Olivier's Richard; this actor has neither the voice nor the shoulders. But let me, like my discerning colleague, congratulate him on being 'as graceful as he is witty and accomplished.' Mr Olivier has had the first-rate notion of making first-rate virtue out of flat necessity. And he has this come-back to any criticism on this point – that Shakespeare has provided excuses for him all over the place. Just as the First Murderer in *Macbeth* talks poetry because Shakespeare was a poet, so this boar has witty bristles because Shakespeare's mind bristled with wit. An ideal Richard will not let you forget the boar; Mr Olivier never suggests him. Serpent, rather. Something spiritually evil, and fascinated by the power to work evil.

As I sat attentive at this admirable performance I seem to see an extraordinary succession of images – Charles II plotting mischief, any old actor's Robert Macaire and Alfred Jingle, any good actor's Iago and even Iachimo, and, above all, a great deal of Irving's Mephistopheles. People still talk of the way in which the Old Man would say about Martha, 'I don't know what's to become of her – *I* won't have her!' Yes, there was a great deal of Irving in Wednesday's performance, in the bite and devilry of it, the sardonic impudence, the superb emphases, the sheer malignity and horror of it. If I have a criticism it is that Mr Olivier takes the audience a little too much into his confidence. Richard is immensely tickled at the virtuosity with which he proposes to take the world-stage. And, in his hero's opening soliloquy, Shakespeare is at great pains to convey this relish. But Mr Olivier makes that speech rather more than something overheard. This Richard means us to overhear; we are positively tipped the wink.

Now are our brows bound with victorious wreaths;
Our bruisèd arms hung up for monuments;
Our stern alarums changed to merry meetings,
Our dreadful marches to delightful measures.
Grim-visaged war hath smooth'd his wrinkled front, I don't think;

Mr Olivier may not say those last three words; his eyebrows certainly signal them.

This Richard coheres from start to finish, and is a complete presentation of the character as the actor sees it and his physical means permit. Yet one has to close one's ears to certain disadvantages. Take that moment when Stanley says 'Richmond is on the seas,' and Richard has his tremendous 'There let him sink, and be the seas on him!' This, surely, must be an occasion for Voice. It was here on Wednesday that old Martha came to mind; that I seemed to hear Irving chuckle, 'There let her sink, and be the seas on her!' It is a moot point whether Richard's 'There is no creature loves me' should or should not crook a finger at pathos. Mr Olivier says 'No' firmly. This Richard is bent on carrying the joke through. And on the note of

> March on, join bravely, let us to't pell-mell;
> If not to heaven, then hand in hand to hell,

he brings the drama to a jaunty, Jingle-esque conclusion. To sum up, I do not think that this is Shakespeare's Richard. It could not be said of this Renaissance villain at the end that 'The bloody dog is dead.' 'Dog' is wrong. What Richmond would say over Mr Olivier's corpse is: 'We have scotch'd the snake *and* kill'd it!' But even if this Richard is not Shakespeare's it is very definitely Mr Olivier's, and I do not propose to forget its mounting verve and sustained excitement.

The production is fair. Mr Burrell, having realized that the Middle Ages were not the Dark Ages, gives us plenty of illumination to see his actors by, though I still can't quite understand why Richard should be crowned in the middle of the night! In one respect only do I fault the production; this is that it is too glittering and too band-boxy. Everybody, like Pinero's French governess, is over-gowned and over-hatted. Indeed, one feels that the whole thing could be turned into ballet at a minute's notice, and I have no doubt that Mr Helpmann would dance Richard to perfection. There is, however, no mistake about Mr Herbert Menges's music, which, without being obtrusively archaic or disgustingly atonal, suggests the fifteenth century.

From the *Pall Mall Gazette*, 11 January, 1900. A report on Herbert Beerbohm-Tree's production of *A Midsummer Night's Dream*:

Mr Tree's most recent achievement is in every sense notable; he has not only given us the finest production of Shakespeare's comedy, but in it he plays Bottom as certainly it has not been played by any actor since Phelps. For a manager, a great production, with all its enormous labour and profuse expenditure, *is*, if it be successful, in itself sufficient cause for triumph; but when the manager is actor too, and finds himself precisely fitted with the part best fitted to display his talent, the result is as legitimate an occasion of pride as when the general has to fight in person, and, like Napoleon at Lodi, himself carries the colours across the bridge. It is not often, we believe, the actor-manager at any theatre is seen at his best; meaning by that, in the part best suited to him. There is something in human nature, more particularly theatrical human nature, which constantly drives it out of the appointed course; Liston wants to play Hamlet, and no one can persuade Sothern he is not a romantic lover. Now Mr Tree is a character-actor, and, probably, the best on the stage; character as dependent on observation, and not on passion or emotion, is the medium best fitted for the display of his talent. In Bottom the Weaver he gets precisely the chance desired; how he avails himself of it, with what richness, and yet delicacy, of humour, will be seen for many nights to come – would be willingly seen by us again and again.

Yet Mr Tree, who has cast himself so perfectly, has in Miss Louie Freear as Puck made a grievous mistake. Miss Freear's notion of Puck is to make of him a sort of male Marchioness; it is, in fact, simply a domestic servant, whose head has been turned by reading dreambooks, indulging in a series of *entrechats*, from kitchen to scullery. It is not even droll, it is merely common, and has no more to do with Shakespeare than would Mr Dan Leno as Oberon. The clumsiness of it is, unfortunately, all the more apparent side by side with the grace and charm of Miss Julia Neilson's King of the Fairies. Her Oberon is truly regal, while the mere fact of her being a woman just differentiates it from humanity. For her singing no praise can be too high; there is a rich thrill in her tones that suggests some gorgeous Eastern bird. We have never heard the bulbul, but if the bulbul could be taught to chant

'I know a bank,' and that the bank of the Tigris, we should imagine it very like Miss Neilson. As Titania, Mrs Tree plays prettily, but is scarcely fairylike. It is a fairy from South Kensington, whose revels are limited to Queen's Gate, and whose rings are to be found in Kensington Gardens. Mrs Tree gives one the notion that Titania has smart friends somewhere, and is only out in the wood because it happens for the time to be a society fad. Nor need even a fairy wear quite so fixed a smile; and its constancy makes one suspect the Fairy Queen's true amiability.

But in the general cast there are few blemishes. Of the quartet of lovers, always, to us, tedious, and surely capable of some compression, Miss Dorothea Baird's Helena is by far the most successful. Miss Baird will probably never make an actress, in the stereotyped sense of the word, but she is always seen with pleasure; just as there are some singers the *cognoscenti* tell us cannot sing, yet who are always preferable to many more highly cultured in the art. Miss Baird has a charm which is happiest in uncultivation; in Helena she manages to convey an impression, one understands better her running after Demetrius (very intelligently played by Mr Gerald Lawrence) where other more gifted actresses would very likely fail. Miss Sarah Brooke's Hermia would be better – it very probably is – if one could do her the justice to get the *Mikado* out of one's head. But Miss Brooke so strongly recalls one of three little maids from school, that for our part, at any rate, we find it impossible. For Mr Lewis Waller we can only say he was, unfortunately, so hoarse as to be well-nigh inaudible; later, no doubt, he will play the part as well as he plays most others. As Theseus, Mr William Mollison was admirable; we cannot tell why, but we can always hear Mr Mollison, whereas with most other actors we have to listen. We imagine the reason to be that Mr Mollison is one of the few actors on the stage who have really learnt to speak; the others, for the most part, only talk. The 'rude mechanicals' were without exception delightful; the Flute of Mr Louis Calvert, the Starveling of Mr Fisher White could not be improved upon; nor were the Snout of Mr Percival Stevens, the Quince of Mr Franklin McLeay, the Snug of Mr E. M. Robson otherwise than excellent. One wishes to see them again at the end of the play. We feel, indeed, that the curtain should not fall on the fairies' stealing out of Theseus' palace after the revels, but on the cheerful yet subdued riot of the Pyramus and Thisbe company, finding their way out through the deserted great hall, after having been properly entertained at supper in the Royal servants' kitchen. After all, the true life of the comedy lies not so much in Oberon and Titania, Theseus and Hippolyta, or in the young lovers, as in the delicious humours of the 'mechanicals,' faithfully sketched – who can doubt it? – from some old Warwickshire friends of the immortal author. In any event, the curtain falls on one of the most delightful Shakespearean productions of our time.

The actress PENELOPE KEITH in an interview with Sheridan Morley told of an experience as a lowly member of the Royal Shakespeare Company in 1963:

Spears, mainly, and crowd scenes in *Julius Caesar*. John Blatchley, the director, said we were all to be real people and say things, so on the first night just as Mark Antony started the speech I said 'Have an ear' and just then everyone in the crowd fell silent and the whole audience heard me and Bernard Levin was jolly rude about me in his notice the next morning. I thought of drowning myself in the Avon but when I went back on the second night the whole green room stood up and cheered because they said nobody in the crowd had ever got a Bernard Levin notice before.*

An unidentified writer describes the most famous role of Sir John Martin-Harvey (1863–1944), actor-manager. On 16 February 1898 he presented himself in *The Only Way*, an adaptation by Freeman Wills of Dickens's *The Tale of Two Cities*:

Success, absolute and indisputable, attended the opening of Mr Martin Harvey's venture last evening. It was a first-night at the

---

*In fact, the reviewer was Kenneth Tynan. 'By way of further deflation, a cackling hag greets the opening lines of "Friends, Romans, countrymen" with the derisive offer: "Here, have an ear!"' *Observer*, 14 April 1963.

Lyceum, though not exactly a Lyceum first-night, for only Sir Henry Irving can invest that great function with its distinguishing attributes. But it was an interesting and attractive occasion nevertheless. A young and clever actor dared to make a bold bid in the foremost of our dramatic houses, and his brave spirit led him on to victory. An author of taste and judgment lent his aid by providing material that was at once sound, honest, and direct. Mr Freeman Wills did not respond to the summons of the audience at the end of the play, and it was explained that modesty forbade. Let us hope that this was the true reason, for the writer has no reason to be ashamed of his work. He has taken a powerful and engrossing novel and planned from it a drama which is clear, distinct, and intelligible; which never loses itself in mysterious byways; which keeps to the high road of unembarrassed lucidity and successively passes the milestones of attention, interest, and success. *The Only Way* will bear compression. If there were moments when it flagged last evening the reason was to be found in the occasional wordiness of the dialogue, and a tendency on the part of the performers to 'drag the time.' This should presently disappear, and then the latest 'drama of the tumbril' will settle down to a period of prosperity. Throughout the five acts not a dissentient note was heard, and, allowing for the friendliness of feeling inseparable from a first-night assembly, the enthusiasm exhibited rang out firm and true. We do not believe that an English audience will ever withhold its approval from sincere and legitimate work. *The Only Way* is necessarily a sad play, and a sad play, badly acted, is the surest and quickest road to disaster. That Mr Martin Harvey succeeded is the more to his credit and to that of his faithful helpers.

As the moth hovers round a naked flame, so is the dramatist fascinated by the grim and gruesome story told in the most dread and dire chapter of French history. Revolution plays will be with us from time to time, so long as our stage endures. The possibilities are high, the interest keen and human, and the surroundings, built up by a practised hand, cannot fail to impart the needed touches of intensity and horror. Dion Boucicault dealt with the subject in an adaptation of Dumas' *Chevalier de la Maison Rouge*, and it was this fact, it is believed, which caused Ben Webster long to hesitate over the production of unlucky Watts Phillips's *Dead Heart*, which is now, by the way, exactly forty years old. Three members of the original cast remain – John Billington, Toole (the perruquier, Toupet), and Mrs Alfred Mellon. It is an old story how the author learned with consternation that this excellent actress was to play Catherine Duval. In her own particular line he had the highest admiration for her, but this part was quite out of it. Apparently Miss Woolgar was of the same opinion, and only on threat of dismissal by the manager did she undertake a character which stands out as one of her most conspicuous and brilliant successes. A few months previously *A Tale of Two Cities* had begun to appear in serial form, and presently a fierce discussion arose, unkind persons asserting that Phillips had stolen his idea from Dickens, an accusation vigorously and loyally repudiated by Webster in a public manifesto, wherein he showed that *The Dead Heart* had been written and paid for years before *A Tale of Two Cities* was published. Over Carton's vicarious sacrifice much ink was shed. It was pointed out that Carlyle, and Lord Lytton in *Zanoni*, had a similar incident. But *The Dead Heart* lived and made a far greater stir in the dramatic world than Tom Taylor's adaptation of Dickens's novel given by Madame Celeste, when she had the Lyceum, in 1860. Here the late John Rouse played Jerry Cruncher, and we confess that, amidst the strain and stress of the tragic tale Mr Freeman Wills presented last evening, we sadly missed the immortal – and immoral – odd man at Tellson's bank. Yet there was one actor at hand who could have pictured him to a nicety. We mean Mr James Taylor – a most experienced and versatile comedian and character actor. The drawback to such a piece as *The Only Way* is the sustained gloom of the story, and our old friend, the humorous body-snatcher, must have proved highly acceptable. Jerry is a being outside the broad considerations of the French Revolution, but he is certainly not beyond the scheme of *A Tale of Two Cities*. In other directions let us remember that the late W. G. Wills and Mr Kyrle Bellew have given us a Marat in *Ninon* and *Charlotte Corday* respectively, and that Mr Joseph Hatton has shown Robespierre in *When Greek Meets Greek*. The old play, *The Black Doctor*, also deals with the Revolution, and will be remembered for the effect of a 'multiple' scene, in which four different actions take place simultaneously.

Mr Wills takes the love of the exiled St Evrémonde for Lucie

Manette, the ruthless vengeance of Ernest Defarge for the murder of his brother and the dishonour of his sister, and carries us, by a natural transition, from England to France, where the noble Carton makes his heroic exit for the sake of the woman he loves. With an excellent eye for contrast, the earlier scenes in London stand out in bold relief against the blood-stained orgies of the Parisian period. From peace we move on to turmoil, and when the author had finished with his opening acts the remaining ones were, to a large extent, certain to 'play themselves.' Hawes Craven's beautiful picture of Dr Manette's garden in Soho carried our thoughts back a quarter of a century to the lovely rural scene at the Lyceum where, in the play of another Wills, Eugene Aram made the expiation of his sin. And the stage-management would have reflected no discredit upon Sir Henry Irving himself. The revolutionary tribunal, cold and merciless, swayed by conflicting waves of passion and indecision, struck upon the spectator with a fearsomeness which bore the best testimony to its dramatic force. Nor did the unsparing realism of the last grim act fail to impress the spectators into absorbed silence. Sidney Carton was no theatrical puppet. With his soft, sad face, lighted up by a new resolve and a new joy; a bright light in his eye, and a sweet hope in his heart, he compelled the tears of the house, and compelled them as much by his own power as by the appealing sentiment of the story. Mr Harvey was careful, throughout the play, never to get out of his depth, and to our thinking the great virtue of his playing lay in his steady avoidance of any attempt to force a point. The Carton of the early scenes was a sufficiently emphasized 'ne'er-do-weel,' without being a raucous-voiced and shouting ruffian, as we have erstwhile seen him represented. He will have a better chance after the blue pencil has eliminated the unnecessary verbiage in the dialogue, and after Mr Holbrook Blinn, perhaps fettered to some extent by fear of Lyceum 'traditions,' has more accurately gauged the pitch of the house. A character like Defarge must be 'let go.' We do not desire any Coghlan exhibition of 'reserved force.' Be it remembered that *The Only Way* is melodramatic in its very conception and essence, and that it never pays to mumble melodrama. Mr Blinn did well, and was anxious not to overact. Only he and some other of the performers should not forget that the man at the back of the gallery is a person with rights which are not to be overlooked.

If there be any doubt on this point, let the players in *The Only Way* take guidance from that accomplished and ever welcome favourite, Miss Marriott. In her we saw one of the 'old school' – the best Jeanie Deans known to this generation, and an enterprising Hamlet long before Sarah Bernhardt thought of the melancholy Dane. 'The Vengeance' gave her small opportunity, but she made the very most of it, and her musical notes were as true and penetrating as ever. A quite unexpected success was achieved by Miss de Silva in the part of Mimi – pretty, pathetic, and delightfully natural – while the veteran, Sam Johnson, lent breadth and significance to pompous Mr Stryver. Mr Taylor was not altogether too well placed as Lorry, but Mr Tyars, in his common and congenial character of president of a court, was perfectly at home. Of Mr Herbert Sleath it may fairly be said that he shows signs of improving in his work, and his Charles Darnay was fairly good. Mr Fred Everill plays Dr Manette with discretion, and Miss Grace Warner, though scarcely realizing our ideas of Lucie, gave signs of careful training received from a clever and painstaking father. Most of the other people are simple sketches on the canvas, though valuable in the general scheme, and when *The Only Way* is rid of redundancies which will permit the dropping of the curtain at an earlier hour than twenty-five minutes to twelve, Londoners will go to see the latest version of *A Tale of Two Cities*. For it shows us that we have devoted young men springing up in our midst, and next to the repeated conquests of ripe experience nothing is more gratifying than the fragrant promise of youth.

KENNETH TYNAN on Laurence Olivier's performance of Coriolanus, 1959:

No actor uses *rubato*, stealing a beat from one line to give to the next, like Olivier. The voice is soft steel that can chill and cut, or melt and scorch. One feels the chill in the icy tirade that begins 'You common cry of curs' and ends 'There is a world elsewhere.' And one is scorched by the gargled snarl of rage with which Olivier rams home, by a wrenching upward inflexion on the last syllable, 'The fires i' th' lowest hell fold in the peo*ple*!' At the close, faithful as ever to the characterization on which he has fixed, Olivier is roused to suicidal frenzy by Aufidius's gibe – 'thou boy of tears.' '*Boy!*' shrieks the overmothered general, in an outburst of strangled fury, and leaps up a flight of precipitous steps to vent his rage. Arrived at the top, he relents and throws his sword away. After letting his voice fly high in the great, swingeing line about how he 'flutter'd your Volscians in *Cor-i-o-li,*' he allows a dozen spears to impale him. He is poised, now, on a promontory some twelve feet above the stage, from which he topples forward, to be caught by the ankles so that he dangles, inverted, like the slaughtered Mussolini. A more shocking, less sentimental death I have not seen in the theatre; it is at once proud and ignominious, as befits the titanic fool who dies it.

The image, and the echo, of this astonishing performance have taken root in my mind in the weeks that have passed since I witnessed it. The dark imprint of Olivier's stage presence is something one forgets only with an effort, but the voice is a lifelong possession of those who have heard it at its best. It sounds, distinct and barbaric, across the valley of many centuries, like a horn calling to the hunt, or the neigh of a battle-maddened charger.

Sir Donald Wolfit was acclaimed as the greatest King Lear of his generation. In my biography of him, *Sir Donald Wolfit CBE: His life and work in the unfashionable theatre* (1971), I attempted to recreate the particular performance which James Agate described as 'the greatest piece of Shakespearean acting I have seen since I have been privileged to write for the *Sunday Times*':

The night of Wednesday 12 April 1944 was misty and damp and chill. London was again under attack, but the weather was shortly to improve and the raids slackened.

Wolfit had taken the Scala Theatre for a thirteen-week season which had begun in February; after nine weeks, he decided to try *King Lear* once more.

He arrived at the theatre with Rosalind at five, dressed in a voluminous brown teddy-bear coat acquired in Canada while touring with Barry Jackson. Black homburg on head, shoulders stooped, the actor advanced towards the stage-door, paused and glanced at nearby bomb damage, appeared to nod gravely as if he understood some symbolic message contained in the ruins, and marched into the theatre.

It being the first performance of the play that season, he went on to the stage, lit by the naked bulbs of working lights, to make sure all was in order. He surveyed the grey set, something like Stonehenge, gazed up at the position of the spotlights, nodded once more, and retired to his dressing room; it was noticed that he was unusually preoccupied.

He undressed and, wrapped in a pink towelling dressing gown, began to make up, painting in the heavy lines on his forehead and about the eyes, whitening his thick bushy eyebrows, highlighting his nose with a broad line. Next came the white beard, then the wig, stuck down with white-hard varnish. As the make-up took form, as wig and beard were fixed in place, and the joins disappeared under the thick grease-paint, so his hands began to tremble, his eyes to narrow and appear rheumy, his head to shake. At last he powdered – Brown and Polson's cornflour – and brushed it off, once more to reveal the aged face of the King. Last, he lined his hands, to age them, too.

With forty-five minutes to go to curtain-up, he called for his dresser. In silence, the clothes were handed to him until at last the heavy cloak sat upon the bent shoulders; the triple coronet was offered and he fixed it securely on his head, nodding and shaking as if with palsy.

When the assistant stage-manager called five minutes to the rise of the curtain, Wolfit slowly descended to the stage, his dresser in attendance, carrying a silver salver upon which stood a moist chamois leather, a glass of Guinness and – rare in war-time – some peeled grapes. Actors who happened to be waiting in the corridors stood aside to allow the little procession to pass; Wolfit nodded to them with an expression of infinite weariness. The silence backstage was oppressive.

He waited in the wings, doing his best not to concern himself with the bustle of activity that precedes the performance; this, in itself, was unusual, for in other plays, no matter how large or wearying the part, he would be hissing last-minute instructions to the stage management, electricians and actors. But not this night; he stood perfectly still with Rosalind, ready as Cordelia, beside him, occasionally glancing at her with a look that seemed to want to make sure that she understood the weight of all the world was upon his shoulders. He talked to no one; members of the company gave him a wide berth if they had to pass. He did not even enquire about the size of the audience; he might be expected to gaze through the peep-hole, but he did not; the house, in fact, was painfully thin, less than half-full.

His stage-director ordered the actors to stand by. The house lights dimmed. Rosabel Watson received her cue, and the trumpet sounded. The curtain rose slowly.

Kent and Gloucester begin. In the wings, Wolfit fidgets with his cloak, sceptre and crown, pulling at his beard, relaxing his neck muscles. Now comes his cue: Eric Maxon, as Gloucester says, 'He hath been out nine years, and away he shall be again.' The trumpet sounds once more. 'The King is coming'.

Lear enters from the extreme down-stage position, and crossing to centre, orders 'Attend the lords of France and Burgundy, Gloucester.' It is a sombre voice, accustomed to command. The King reaches centre and turns his back on the audience, pauses, his head shaking almost imperceptibly, and then advances towards his throne; once seated, he commences the division of his kingdom, which the actor believes to be the first step in the betrayal of Kingship upon which the tragedy is built.

How gentle but firm he is with Goneril, as if making himself more affectionate than is his wont; and so with Regan, more indulgent perhaps, yet no less certain of his authority. To Cordelia, he invites her honesty by a slight descent into sentimentality. Her reply halts him. 'Nothing will come of nothing' is uttered with a contempt for her sincerity. Her banishment is delivered as if Lear pronounces on behalf of some primeval, barbaric power. The King is set on his path, obstinate, angry, unreasonable.

It is a gentle Lear who toys with the disguised Kent, an indulgent King who is amused by the Fool, played by Richard Goolden almost as old as his master. At the first insult delivered by Oswald, Lear is incredulous.

LEAR: My lady's father? my lord's knave, you whoreson dog, you slave, you cur!
OSWALD: I am none of this, my lord, I beseech you pardon me.
LEAR: Do you bandy looks with me, you rascal?

And with sudden savagery, the King reveals his whip – Ayrton's whip – and flays the insolent steward, punishing him out of a savage, determined impulse. But in the scene that follows with the Fool, Lear's mood reflects his concern for his own frail position, pre-occupied with the unexpected hardening of his eldest daughter's affections. His temper is unpredictable; the whip dangles by his side, twitching dangerously from time to time. His tongue lashes round 'No lad, teach me'; 'Dost call me fool, boy?' is puzzled, but not without venom; the relationship between King and Fool is founded on love and compassion, which deepens as the scene proceeds, as if the King, sensing his alienation, admits the wise clown to Cordelia's place in his heart.

The King's fury with Goneril is at first a show of paternal wrath, but as the scene gains momentum, so the actor's reshaping of the text begins to work to his advantage, for he has built slowly and carefully to the hideous curse upon Goneril:

> Into her womb convey sterility,
> Dry up in her organs of increase,
> And from her derogate body never spring
> A babe to honour her! If she must teem,
> Create her child of spleen, that it may live
> And be a thwart disfeatur'd torment to her,
> Let it stamp wrinkles in her brow of youth,
> With cadent tears fret channels in her cheeks,
> Turn all her mother's pains and benefits
> To laughter and contempt, that she may feel
> How sharper than a serpent's tooth it is
> To have a thankless child!

And from the air, arms upstretched, Lear clutches the physical parcel, as it were, of his savage imprecation, pulls it down and then, to be rid of it, hurls it at his ingrate daughter.

When the King next appears it is with the Fool and Kent, and he cannot keep from his voice a growing, agonizing hurt, the pain of rejection. 'O let me not be mad, not mad, sweet heaven! Keep me in temper. I would not be mad!' It is spoken like the first distant echo of the wind; it is a vocal intimation of the storm; the thunder breaks from him on seeing Kent in the stocks. 'By Jupiter, I swear no,' is not idly spoken; it rumbles. Now the passion, the fury, the pain increase. In the scene with Regan, the old man is consumed with emotion, bordering on self-pity. 'I can scarce speak to thee,' he utters crying; tears are on the actor's cheeks. But the mood changes. Regan begins to advise her father on how he should behave; his response, 'Say, how is that?' contains danger, which quickly turns to incredulity at his daughter's persistence, then to irony, from irony once more to fury. It is an incredible display of shifting mood and emotion. 'How came my man i' the stocks?' he demands in a pathetic attempt to regain authority. The actor has laid the seeds of the King's madness in the instability of the old man's passions. The appeal to the gods, 'If you do love old men' is an appeal for sanity.

But Lear is more than a father spurned by ungrateful and ambitious children, more than a man whose reason is endangered. 'I gave you all,' he cries, and the actor speaks the line as though aware for the first time of the enormity of his own self-betrayal: it is the King, stripped bare of power and authority. His strength is drained in the argument concerning the number of his retinue, and again he is no more than man, aged, helpless. He turns his back on the audience, crouching low, sobbing into his hands. Regan asks, 'What need one?' Now cries the wind: 'O reason not the need' it pleads, and the actor's voice is burdened with piercing, whining overtones, then is entrapped in despair, '. . . let not women's weapons, water-drops, Stain my man's cheeks!' The vocal thunder cracks. 'No, you unnatural hags' is accompanied by an electrifying effect: Lear's cloak, a wide full circle, swirls in a petrified arc as the King turns upon his daughters, and the actor embarks on the major climax of Lear's mounting crisis.

I will have such revenges on you both
That all the world shall – I will do such things, –
What they are, yet I know not, but they shall be
The terrors of the earth. You think I'll weep;
No, I'll not weep: I have full cause of weeping.
But this heart shall break into a hundred thousand flaws,
Or ere I'll weep. O fool, I shall go mad!

The 'terrors of the earth', delivered in the nasal register, harsh and grating, is echoed by a thunderclap which seems to arrest the King's anger, for it is the gentle, pitiful frailty of 'O fool, I shall go mad' that finally takes him out onto the heath.

The storm that night was not, nor on any subsequent night would ever be, loud enough to drown the actor's voice which soars above wind and thunder and rain. 'Blow, winds, and crack your cheeks! rage! blow!' he commands, daring the elements, taunting them to overwhelm him. The actor has ascended into the cosmos. He obeys Granville Barker's injunction, 'Lear *is* the storm'. With Kent and Fool crouching at his feet, he stands against a tall obelisk, bathed in white light, the tempest in his mind communing with the outraged elements:

Let the great gods,
That keep this dreadful pother o'er our heads,
Find out their enemies now.

cracks like a mighty lightning flash and the power is spent; tones of child-like simplicity enter the actor's voice, so bereft of reason and majesty; all that remains is naked man, a tormented soul, sheltering in the hovel. 'Wilt break my heart?' asks Lear, before entering; it is not a king's question in the actor's reading, but man's, base and brought low, humiliated, humbled. For the actor is playing, too, for the scene that is to come with blind Gloucester. 'Ay, every inch a king,' jogs Lear's ancient memory of some glorious past. 'I am a king, my masters, you know that,' has a forlorn, hollow dignity, as the actor pulls the two knights with whom he plays the scene, to their knees, demanding of them meaningless obeisance. The more pitiful still the exit: 'Nay, if you get it, you shall get it with running. Sa, sa, sa, sa,' comes like an infantile game, devoid of reason, begging compassion.

The actor achieves sublime peace in his waking after the storm; an untroubled calm pervades his person. For one terrible moment he leads all to believe he may have regained his sanity as he recognizes his Cordelia, but the hope passes.

The physical test of the actor is still to come and, incredibly, he has voice to rend the air. 'Howl! Howl! Howl!' catches yet again the wind, but it is the final terror. He carries Cordelia, the rope hanging from her neck; he places her on the ground, touches her face with infinite gentleness, distractedly tugs at the rope, and strokes her face.

> And my poor fool is hang'd! No, no life!
> Why should a dog, a horse, a rat, have life,
> And thou no breath at all? O thou wilt come
> No more; never, never, never, never, never.

The actor treats the finality as if seeking a dark, awesome vision of eternity. The tragedy of King Lear has come almost to its end:

> The oldest hath borne most; we that are young
> Shall never see so much, nor live so long.

The solemn chords of the dead march are heard; the curtain falls.

The atmosphere back-stage had, all through the performance, been infected with auspicious excitement. Wolfit, when not on stage, behaved with strange, unaccustomed remoteness. Even during his change of cloak, which was always performed by Rosalind, he said nothing to her, but she could feel an unfamiliar tension in every muscle of his back.

The few in the audience that night bellowed their acclaim loud enough for twice their number. The shouts of 'bravo', the cheers, were an acknowledgement of a momentous performance. As Wolfit stood waiting for his turn to bow, he dabbed at his face with the moist chamois leather, downed the last drop of Guinness – he had drunk and sweated out eight bottles that evening. At last, his turn came: as was his custom, he pounded the curtain with his fist ('let 'em know you're coming' he used to say) and stepped out through the opening, into the light, clutching the curtain for support. The volume of acclaim washed over him; the actor who had not surrendered to the storm, surrendered now to his public. Wearily, he raised a hand for silence – it came at once. In a spent voice he offered his thanks for the way they had received 'the greatest tragedy in our language'. Exhausted, he withdrew, the sound of renewed cheering still ringing in his ears.

In the privacy of his dressing room, he undressed, unstuck beard and wig and, holding on to the back of a chair, instructed his dresser to sprinkle surgical spirit over his back and to rub hard with a towel. That night the actor slept well.

JAMES AGATE's genius was inspired by his knowledge, experience and breadth of taste. He had seen Irving and Sarah Bernhardt. He was able to admire actors as diverse in style as Olivier and Gielgud, or Richardson and Wolfit. He was a prolific and brilliant diarist. He hardly every damned without reason. From the *Sunday Times*, 1931:

Miss Peggy Ashcroft was the Rosalind, and that young lady gave us all that is left after taking away the poetry, the depth of feeling, and what I should like to call the lineage of the part. Rosalind . . . in plain words must have style. Miss Ashcroft made her a nice little girl in a wood.

In September 1945 Sir Ralph Richardson (1902–1983) played Falstaff in *Henry IV, Part II*, at the New Theatre in the famous Old Vic Season which he and Olivier led. JAMES AGATE in the *Sunday Times*:

'England,' announces the programme. And who is to set the first half of this great play in its country and period? Not, one thinks, the wan and shaken King, nor yet his priggish, pragmatical son; and surely the Percys and the Mortimers, Douglases and Glendowers have long been piffle before the wind of time. Does anybody really care what wars were happening, or what river comes cranking in whom? In the second half . . . but stay a moment. It is as idle to exalt the second half of this play over the first as to prefer October to June, nip to flame; the first is a play for boys; the second is for old boys. To return to the spirit, sense, sound, sight, feel, and taste of England. In the second part Shakespeare permits himself a whole company of Englanders – the country justices, the recruits, the old sweats, a tavern hostess drawn at full length, and that immortal harlotry Doll Tearsheet. All these surround Falstaff, who, in the first part, must bear the brunt alone. Can the actor essaying Falstaff do it? 'Ay,' we answer for Richardson, 'and twenty such!' Meaning that in this brain it snows of twenty Englands.

Hazlitt tells us of Liston that 'his jaws seem to ache with laughter; his eyes look out of his head with wonder; his face is unctuous all over and bathed with jests; the tip of his nose is tickled with conceit of himself, and his teeth chatter in his head in the eager insinuation of a plot; his forehead speaks, and his wig (not every particular hair, but the whole bewildered bushy mass) stands on end as life were in it.' In the past I have had occasion to indicate, regretfully, the roles Mr Richardson could not fill. Roles to which he brought no more than the competence of a fine actor labouring at the uncongenial. Now at last comes the time when I can legitimately quote the great critic, again on Liston, 'He does some characters but indifferently, others respectably; when he *puts himself whole* into a jest, it is unrivall'd.'

Mr Richardson put himself whole on Wednesday night into the great joke which is Falstaff. He had everything the part wants – the exuberance, the mischief, the gusto, in a word. Falstaff is more than a 'stuffed cloak-bag of guts.' He is also 'reverend vice' and 'grey iniquity.' Meaning two things. First, that the old toper, sorner, fribble still keeps some of his fallen day about him; second, that he is conscious of his own enormities. Would it be true to say of this Falstaff that he has 'more comic humour, more power of face and a more genial and happy vein of folly, than any other we remember'? Yes, but for Weir, whose Falstaff I saw fifty years ago and about which I read next morning: 'It is impossible to describe the drollery of this voice, or the most ludicrous impression which it gives of a periodical overflow and escape of sound from some perpetual roar in the interior of the actor's person. . . . Mr Weir succeeds brilliantly in filling his audience early on with the central idea of the character, and from then onward one is inclined at every moment of his presence on the stage, even when he is silent or doing little, to break into uncontrollable fits of laughter merely at the picture of such a man walking and talking.' Well, what does it matter, Weir or Richardson? The new Falstaff is a piece of great acting in its own day, and right from the Rowlandson-like legs up past the obstreperous hurdle of belly to that contumacious, unsanctified halo.

Hotspur is not a first-rate part, being little more than a trumpet solo and in the 'pluck bright honour' speech a coach-horn tootle. Mr Olivier does with it what he can and more than anybody in my time has done, humanizing the heroics and at the end touching the whole to a noble pathos. It was a stroke of genius to make the bright youth stammer only at the letter 'w,' so that his last words become 'and food for w–,' immediately taken up by the Prince's 'for worms, brave Percy.' Mr Michael Warre is not yet up to the Prince's weight; this stripling would have got the better of Hotspur only on the theory that ash can tilt successfully at oak. Mr Nicholas Hannen bore himself with great dignity as the King, and I liked very much Mr George Relph's Worcester. A noble, well-conceived setting by Mr Gower Parks, good costumes by Mr Roger Furse, first-rate evocative music by Mr Herbert Menges, and a production by Mr John Burrell which would leave even the captious nothing to cavil at. In short, the Old Vic has made magnificent re-entry.

The first act of *The Seagull* by ANTON CHEKHOV ends with Masha and Dorn, the doctor, alone:

> MASHA: Oh, I'm so unhappy! Nobody knows how unhappy I am. (*Leaning her head against his breast; softly.*) I love Konstantin.
> DORN: How distraught they all are! How distraught! And what a quantity of love about! . . . It's the magic lake! (*Tenderly.*) But what can I do, my child? Tell me, what can I do? What?
>
> CURTAIN

On the first night, 17 December 1898, what happened next is described by
STANISLAVSKY, who played the writer Trigorin, in *The Seagull* produced by
Stanislavsky:

There was a gravelike silence. Olga Knipper fainted on stage. All of us
could hardly keep our feet. In the throes of despair we began moving to
our dressing rooms. Suddenly there was a roar in the auditorium, and
a shriek of joy or fright on the stage. The curtain was lifted, fell, was
lifted again, showing the whole auditorium our amazed and
astounded immovability. It fell again, it rose; it fell, it rose, and we
could not even gather sense enough to bow. Then there were
congratulations and embraces like those of Easter night, and ovations
to Lilina, who played Masha, and who had broken the ice with her last
words, which tore themselves from her heart, moans washed with
tears. This it was that held the audience mute for a time before it began
to roar and thunder in mad ovation. We were no longer afraid of
sending a telegram to our dear and beloved friend and poet.

NOËL COWARD, from the first volume of his autobiography, *Present Indicative*,
1937 (Basil is the director Basil Dean):

The two principal parts in *Sirocco* were played by Ivor Novello and
Frances Doble, and the only theatre available was Daly's, which had
housed nothing but musical comedies for many years.

Basil took infinite pains over the production, and although the *festa*
scene in the second act was considered by some to be over-elaborate, I
personally thought it a superb piece of ensemble work.

Ivor was a difficult proposition. Although his looks were marvellous
for the part, and his name, owing to film successes, was a big draw, his
acting experience in those days was negligible. I must say, however,
that he worked like a slave and endeavoured, to the best of his ability,
to do everything that Basil told him. Unlike Nigel Bruce, he was not in
the least fussed or nerve-stricken and, although Basil at various times
brought up all his artillery, gentle sarcasm, withering contempt, sharp
irascibility, and occasionally full-throated roaring, Ivor remained

unimpressed, behaving on the whole gaily, as though he were at a party.

Frances Doble was frankly terrified from beginning to end. She looked lovely, but, like Ivor, lacked technique. On the whole she gave a good performance, although it ultimately transpired that neither she nor Ivor had at that time strength or knowledge enough to carry those two very difficult parts. The play, I think, was fairly good. The characterization was clear, and although the story was a trifle thin in texture, it seemed to me that it should be strong enough to hold.

On the evening of the first performance Mother, Gladys, Jack and I, elaborately dressed and twittering with nerves, dined at the Ivy. Abel, the proprietor, stood us champagne cocktails, and we drove to the theatre in good time to go backstage and wish everybody success.

When we went into the box I noticed, over the squeaking and scraping of the refined quintet in the orchestra pit, the familiar sound of restlessness in the upper parts of the house. The gallery was jammed – mostly, I suspected, with Ivor's film fans. The atmosphere in the theatre was certainly uneasy, and when the house lights went down, my heart went down with them.

Probably nobody not connected with the theatre could appreciate fully the tension and strain of that dreadful evening. The first night of any play is uncomfortable enough for those who are intimately concerned with it.

And in the case of *Sirocco* it was a losing battle from the word 'Go!'

The first act was received dully. Ivor got a big reception from the gallery when he came on; apart from that there was nothing but oppressive stillness, broken, only very occasionally, by two or three half-hearted titters on certain comedy lines.

The curtain fell to scattered applause, and in the orchestra pit a quintet, with almost shocking vivacity, struck up the Henry the VIII dances. G. B. Stern came to my box and said that she was sitting at the back of the stalls close to the pit, and that there was going to be trouble.

Jack's face assumed a slightly greenish tinge, Gladys's chin shot up so high that I was afraid she would rick her neck. Mother, unaware of impending disaster, waved to Madame Novello Davies at the opposite side of the theatre, and the second act started.

The storm broke during Ivor's love scene with Bunny Doble. The gallery shrieked with mirth and made sucking sounds when he kissed her, and from then onwards proceeded to punctuate every line with catcalls and various other animal noises.

The last act was chaos from beginning to end. The gallery, upper circle and pit hooted and yelled, while the stalls, boxes and dress circle whispered and shushed. Most of the lines weren't heard at all. Ivor and Bunny and the rest of the cast struggled on doggedly, trying to shut their ears to the noise and get the torture done with as quickly as possible.

The curtain finally fell amid a bedlam of sound, and even Mother, who was slightly deaf, was forced to realize that all was not quite as it should be. I remember her turning to me in the darkness and saying wistfully: 'Is it a failure?'

I replied, without quibbling, that it was probably the bloodiest failure in the history of English theatre, and rushed through the pass door on to the stage.

During the first act I had felt utterly miserable. The sense of hostility was strong in the house and I knew it was directed against me. The second-act commotion jumped me from misery into angry, and by the last act I was in a white-hot fury. I don't ever remember being so profoundly enraged in my whole life. I could think of no way to account for this violent change of public feeling towards me. The failure of *Home Chat* had not been important enough to cause it, and *Sirocco* as a play, although far from perfect, was at least superior in quality and entertainment value to many plays running successfully in London at the moment.

Whether or not the demonstration was organized by personal enemies I neither knew nor cared; I was conscious only of an overwhelming desire to come to grips in some way or other with that vulgar, ill-mannered rabble. When I reached the side of the stage, Basil, who never attended first nights of his own productions, and had been quietly dining somewhere, was standing in the prompt corner smiling and ringing the curtain up and down. From where we stood, the tumult in the front of the house might conceivably be mistaken for cheering and he, having no idea of the horrors of the evening, was happily convinced that it was.

I quickly disillusioned him and walked on to the stage. Without once looking at the audience I went along the frightened line of the company to the centre, shook hands with Ivor, kissed Bunny Doble's hand, presenting my behind to the public as I did so, and walked off again.

This, as I expected, increased the booing ten thousandfold. I whispered hurriedly to Basil that I was going on again and that he was to take the curtain up and keep it up until I gave him the signal. If we were to have a failure I was determined that it should be a full-blooded one.

I went on again and stood in the centre, a little in front of Bunny and Ivor, bowing and smiling my grateful thanks to the angriest uproar I have ever heard in a theatre. They yelled abuse at me, booed, made what is known in theatrical terms as 'raspberries,' hissed and shrieked. People stood up in the stalls and shouted protests, and altogether the din was indescribable.

It was definitely one of the most interesting experiences of my life and, my anger and contempt having reduced me to a cold numbness, I was able almost to enjoy it.

I stood there actually for about seven minutes until their larynxes became raw and their breath failed and the row abated a little. Then someone started yelling 'Frances Doble'; it was taken up, and she stepped forward, the tears from her recent emotional scene still drying on her face and in the sudden silence following what had been the first friendly applause throughout the whole evening, said in a voice tremulous with nerves: 'Ladies and gentlemen, this is the happiest moment of my life.'

I heard Ivor give a gurgle behind me and I broke into laughter, which started a fresh outburst of booing and catcalls. Bunny stepped back, scarlet in the face, and I signalled to Basil to bring the curtain down.

Ivor's behaviour all through was remarkable. He had played a long and strenuous part in the face of dreadful odds without betraying for an instant that he was even conscious of them, and at the end, with full realization that all his trouble and hard work had gone for less than nothing, his sense of humour was still clear and strong enough to enable him to make a joke of the whole thing. Nor was he apparently in the least ruffled by the inevitable Press blast the next day. He made no complaints, attached no blame or responsibilities to anyone, and accepted failure with the same grace with which he has always accepted success.

The evening for me, however, was not quite over. The fireman sent a message to me in Ivor's dressing-room where we were all drinking champagne in a state of dazed hysteria, to say that there was a hostile crowd outside the stage door and that it would be wiser for me to leave by the front of the house. This information refuelled my rage and I went immediately up to the stage door. The alley was thronged with people who yelled when I appeared. I surveyed them for a moment from the steps, wearing what I hoped was an expression of utter contempt, and then pushed my way through to the car. Several of them spat at me as I passed, and the next day I had to send my evening coat to the cleaners.

HILAIRE BELLOC (1870–1953), a man of letters but not of the theatre, wrote 'The World's A Stage' in 1923:

I

The world's a stage. The light is in one's eyes.
The Auditorium is extremely dark.
The more dishonest get the larger rise;
The more offensive mark the greater mark.
The women on it prosper by their shape,
Some few by their vivacity. The men,
By tailoring in breeches and in cape.
The world's a stage – I say it once again.

The scenery is very much the best
Of what the wretched drama has to show,
Also the prompter happens to be dumb.
We drink behind the scenes and pass a jest
On all our folly; then, before we go
Loud cries for 'Author' . . . but he doesn't come.

2

The world's a stage – and I'm the Super man,
And no one seems responsible for salary.
I roar my part as loudly as I can
And all I mouth I mouth it to the gallery.
I haven't got another rhyme in 'alery';
It would have made a better job, no doubt,
If I had left attempt at Rhyming out,
Like Alfred Tennyson adapting Malory.

The world's a stage, the company of which
Has very little talent and less reading:
But many a waddling heathen painted bitch
And many a standing cad of gutter breeding.
　　　We sweat to learn our book: for all our pains
　　　We pass. The Chucker-out alone remains.

3

The world's a stage. The trifling entrance fee
Is paid (by proxy) to the registrar.
The Orchestra is very loud and free
But plays no music in particular.
They do not print a programme, that I know.
The cast is large. There isn't any plot.
The acting of the piece is far below
The very worst of modernistic rot.

The only part about it I enjoy
Is what was called in English the Foyay.
There will I stand apart awhile and toy
With thought, and set my cigarette alight;
And then – without returning to the play –
On with my coat and out into the night.

WILLIAM SHAKESPEARE, the Epilogue to *A Midsummer Night's Dream*, *c.* 1600:

If we shadows have offended,
Think but this, and all is mended,
That you have but slumb'red here
While these visions did appear.
And this weak and idle theme,
No more yielding but a dream,
Gentles, do not reprehend
If you pardon, we will mend.
And, as I am an honest Puck,
If we have unearned luck
Now to scape the serpent's tongue,
We will make amends ere long;
Else the Puck a liar call.
So, good night unto you all.
Give me your hands, if we be friends,
And Robin shall restore amends.

5

After the Performance

There are several rituals that follow the fall of the final curtain: the rush backstage to see the performers – a difficult moment if things have not gone well; the parties of various kinds about which little is written; and, of course, the reviews.

Drama critics are seldom if ever popular; some, it is true, are greatly loved after they die. While they practise their craft they are vilified and disparaged by those whom they criticize. The most common attack is to say they write badly.

The English tradition of dramatic criticism dates back to the Restoration, although one of the few hard facts known about William Shakespeare is that he received at least one bad review.

The theatre at its best invades memory and consciousness. As a result actors and actresses, the interpreters of dreams, often find a place deep in people's affections. Much has been written about their exits from the scene.

NIGEL Planer, writing as Nicholas Craig, from *I, An Actor*, 1988:

If actors are a noble priestly caste of fakir magician poets with the theatre as their temple and the stage their altar, the Chinese restaurant is where they have their dinner after the show.

JOHN OSBORNE (b. 1929), in the second volume of his autobiography, *Almost a Gentleman*, describes the party after the first night of *The Entertainer*, 10 April 1957, in which Laurence Olivier played the leading part of Archie Rice. (Vivien is Vivien Leigh, then Olivier's wife; Mary is Mary Ure, then Osborne's wife.)

Olivier's presence and the sense of occasion persuaded the notoriously mean management of the Court to allow us the stage and a few bottles of extremely cheap wine for a party. The band played, stage-hands and actors danced and drank. Vivien sang rather sweetly. Mary sang 'Bonny Mary of Argyll.' Richard Pasco and I sang 'Don't be afraid to sleep with your sweetheart', and I forgot the words. Olivier went through his routines from the play. He was happy. He knew he had created a remarkable memory for everyone.

During the early hours, he saw me slumped and buzzed in the stalls. He came over and put his arm around me. 'Whatever you do, dear heart, *don't* ever, ever, get into trouble with the Income Tax Man. Buy certificates.' He sounded like, he still *was*, Archie.

LAURENCE OLIVIER is reported to have had an infallible formula when going backstage to see actors. He would pop his head round the dressing-room door and say:

'My name is Laurence Olivier. Thank you,' and go.

W. S. GILBERT (1836–1911), also had a stock-phrase when visiting actors backstage:

My dear fellow, *good* isn't the word!

IN *Sprezz: The Art of Effortless Superiority* (1985), JANEY PREGER offered specific advice on what to say about plays and playwrights.

When invited to express an opinion about a play, never say, 'I quite liked it,' or 'Not really my cup of tea.' If in doubt, select your critical barbs from the following quiver:

ALAN AYCKBOURN	– 'Mrs Dale's Diary' as rewritten by Cecil B. De Mille.
AMERICAN COMEDY	– Ramshackle.
STEPHEN BERKOFF	– He won't be happy until actors learn to speak through their bottoms.
ALAN BLEASDALE	– Overripe.
EDWARD BOND	– Shows how low you have to sink to repel an audience.
BERTHOLD BRECHT	– I've heard of alienation but this is ridiculous.
ANTON CHEKHOV	– Too much pathos, not enough threat.
T. S. ELIOT	– Philosophically an antithesis rather than a synthesis.
FARCE	– Lacks repose.
FEMINIST DRAMA	– Unforgivably masculine.

TREVOR GRIFFITHS	– The sort of writer who demonstrates solidarity with the workers by licking his plate at the Ritz.
RONALD HARWOOD	– Sags in the middle. Also at both ends.
HENRIK IBSEN	– Nobody seems to realise he was writing comedy.
ARTHUR MILLER	– Presents truisms as truth.
MUSICAL	– Pre-pubertal.
JOHN OSBORNE	– Too loud.
HAROLD PINTER	– Writes for the ear, not the eye.
STEPHEN POLIAKOFF	– All the resonance of a concrete violin.
DENNIS POTTER	– Too easily shocked by himself. and Too much treacle, not enough brimstone.
J. B. PRIESTLEY	– Underrated by the actors, overrated by the audience.
FREDERICK RAPHAEL	– A ventriloquist with a broken doll.
TERENCE RATTIGAN	– Gave the well-made play a bad name. and The gloss of mahogany-finish Formica.
RESTORATION DRAMA	– A timid version.
WILLY RUSSELL	– Soap opera.
PETER SCHAEFFER	– Writes for the eye, not the ear.
W. SHAKESPEARE	– Should be played as though it's noon in the desert. This production made it midnight.
GEORGE BERNARD SHAW	– Phony paradoxes strung together like onions.
NEIL SIMON	– Rots the teeth.
OSCAR WILDE	– Phony paradoxes strung together like pearls.

DR SAMUEL JOHNSON (1709–84), in his *Dictionary* of 1755 gives the following definition:

Criticism (from *Critic*): Criticism, as it was first instituted by Aristotle, was meant a standard of judging well.

The only bad review for Shakespeare was by ROBERT GREENE (c. 1560–92), a university playwright. He wrote in a pamphlet on his deathbed:

There is an upstart crow, beautified with our feathers, that with his *Tygers heart wrapt in a Players hide* supposes he is as well able to bombast out a blank verse as the best of you; and, being an absolute *Johannes Factotum*, is in his own conceit the only Shake-scene in a country.

The art of recreating the feeling of a performance has largely vanished. Contemporary critics go in for Lit. Crit. rather than making any attempt to tell the reader what it was like to be in the audience of a theatre on a particular night. The last drama critic who could vividly describe what he saw on the stage was KENNETH TYNAN for the *Observer*. Here he catches the styles of three leading actors:

Whenever I see *The Merchant of Venice*, I while away the blanker bits of verse by trying to pull the play together in my mind. Does Shylock stand for the Old Testament (an eye for an eye, etc.) and Portia for the New (mercy, etc.)? And if so, what does that make Antonio, the shipping magnate whose bond unites the two plots? Does he represent the spirit of Protestantism? These metaphysical hares chase each other round and round; and when I have done, the play remains the curate's egg it always was. Or, rather, the rabbi's egg, because so much depends on Shylock. Which brings us to the Problem of Michael Redgrave, now, as always, at the turning-point of his career.

The difficulty about judging this actor is that I have to abandon all my standards of great acting (which include relaxation and effortless command) and start all over again. There is, you see, a gulf fixed between good and great performances; but a bridge spans it, over which you may stroll if your visa is in order. Mr Redgrave, ignoring this, always chooses the hard way. He dives into the torrent and tries to swim across, usually sinking within sight of the shore. Olivier pole-vaults over in a single animal leap; Gielgud, seizing a parasol, crosses by tight-rope; Redgrave alone must battle it out with the current. The ensuing spectacle is never dull, but it can be very painful to watch.

J. B PRIESTLEY (1894–1984), from a letter to the broadcaster Robert Robinson:

I have just joined the board of the National Theatre – about which I have many grave doubts – and if I should propose, as I might in the fairly near future, that Tynan should go, probably I'll be told this is because he says 'fuck' in public . . . The trouble about Tynan, who is a clever chap who can write, is that he doesn't really care about the Theatre, which he uses as a trampoline for his ego.

DOROTHY PARKER (1893–1967), reviewed the theatre for *Vanity Fair* and the *New Yorker*. She was a killer. On Tolstoy's *Redemption*, in 1918:

It isn't what you might call sunny. I went into the Plymouth Theatre a comparatively young woman, and I staggered out of it three hours later, twenty years older, haggard and broken with suffering.

And on a British import, in the *New Yorker*, 1931:

Now that you've got me right down to it, the only thing I didn't like about *The Barrets of Wimpole Street* was the play.

GEORGE BERNARD SHAW from the Epilogue to *Fanny's First Play*:

You don't expect me to know what to say about a play when I don't know who the author is, do you?

Dame Ellen Terry (1847–1928) was a great actress from an illustrious theatrical family. (Sir John Gielgud is her grand-nephew, Gordon Craig, the designer, was her illegitimate son.) She was Henry Irving's leading lady at the Lyceum. Beautiful and versatile, she was adored by G. B. Shaw and others. From the *Stage*, the theatrical newspaper, 4 January, 1889:

It is difficult to speak of the Lady Macbeth of Miss Terry. So perfect has she been in everything else at the Lyceum that we are loath to differ from her admirers upon the merits of a performance that has evidently been the outcome of great labour and perseverance. Miss Terry has based her entire reading of the character upon the supposition that Macbeth is loved by his wife, that all her evil promptings are but the outcome of her loving thought for his future; and it must be owned that Miss Terry in following out this theory plays the part in a generally consistent manner. But the question arises, did such a love exist? There is no mention of it in the play. Macbeth frequently addresses his wife in endearing terms: her dialogue, on the other hand, displays no love for her lord and master. What little affection she may have comes from ambition, and it is but as ambition's slave that she urges her husband on to the bitter end – not that he may benefit, but that she may rule. It may be questioned if a loving, tender wife such as Miss Terry brings before us could invoke the aid of the spirits to unsex her, to fill her with direst cruelty, and 'stop up the access and passage to remorse.' Could such a woman laugh and jeer at her husband's fears after the murder is done? Could she take the daggers from his hands and carefully smear the faces of the grooms with the dripping blood? Miss Terry's performance is most interesting, graceful, and at times most poetical, but it does not suggest the author's creation. The sleep-walking scene is full of charm by reason of Miss Terry's personality. She looks like a beautiful picture, the conception of a poetic mind. But her pure white clinging garments and pain-strained face call for admiration rather than pity and awe.

Attributed to GROUCHO MARX (1895–1977):

I didn't like the play but then I saw it under adverse conditions – the curtain was up.

ELIZABETH BOWEN, writing in *Night and Day*, August 1937:

There is a lot to be said for *Wanted For Murder*, the melodrama with which the Lyceum is now reverting to tradition. It features the homicidal pervert, today an established favourite on the English stage; and it infuses into the story of his downfall a proper and portentous urgency. And yet this melodrama is like most veal and ham pies; there isn't enough ham.

SIR MAX BEERBOHM was G. B. Shaw's successor on the *Saturday Review*. From *Around Theatres*, 1924:

I have often wondered why Sydney Smith said he 'would as soon speak disrespectfully of the Equator.' After all, the Equator is a mere geographical expression. It casts no weird spell of awe over mankind.

On the contrary, seafarers, when they come to it, put on false noses and play practical jokes. For 'Equator' read 'Duse,' and then the remark has point. There never was an influence so awe-inspiring as Duse. At her coming, all the voices of the critics are hushed. Or rather, they are uplifted in unisonant dithyrambus. The heaven is rent with superlatives. And these are not the bright little superlatives we flick at Sarah – imagine any one calling Duse 'Eleonora'! – but superlatives of a solemn, almost religious, order. The heaven is rent, and the entrances to the theatre are forthwith besieged by great concourses of people who don't know a word of Italian. Night by night, the English public sits solemnly at the Lyceum (having paid higher prices than it pays for a play in its own language), tremendously bored, tremendously edified. Whatever Duse may be in her own country, here she is a national institution, nay! a supernatural phenomenon, making for righteousness. If a fiery chariot were seen waiting outside the stage-door, no one would be much surprised.

Last week I said that I would write about Duse as soon as I had 'seen her whole repertoire.' That sounded a little pompous, perhaps; as though I were loth to deliver judgment until the whole bulk of the evidence had been adduced. As a matter of fact, it was merely cowardly procrastination. I wished to put off the evil hour of confessing that I could not bow down before the demi-goddess. There are three ways of raving about an actress. One way is to rave about her technique; another, to rave about her conception of the part she is playing; another, to rave about her personality. Well! I am debarred from the first way by the simple fact that I know no more Italian than did poor Mrs Plornish. This disability is the more humiliating for me, in that I am, evidently, the only critic who labours under it. All the other critics understand the language perfectly; else they would not be able to tell us unanimously that Duse's technique is beyond reproach. The technique of acting lies in the relation of the mime's voice, gesture and facial expression to the words by him or her spoken. Obviously, if those words are for you so much gibberish, you cannot pass any judgment on the mime's technique. You look on, and you see certain movements of the mime's face and hands, and you hear certain inflections of the mime's voice, but I defy you to know whether they are the right movements, the right inflections. You have to take them on trust. I am willing to take Duse's technique on trust, but I cannot rave about it: I can but consume myself with envy of my colleagues, and wish I had made a better use of my opportunities for learning Italian.

❦

CHARLES DICKENS, from *Great Expectations*. Pip and his friend, Herbert Pockett, having seen Mr Wopsle as Hamlet, decide to go backstage.

We had made some pale efforts in the beginning to applaud Mr Wopsle; but they were too hopeless to be persisted in. Therefore we had sat, feeling keenly for him, but laughing, nevertheless, from ear to ear. I laughed in spite of myself all the time, the whole thing was so droll; and yet I had a latent impression that there was something decidedly fine in Mr Wopsle's elocution – not for old associations' sake, I am afraid, but because it was very slow, very dreary, very up hill and down-hill, and very unlike any way in which any man in any natural circumstances of life or death ever expressed himself about anything. When the tragedy was over, and he had been called for and hooted, I said to Herbert, 'Let us go at once, or perhaps we shall meet him.'

We made all the haste we could downstairs, but we were not quick enough either. Standing at the door was a Jewish man with an unnatural heavy smear of eyebrow, who caught my eyes as we advanced, and said, when we came up with him:

'Mr Pip and friend?'

Identity of Mr Pip and friend confessed.

'Mr Waldengarver,' said the man, 'would be glad to have the honour.'

'Waldengarver?' I repeated – when Herbert murmured in my ear, 'Probably Wopsle.'

'Oh!' said I. 'Yes. Shall we follow you?'

'A few steps, please.' When we were in a side alley, he turned and asked, 'How do you think he looked? – *I* dressed him.'

I don't know what he had looked like, except a funeral; with the

207

addition of a large Danish sun or star hanging round his neck by a blue ribbon, that had given him the appearance of being insured in some extraordinary Fire Office. But I said he had looked very nice.

'When he come to the grave,' said our conductor, 'he showed his cloak beautiful. But, judging from the wing, it looked to me that when he see the ghost in the queen's apartment, he might have made more of his stockings.'

I modestly assented, and we all fell through a little dirty swing door, into a sort of hot packing-case immediately behind it. Here Mr Wopsle was divesting himself of his Danish garments, and here there was just room for us to look at him over one another's shoulders, by keeping the packing-case door, or lid, wide open.

'Gentlemen,' said Mr Wopsle, 'I am proud to see you. I hope, Mr Pip, you will excuse my sending round. I had the happiness to know you in former times, and the Drama has ever had a claim which has ever been acknowledged, on the noble and the affluent.'

Meanwhile, Mr Waldengarver, in a frightful perspiration, was trying to get himself out of his princely sables.

'Skin the stockings off, Mr Waldengarver,' said the owner of that property, 'or you'll bust 'em. Bust 'em and you'll bust five-and-thirty shillings. Shakspeare never was complimented with a finer pair. Keep quiet in your chair now, and leave 'em to me.'

With that, he went upon his knees, and began to flay his victim; who, on the first stocking coming off, would certainly have fallen over backward with his chair, but for there being no room to fall anyhow.

I had been afraid until then to say a word about the play. But then, Mr Waldengarver looked up at us complacently, and said:

'Gentlemen, how did it seem to you, to go, in front?'

Herbert said from behind (at the same time poking me), 'capitally.' So I said 'capitally.'

'How did you like my reading of the character, gentlemen?' said Mr Waldengarver, almost, if not quite, with patronage.

Herbert said from behind (again poking me), 'massive and concrete.' So I said boldly, as if I had originated it, and must beg to insist upon it, 'massive and concrete.'

'I am glad to have your approbation, gentlemen,' said Mr Waldengarver, with an air of dignity, in spite of his being ground against the wall at the time, and holding on by the seat of the chair.

'But I'll tell you one thing, Mr Waldengarver,' said the man who was on his knees, 'in which you're out in your reading. Now mind! I don't care who says contrary; I tell you so. You're out in your reading of Hamlet when you get your legs in profile. The last Hamlet as I dressed, made the same mistakes in his reading at rehearsal, till I got him to put a large red wafer on each of his shins, and then at that rehearsal (which was the last) I went in front, sir, to the back of the pit, and whenever his reading brought him into profile, I called out "I don't see no wafers!" And at night his reading was lovely.'

Mr Waldengarver smiled at me, as much to say 'a faithful dependent – I overlook his folly;' and then said aloud, 'My view is a little classic and thoughtful for them here; but they will improve, they will improve.'

Herbert and I said together, Oh, no doubt they would improve.

'Did you observe, gentlemen,' said Mr Waldengarver, 'that there was a man in the gallery who endeavoured to cast derision on the service – I mean, the representation?'

We basely replied that we rather thought we had noticed such a man. I added, 'He was drunk, no doubt.'

'Oh dear, no, sir,' said Mr Wopsle, 'not drunk. His employer would see to that, sir. His employer would not allow him to be drunk.'

'You know his employer?' said I.

Mr Wopsle shut his eyes, and opened them again; performing both ceremonies very slowly. 'You must have observed, gentlemen,' said he, 'an ignorant and a blatant ass, with a rasping throat and a countenance expressive of low malignity, who went through – I will not say sustained – the role (if I may use a French expression) of Claudius King of Denmark. That is his employer, gentlemen. Such is the profession!'

Without distinctly knowing whether I should have been more sorry for Mr Wopsle if he had been in despair, I was so sorry for him as it was, that I took the opportunity of his turning round to have his braces put on – which jostled us out at the doorway – to ask Herbert what he thought of having him home to supper? Herbert said he thought it would be kind to do so; therefore I invited him, and he went to Barnard's with us, wrapped up to the eyes, and we did our best for him, and he sat until two o'clock in the morning, reviewing his success and developing his plans. I forgot in detail what they were, but I have a general recollection that he was to begin with reviving the Drama, and to end with crushing it; inasmuch as his decease would leave it utterly bereft and without a chance or hope.

SAMUEL BUTLER (1612–80), poet and satirist, *Upon Critics Who Judge of Modern Plays Precisely by the Rules of the Ancients*, 1678:

> Who ever will regard poetic fury,
> When it is once found idiot by a jury;
> And ev'ry pert and arbitrary fool
> Can all poetic licence over-rule;
> Assume a barbarous tyranny to handle
> The Muses worse than Ostrogoth and Vandal;
> Make 'em submit to verdict and report,
> And stand or fall to th' orders of a court?
> Much less be sentenced by the arbitrary
> Proceedings of a witless plagiary,
> That forges old records and ordinances
> Against the right and property of fancies,
> More false and nice than weighing of the weather
> To th' hundredth atom of the lightest feather;
> Or measuring of air upon Parnassus
> With cylinders of Torricellian glasses;
> Reduce all Tragedy, by rules of art,
> Back to its antique theatre, a cart;
> And make them henceforth keep the beaten roads
> Of reverend choruses and episodes;
> Reform and regulate a puppet-play,
> According to the true and ancient way;
> That not an actor shall presume to squeak,
> Unless he have a licence for 't in Greek;
> Nor Whittington henceforward sell his cat in

Plain vulgar English, without mewing Latin:
No pudding shall be suffer'd to be witty,
Unless it be in order to raise pity;
Nor Devil in the puppet-play b' allow'd
To roar and spit fire, but to fright the crowd,
Unless some god or demon chance t' have piques
Against on ancient family of Greeks;
That other men may tremble, and take warning,
How such a fatal progeny they're born in.
For none but such for Tragedy are fitted,
That have been ruin'd only to be pity'd;
And only those held proper to deter,
Who've had th' ill luck against their wills to err.
Whence only such as are of middling sizes,
Between morality and venial vices,
Are qualify'd to be destroy'd by Fate,
For other mortals to take warning at . . .
   These are the reformations of the Stage,
Like other reformations of the age,
On purpose to destroy all wit and sense,
As th' other did all law and conscience. . . .
   An English poet should be try'd b' his peers,
And not by pedants and philosophers,
Incompetent to judge poetic fury,
As butchers are forbid to be of a jury;
Besides the most intolerable wrong
To try their matters in a foreign tongue. . . .
Enough to furnish all the lewd impeachers
Of witty Beaumont's poetry and Fletcher's;
Who, for a few misprisions of wit,
Are charged by those who ten times worse commit;
And, for misjudging some unhappy scenes,
Are censured for 't with more unlucky sense;

When all their worst miscarriages delight,
And please more, than the best that pedants write.

JAMES THURBER (1894–1961), the American writer and cartoonist, said of one
play:

It had only one fault. It was kind of lousy.

JEREMY COLLIER (1656–1726), pamphleteer, famed for an attack on the theatre
published in 1697–8. He also attacked Thomas D'Urfey (1653–1723) for his play
Don Quixote:

He diverts the ladies with the charming rhetoric of *snotty-nose, filthy
vermin in the beard, nitty jerkin, louse-snapper, and letter in the
chamber pot*; and with an abusive description of a countess, and a
rude story of a certain lady with some other varieties of this kind too
coarse to mention . . . There is more of physic than comedy in such
sentences as these. *Crocus metallorum* will scarce turn the stomach
more effectively.

In March 1931 DOROTHY PARKER saw a production of *Give Me Yesterday* by A.
A. Milne (1882–1956) starring Louis Calhern. From her *New Yorker* review:

In a shifting, sliding world, it is something to know that Mr A. A.
('Whimsy-the-Pooh') Milne stands steady. He may, tease that he is,
delude us into thinking for a while that he has changed, that we are all
grown up now . . . and then, suddenly as the roguish sun darting from
the cloud, or the little crocus popping into bloom, or the ton of coal

clattering down the chute, he is our own Christopher Robin again, and everything hippity-hoppity as of old.

. . . My dearest dread is the word 'yesterday' in the name of a play; for I know that sometime during the evening I am going to be transported, albeit kicking and screaming, back to the scenes and costumes of a tenderer time. And I know, who show these scars to you, what the writing and the acting of these episodes of tenderer times are going to be like. I was not wrong, heaven help me, in my prevision of the Milne work. Its hero is caused, by a novel device, to fall asleep and a-dream; and thus he is given yesterday. Me, I should have given him twenty years to life.

Give Me Yesterday . . . opens in the sunlit drawing-room of the Cavendish Square house of one of those cabinet ministers. The cabinet minister is . . . not happy; his wife is proud, cold, and ambitious; his daughter is a Bright Young Thing; his son has gone Socialist; and, to crown all, it is rumoured that Mowbray is to be appointed to the coveted position of Chancellor of the Exchequer. 'Ah,' I said to myself, for I love a responsive audience, 'so it's one of those plays. All right, it's one of those plays. At least we have no Christopher Robins cocking their heads on the lawn.' For a moment you see, I had forgotten the title, and hope tormented me.

Well. At the end of the first act, the cabinet minister is leaning back in a chintz-covered chair, conning the speech he is to deliver in Yorkshire, and murmuring drowsily, 'The place of my boyhood. Ah, happy days, happy, happy days.' *Then* I knew we were all gone.

In the second act, the cabinet minister has made that speech and is, for the night, back in the little bedroom in Yorkshire where, as a boy, he spent the nights of his holidays. It appears that his boyhood sweetheart, Sally – called, by Mr Louis Calhern, who has gone British or something, 'Selly' . . . had used to occupy the adjoining room, and he had had a nasty habit of tapping on the wall between, to communicate with her. The code was not essentially difficult. There was one tap for 'a', two for 'b' and so on. I ask you, kind reader, but to bear this in mind for rougher times.

The cabinet minister stretches himself out on his old bed, and slips picturesquely into slumber. Darkness spreads softly over the stage, save for a gentle blue beam on Mr Calhern. Music quivers; then come lights. Then there appear two – not one, but two – Christopher Robins, each about eleven years of age and both forced, poor kids, to go quaintsy-waintsy in doings about knights and squires and beauteous maidens . . . For a few minutes, everything is so cute that the mind reels. Then the cabinet minister himself gets into the dream – I do not pretend to follow the argument – and meets up with his boyhood sweetheart, who wears, and becomingly, the dress of her day. And then, believe it or not, things get worse.

The cabinet minister talks softly and embarrassingly to Sally – 'Ah, Selly, Selly, Selly' – but that is not enough. He must tap out to her, on the garden wall, his message, though she is right beside him. First he taps, and at the length it would take, the letter 'I'. Then he goes on into 'l' and, though surely everyone in the audience has caught the idea, he carries through to 'o'. 'Oh, he's not going on into "v",' I told myself. 'Even Milne wouldn't do that to you.' But he did. He tapped on through 'v' and then did an 'e'. 'If he does "y",' I thought, 'I'm through.' And he did. So I shot myself.

It was, unhappily, a nothing – oh, a mere scratch – and I was able to sit up and watch the dream go on . . . All the Cavendish Square characters of the first act march in . . . They force the minister to don a chancellor's robe, and line themselves up between him and his little new-found love. Sadly she vanishes, leaving him wildly shrieking her name . . .

In the next scene, our hero appears with his coat on – to get it over to the audience, one presumes, that he is no longer in bed and asleep – and meets, after all the years, the Selly of his youth, sitting on the steps of the garden wall, just as she used to sit. She is married, for she had had to make something of her life when ambition called him away from her; but she is not, it seems, heppy either. They will fly together, but the cabinet minister, leashed by caution, must first take time to settle his affairs. He will come back for her, he tells her, in a week . . .

The final act takes us all back, two days later, to Cavendish Square. The minister, transformed by love and hope into a new and somewhat stressfully tender man, has started cleaning up his affairs by sending his resignation to the Prime Minister. All seems set for his return to the Real Things of Life. Then comes word that Mowbray is not, after all, to be Chancellor of the Exchequer; and right after that, little to my surprise, arrives the letter from the Prime Minister asking our hero if he won't please come over and be Chancellor. It is the job he always wanted (P.S. He got it) and it comes to him, oh, irony, irony, just at the time he was about to get away from it all. For several minutes, Mr Calhern must, with no other aid than that of his face and his clenching right hand, show us a man torn, a man in agonies of indecision. But he has been too long bound by the thongs of success. ('Success,' people keep remarking, always portentously, throughout the play, 'closes in.') The daring has been squeezed out of him. The play ends with him sitting at his desk, one hand tapping out 'Good-bye dear' – what a man; he must have had woodpecker blood in him! – while the other grasps the pen with which he is to write his acceptance of his Chancellorship.

Now I have gone into this opus at such dreary length not only out of masochism, but from bewilderment. On the morning after its unveiling, the critics of the daily papers went into a species of snake-dance over its magnificence. 'A deeply moving drama on a human topic,' they said . . . Ladies and gentlemen, I have told you the tale of the play they saw. My case rests . . .

Attributed to ORSON WELLES (1915–85):

Every actor in his heart believes everything bad that's printed about him.

BERNARD LEVIN (b. 1928), journalist and author, in the *Daily Express*, 1959:

I think *The Amorous Prawn* is perhaps the most grisly, glassy-eyed thing I have encountered in the theatre for a very long time, and even outside the theatre its like is rarely met with except on a fishmonger's slab, and now I feel very ill indeed, and would like to lie down.

Before doing so, I should say that *The Amorous Prawn* is a farce made out of cobwebs and mothballs, my old socks, empty beer bottles, copies of *The Strand Magazine*, dust, holes, mildew, and Mr Ben Travers's discarded typewriter ribbons . . .

And now I really *must* go and lie down, and I hope I shall feel better in the morning.

Count Leo Tolstoy (1828–1910) on *The Seagull* by Anton Chekhov:

Nonsense. Utterly worthless. It is written just as Ibsen writes his plays.

Also attributed to Tolstoy is the following remark which he is supposed to have made to Chekhov:

Anton Pavlovich, Shakespeare's plays are bad, but yours are worse.

William Hazlitt (1778–1830) in the *Examiner*, 5 May 1816, on John Philip Kemble's (1757–1823) performance in *A New Way to Pay Old Debts* by Philip Massinger (1583–1639/40):

Why they put Mr Kemble into the part of Sir Giles Overreach, we cannot conceive; we should suppose he would not put himself there. Malvolio, though cross-gartered, did not set himself in the stocks. No doubt, it is the Manager's doing, who by rope-dancing, fire-works, play-bill puffs, and by every kind of quackery, seem determined to fill their pockets for the present, and disgust the public in the end, if the public were an animal capable of being disgusted by quackery. But

> Doubtless the pleasure is as great
> In being cheated, as to cheat.

We do not know why we promised last week to give some account of Mr Kemble's Sir Giles, except that we dreaded the task then; and certainly our reluctance to speak on the subject has not decreased, the more we have thought upon it since. We have hardly ever experienced a more painful feeling than when, after the close of the play, the sanguine plaudits of Mr Kemble's friends, and the circular discharge of hisses from the back of the pit that came 'full volley home' – the music struck up, the ropes were fixed, and Madame Sach ran up from the stage to the two shilling gallery, and then ran down again, as fast as her legs could carry her, amidst the shouts of pit, boxes and gallery!

> So fails, so languishes, and dies away
> All that this world is proud of. . . .
> Perish the roses and the crowns of kings,
> Sceptres and palms of all the mighty.

We have marred some fine lines of Mr Wordsworth on the instability of human greatness, but it is no matter; for he does not seem to understand the sentiment himself. Mr Kemble, then having been thrust into the part, as we suppose, against his will, run the gauntlet of public opinion in it with a firmness and resignation worthy of a Confessor. He did not once shrink from his duty, nor make one effort to redeem his reputation, by 'affecting a virtue when he knew he had it not.' He seemed throughout to say to his instigators, *You have thrust me into this part, help me out of it, if you can; for you see, I cannot help myself.* We never saw signs of greater poverty, greater imbecility, and decrepitude in Mr Kemble, or in any other actor: it was Sir Giles in his dotage. It was all 'Well, well,' and 'If you like it, have it so,' an indifference and disdain of what was to happen, a nicety about his means, a coldness as to his ends, much gentility and little nature. Was this Sir Giles Overreach? Nothing could be more quaint and out-of-the-way. Mr Kemble wanted the part to come to him, for he would not go out of himself into the part. He is in fact as shy of committing himself with nature, as a maid is of committing herself with a lover. All the proper forms and ceremonies must be complied with, before 'they two can be made one flesh.' Mr Kemble sacrifices too much to decorum. He is chiefly afraid of being contaminated by too close an identity with the characters he represents. This is the greatest vice in an actor, who ought never to *bilk* his part. He endeavours to raise Nature to the dignity of his own person and demeanour, and declines with a graceful smile and a wave of the hand the ordinary services she might do him. We would advise him by all means to shake hands, to hug her close, and be friends, if we did not suspect it was too late – that the lady owing to this coyness has eloped, and is now in the situation of Dame Hellenore among the Satyrs. The outrageousness of the conduct of Sir Giles is only to be excused by the violence of his passions and the turbulence of his character. Mr Kemble inverted this conception, and attempted to reconcile the character by softening down the actions. He 'aggravated the part so, that he would seem like any sucking dove.' For example, nothing could exceed the coolness and sang-froid with which he raps Marall on the head with his cane, or spits at Lord Lovell: Lord Foppington himself never did any commonplace indecency more insipidly. The only passage that pleased us, or that really called forth the powers of the actor, was his reproach to Mr Justice Greedy; 'There is some fury in that *Gut*.' The indignity of the word called up all the dignity of the actor to meet it, and he guaranteed the word, though 'a word of naught,' according to the letter and spirit of the convention between them, with a good grace, in the true old English way. Either we mistake all Mr Kemble's excellences, or they all disqualify him for this part. Sir Giles hath a devil; Mr Kemble has none. Sir Giles is in a passion; Mr Kemble is not. Sir Giles has no regard to appearances; Mr Kemble has. It has been said of the Venus de Medicis, 'So stands the statue that enchants the world,' the same might have been said of Mr Kemble. He is the very still life and statuary of the stage; a perfect figure of a man; a petrifaction of sentiment, that heaves no sigh and sheds no tear; an icicle upon the bust of tragedy. With all his faults, he has powers and faculties which no one else on the stage has; why then does he not avail himself of them, instead of throwing himself upon the charity of criticism? Mr Kemble has given the public great, incalculable pleasure; and does he know so little of the ingratitude of the world as to trust to their generosity? He must be sent to Coventry – or St Helena!

EUGENE FIELD, an American critic, reviewing in the Denver *Tribune* Creston Clark's King Lear, *c.* 1880:

He played the king as though under momentary apprehension that someone else was about to play the ace.

GEORGE BERNARD SHAW on *The Manxman* by Wilson Barrett, adapted from the novel by Hall Caine, at the Shaftesbury Theatre in 1895:

In the bill *The Manxman* is described as 'adapted from Hall Caine's celebrated novel.' Who is Hall Caine? How did he become celebrated? At what period did he flourish? Are there any other Manx authors of calibre? If there are, the matter will soon become serious; for if that gift of intolerably copious and intolerably common imagination is a national characteristic of the Isle of Man, it will swamp the stage with Manx melodrama the moment the islanders pick up the trick of writing for the stage.

Whether the speeches in *The Manxman* are interpolated Wilson Barrett or aboriginal Hall Caine I cannot say, as I have not read the celebrated novel, and am prepared to go to the stake rather than face the least chapter of it. But if they correctly represent the colloquial habits of the island, the Manx race are without a vernacular . . . In the Isle of Man you do not use the word 'always': you say 'Come weal come woe, come life come death'. The most useful phrases for the tourist are, 'Dust and ashes, dust and ashes', 'Dead sea fruit', 'The lone watches of the night', 'What a hell is conscience', 'The storm clouds are descending and the tempest is at hand' and so on. The Manx do not speak of a little baby, but of a baby 'fresh from God'. Their philosophy is that 'love is best – is everything – is the cream of life – better than worldly success'; and they conceive woman – or, as they probably call her, 'the fair sex' – as a creature 'giving herself body and soul, never thinking what she gets by it. That's the glory of a Woman!' And the Manx woman rather deserves this. Her idea of pleasantry is to sit on a plank over a stream dangling her legs; to call her swain's attention to her reflection in the water; and then, lest he should miss the coquetry of the exhibition, to cut off the reflected view of her knees by wrapping her skirt round her ankles in a paroxysm of reflected bashfulness. And when she sprains her ankle, and the gentleman tenders some surgical aid, she requests him to turn his head the other way. In short, the keynote of your perfect Manxman is tawdry vulgarity aping the heroic, the hearty, the primevally passionate, and sometimes, though here the show of vigour in the affectation tumbles into lame ineptitude, the gallant and humorous . . .

As to the acting, most of the sixteen parts are so indefinite in spite of their potentous names – Black Tom, Ross Christian, Jemmy Lord and so on – that there is nothing to act in them . . . Professional methods were . . . illustrated by Mr Hamilton Knight as the Manxsome governor. He, having to leave the stage with the innocent words 'Come and see us as soon as you can', shewed us how the experienced hand can manufacture an effective exit. He went to the door with the words 'Come and see us soon.' Then he nerved himself; opened the door; turned dauntlessly; and with raised voice and sparkling eyes hurled the significant words 'as you can' in the teeth of the gallery . . .

Mr Lewis Waller managed to get a moment of real acting into the end of the first act, and then relapsed into nonsensical solemnity for the rest of the evening. I do not know what he was thinking of; but it can hardly have been of the play. He delivered his lines with the automatic gravity of a Brompton Cemetery clergyman repeating the burial service for the thousandth time. He uttered endless strings of syllables; but he did not divide them into words, much less phrases. 'Icannotwillnotlistentothis I won'thearofit,' was the sort of thing he inflicted on us for three mortal acts. As to Miss Florence West, if she persists in using her privilege as the manager's wife to play melodramatic heroines, she will ruin the enterprise . . .

WILLIAM ARCHER (1856–1924), dramatic critic and translator of Ibsen, from his review of *Arms and the Man* by G. B. Shaw, in the *World*, April 1894:

I begin positively to believe that [Shaw] may one day write a serious and even an artistic play, if he will only repress his irreverent whimsicality, try to clothe his character-conceptions in flesh and

blood, and realize the difference between knowingness and knowledge.

STANLEY KAUFFMANN, an American critic, on the New York production of *Jesus
Christ Superstar*, 1971:

The Christ figure was conventional enough: white gown, long fair hair
with a center part, and trim beard. But Mary Magdalene was
apparently just out of *Hair*, the Pilate had been watching Basil
Rathbone on late-night TV, and the Judas, who was less Iscariot than
a reincarnation of St Vitus, revealed himself at last in a sparkling silver
jockstrap. They were all surrounded at times by writhing dancers and
singers inherited from vintage Cecil B. De Mille . . .

Jews, Catholics, Protestants of the world, relax. The religious crisis
of our time is not at the Mark Hellinger theatre, only some of the Jesus
Generation. I admit that they are sickening. Imagine a lot of people
who think that love means licking everyone like a puppy, and true
Christian belief will make life easier!!! Sometimes one does indeed feel
like crying, 'Savonarola, where are you, now that we need you?' But
Jesus Christ Superstar will flow on, if only at syrup's pace. Religion
and atheism will both survive it.

GEORGE BERNARD SHAW on *Julius Caesar* by Shakespeare, in the *Saturday
Review*, January 1898:

It is impossible for even the most judiciously minded critic to look
without a revulsion of indignant contempt at this travestying of a great
man as a silly braggart, whilst the pitiful gang of mischief-makers who
destroy him are lauded as statesmen and patriots. There is not a single
sentence uttered by Shakespeare's Julius Caesar that is, I will not say
worthy of him, but worthy of an average Tammany boss. Brutus is

nothing but a familiar type of English preacher: politically he would hardly impress the Thames Conservancy Board . . .

DOROTHY PARKER writing in the *New Yorker* of a play called *The Lake*, 1933:

Go to the Martin Beck Theater and watch Katherine Hepburn run the gamut of emotions from A to B.

SAMUEL PEPYS, 6 January 1663:

So to my brother's, where Creed and I and my wife dined with Tom, and after dinner to the Duke's house, and there saw *Twelfth Night* acted well, though it be but a silly play and not relating at all to the name or day. Thence Mr Battersby (the apothecary), his wife and I and mine by coach together and setting him down at his house, he paying his share, my wife and I home, and found all well, only myself somewhat vexed at my wife's neglect in leaving of her scarf, waistcoat, and night-dressings in the coach today that brought us from Westminster, though I confess she did give them to me to look after, yet it was her fault not to see that I did take them out of the coach. I believe it might be as good as 25s loss or thereabouts.

HENRY JAMES (1843–1916) writing in *Scribners Monthly* on Ellen Terry as Portia, 1881:

Her manner of dealing with the delightful speeches of Portia, with all their play of irony, of wit and temper, savours, to put it harshly, of the schoolgirlish. We have ventured to say that her comprehension of a character is sometimes weak, and we may illustrate it by a reference to her whole handling of this same opportunity. Miss Terry's mistress of Belmont giggles too much, plays too much with her fingers, is too free and familiar, to osculatory, in her relations with Bassanio. The mistress of Belmont was a great lady, as well as a tender and clever woman; but this side of the part quite eludes the actress, whose deportment is not such as we should expect in the splendid spinster who has princes for wooers. When Bassanio has chosen the casket which contains the key of her heart, she approaches him, and begins to pat and stroke him. This seems to us an appallingly false note. 'Good heavens, she's touching him!' a person sitting next to us exclaimed – a person whose judgment in such matters is always unerring.

It may be that Henrik Ibsen (1828–1906) received more bad reviews than any other playwright. Here are some on *Ghosts*, first published in an edition of 10,000 copies in 1881:

Ghosts is a repulsive pathological phenomenon which, by undermining the morality of our social order, threatens its foundations.

Complete silence would, in our opinion, be the most fitting reception for such a work. *Ghosts* is the most unpleasant book we have read for a long while.

The book has no place on the Christmas table of any Christian home.

The play is one of the filthiest things ever written in Scandinavia.

The play, after it was performed in London at the Royalty Theatre in March 1891, was the subject of a leading article in the *Daily Telegraph*:

Ay! The play performed last night is 'simple' enough in plan and purpose, but simple only in the sense of an open drain; of a loathsome sore unbandaged; of a dirty act done publicly; or of a lazar-house with all its doors and windows open.

And after the same performance, CLEMENT SCOTT (1841–1904) in the *Illustrated London News*:

... in all my experience of the stage ... I have seldom known a 'cheekier' move than the opening of the Royalty Theatre ... with a play that has not passed the censorship, and that play none other than the revolting *Ghosts* of the Scandinavian Ibsen. But the 'cheek' does not end there, by any means. It goes on to imply that our poor, neglected and degraded stage, having no literature of its own, and fettered up with the shackles of what the revolutionaries call 'conventionality', is to be taught what literature is with the aid of a dull, verbose preacher, and to learn what freedom is by means of a play that may be obnoxious to many men, and that cannot possibly be discussed in all its morbid details in any mixed assembly of men and women.

A Doll's House fared little better. CLEMENT SCOTT again, in the *Sporting and Dramatic News*, 1889:

It is as though someone had dramatized the cooking of a Sunday dinner (no bad subject for a play, one might think nowadays).

And JAMES AGATE in the *Sunday Times* on a later production in 1930:

A Doll's House has no modern application because the modern Nora would simply tell Helmer to stop being daft.

GEORGE BERNARD SHAW on Henry Irving's performance in *A Story of Waterloo* by Arthur Conan Doyle, at the Lyceum Theatre, 1895 (from the *Saturday Review*, 11 May 1895):

It was Mr Grant Allen, I think, who familiarized us with the fact that all attempts to sustain our conduct at a higher level than is natural to us produce violent reactions. Was there not a certain African divine, the Reverend Mr Creedy, who tamed the barbarian within him and lived the higher life of the Caledonian Road for a while, only to end by 'going Fantee' with a vengeance? This liability to reaction is a serious matter for the actor – not, perhaps, for the actor of villains, who becomes by reaction the most amiable of men in private life, but certainly for the actor of heroes, who is occasionally to be found off the stage in a state of very violent reaction indeed. But there are some actors – not many, but some – who have solid private characters which stand like rocks in the midst of the ebb and tide of their stage emotions; and in their case the reaction must take place in their art itself. Such men, when they have to be unnaturally dignified on the stage, cannot relieve themselves by being ridiculous in private life, since the good sense of their private characters makes that impossible to them. When they can bear it no longer, they must make themselves ridiculous on the stage or burst. No actor suffers from the tyranny of this grotesque necessity more than Mr Irving. His career, ever since he became a heroic actor, has been studded by relapses into the most impish buffoonery. I remember years ago going into the Lyceum Theatre under the impression that I was about to witness a performance of Richard III. After one act of that tragedy, however, Mr Irving relapsed into an impersonation of Alfred Jingle. He concealed piles of sand- wiches in his hat; so that when he afterwards raised it to introduce himself as 'Alfred Jingle, Esq., of No Hall, Nowhere,' a rain of ham and bread descended on him. He knelt on the stage on one knee and seated Miss Pauncefort (the spinster aunt) on the other, and then upset himself and her, head over heels. He beat a refractory horse with a bandbox; inked the glimpses of shirt that appeared through the holes in his coat; and insulted all the other characters by turning their coats back with the idiotic remark, 'From the country, sir?' He was not acting: nothing less like the scenes created by Dickens could possibly have been put on the stage. He was simply taking his revenge on Shakespear and himself for months of sustained dignity. Later on we had the same phenomenon repeated in his Robert Macaire. There was, and, I suppose, still is in the market a version of that little melodrama by Mr Henley and the late Louis Stevenson which was full of literary distinction; but Mr Irving stuck to the old third-class version, which gave him unlimited scope for absurdity. He made one or two memorable effects in it: a more horribly evil-looking beast of prey than his Macaire never crossed the stage; and I can recall a point or two where the feeling produced was terrible. But what Mr Irving enjoyed, and obviously what attracted him in the business, was rushing Mr Weedon Grossmith upstairs by the back of the neck, breaking plates on his stomach, standing on a barrel boyishly pretending to play the fiddle, singing a chanson to an accompaniment improvised by himself on an old harpsichord, and, above all – for here his glee attained its climax – inadvertently pulling a large assortment of stolen handker-chiefs out of his pocket whilst explaining matters to the police officer, and clinching his account by throwing one into his hat, which, having no crown, allowed it to fall through to the floor. This alternation of the grotesque, the impish, the farcical, with the serious and exalted, is characteristic of the nineteenth century. Goethe anticipated it in his Faust and Mephistopheles, obviously two sides of the same character; and it was in the foolish travesty of Faust perpetrated by Wills that Mr Irving found a part in which he could be melodramatic actor, mocker, and buffoon all in one evening. Since then he has had a trying time of it. Becket on top of Wolsey was enough to provoke a graver man to go Fantee; and Lear followed Becket. But when King Arthur capped Lear, all of us who knew Mr Irving's constitution felt that a terrific reaction must be imminent. It has come in the shape of Don Quixote, in which he makes his own dignity ridiculous to his heart's content. He rides a slim white horse, made up as Rozinante with painted hollows just as a face is made up; he has a set of imitation geese waggling on springs to mistake for swans; he tumbles about the stage with his legs in the air; and he has a single combat, on refreshingly indecorous provocation, with a pump. And he is perfectly happy. I am the last person in the world to object; for I, too, have something of that aboriginal need for an occasional carnival in me. When he came before the curtain at the end, he informed us, with transparent good faith, that the little play practically covered the whole of Cervantes' novel, a statement which we listened to with respectful stupefaction. I get into trouble often enough by my ignorance of authors whom every literate person is expected to have at his fingers' ends; but I believe Mr Irving can beat me hollow in that respect. If I have not read Don Quixote all through, I have at least looked at the pictures; and I am prepared to swear that Mr Irving never got beyond the second chapter.

Anyone who consults recent visitors to the Lyceum, or who seeks for information in the Press as to the merits of Mr Conan Doyle's Story of Waterloo, will in nineteen cases out of twenty learn that the piece is a trifle raised into importance by the marvellous acting of Mr Irving as Corporal Gregory Brewster. As a matter of fact, the entire effect is contrived by the author, and is due to him alone. There is absolutely no acting in it – none whatever. There is a make-up in it, and a little cheap and simple mimicry which Mr Irving does indifferently because he is neither apt not observant as a mimic of doddering old men, and because his finely cultivated voice and diction again and again rebel against the indignity of the Corporal's squeakings and mumblings and vulgarities of pronunciation. But all the rest is an illusion produced by the machinery of 'a good acting play,' by which is always meant a play that requires from the performers no qualifications beyond a plausible appearance and a little experience and address in stage business. I had better make this clear by explaining the process of doing without acting as exemplified by A Story of Waterloo, in which Mr Conan Doyle has carried the art of constructing an 'acting' play to such an extreme that I almost suspect him of satirically revenging himself, as a literary man, on a profession which has such a dread of 'literary plays.' (A 'literary play,' I should explain, is a play that the actors have to act, in opposition to the 'acting play,' which acts them.)

Before the curtain rises, you read the playbill; and the process commences at once with the suggestive effect on your imagination of 'Corporal Gregory Brewster, age eighty-six, a Waterloo veteran,' of 'Nora Brewster, the corporal's grandniece,' and of 'Scene – Brewster's lodgings.' By the time you have read that, your own imagination, with the author pulling the strings, has done half the work you afterwards give Mr Irving credit for. Up goes the curtain; and the lodgings are before you, with the humble breakfast table, the cheery fire, the old man's spectacles and bible, and a medal hung up in a frame over the chimney-piece. Lest you should be unobservant enough to miss the significance of all this, Miss Annie Hughes comes in with a basket of butter and bacon, ostensibly to impersonate the grandniece, really to carefully point out all these things to you, and to lead up to the entry of the hero by preparing breakfast for him. When the background is sufficiently laid in by this artifice, the drawing of the figure commences. Mr Fuller Mellish enters in the uniform of a modern artillery sergeant, with a breech-loading carbine. You are touched: here is the young soldier come to see the old – two figures from the Seven Ages of Man. Miss Hughes tells Mr Mellish all about Corporal Gregory. She takes down the medal, and makes him read aloud to her the press-cutting pasted beside it which describes the feat for which the medal was given. In short, the pair work at the picture of the old warrior until the very dullest dog in the audience knows what he is to see, or to imagine he sees, when the great moment comes. Thus is Brewster already created, though Mr Irving has not yet left his dressing room. At last, everything being ready, Mr Fuller Mellish is packed off so as not to divide the interest. A squeak is heard behind the scenes: it is the childish treble that once rang like a trumpet on the powder-waggon at Waterloo. Enter Mr Irving, in a dirty white wig, toothless, blear-eyed, palsied, shaky at the knees, stooping at the shoulders, incredibly aged and very poor, but respectable. He makes his way to his chair, and can only sit down, so stiff are his aged limbs, very slowly and creakily. This sitting down business is not acting: the callboy could do it; but we are so thoroughly primed by the playbill, the scene-painter, the stage-manager, Miss Hughes and Mr Mellish, that we go off in enthusiastic whispers, 'What superb acting! How wonderfully he does it!' The corporal cannot recognize his grandniece at first. When he does, he asks her questions about children – children who have long gone to their graves at ripe ages. She prepares his tea: he sups it noisily and ineptly, like an infant. More whispers: 'How masterly a touch of second childhood!' He gets a bronchial attack and gasps for paregoric, which Miss Hughes administers with a spoon, whilst our faces glisten with tearful smiles. 'Is there another living actor who could take paregoric like that?' The sun shines through the window: the old man would fain sit there and peacefully enjoy the fragrant air and life-giving warmth of the world's summer, contrasting so pathetically with his own winter. He rises, more creakily than before, but with his faithful grandniece's arm fondly supporting him. He dodders across the stage, expressing a hope that the flies will not be too 'owdacious,' and sits down on another chair with his joints crying more loudly than ever for some of the oil of youth. We feel that we could watch him sitting down for ever. Hark! a band in the street without. Soldiers pass: the old warhorse snorts feebly, but complains that bands dont play so loud as they used to. The band being duly exploited for all it is worth, the bible comes into play. What he likes in it are the campaigns of Joshua and the battle of Armageddon, which the poor dear old thing can hardly pronounce, though he had it from 'our clergyman.' How sweet of the clergyman to humor him! Blessings on his kindly face and on his silver hair! Mr Fuller Mellish comes back with the breechloading carbine. The old man handles it; calls it a firelock; and goes crazily through his manual with it. Finally, he unlocks the breech, and as the barrel drops, believes that he has broken the weapon in two. Matters being explained, he expresses his unalterable conviction that England will have to fall back on Brown Bess when the moment for action arrives again. He takes out his pipe. It falls and is broken. He whimpers, and is petted and consoled by a present of the sergeant's beautiful pipe with 'a hamber mouthpiece.' Mr Fuller Mellish, becoming again superfluous, is again got rid of. Enter a haughty gentleman. It is the Colonel of the Royal Scots Guards, the corporal's old regiment. According to the well-known custom of colonels, he has called on the old pensioner to give him a five-pound note. The old man, as if electrically shocked, staggers up and desperately tries to stand for a moment at 'attention' and salute his officer. He collapses, almost slain by the effort, into his chair, mumbling pathetically that he 'were a'most gone that time, Colonel.' 'A masterstroke! who but a great actor could have executed this heart-searching movement?' The veteran returns to the fireside: once more he depicts with convincing art the state of an old man's joints. The Colonel goes; Mr Fuller Mellish comes; the old man dozes. Suddenly he springs up. 'The Guards want powder; and, by God, the Guards shall have it.' With these words he falls back in his chair. Mr Fuller Mellish, lest there should be any mistake about it (it is never safe to trust the intelligence of the British public), delicately informs Miss Hughes that her granduncle is dead. The curtain falls amid thunders of applause.

Every old actor in whose hands this article falls will understand perfectly from my description how the whole thing is done, and will wish that he could get such Press notices for a little hobbling and piping, and a few bits of mechanical business with a pipe, a carbine, and two chairs. The whole performance does not involve one gesture, one line, one thought outside the commonest routine of automatic stage illusion. What, I wonder, must Mr Irving, who of course knows this better than anyone else, feel when he finds this pitiful little handful of hackneyed stage tricks received exactly as if it were a crowning instance of his most difficult and finest art? No doubt he expected and intended that the public, on being touched and pleased by machinery, should imagine that they were being touched and pleased by acting. But the critics! What can he think of the analytic powers of those of us who, when an organized and successful attack is made on our emotions, are unable to discriminate between the execution done by the actor's art and that done by Mr Conan Doyle's ingenious exploitation of the ready-made pathos of old age, the ignorant and maudlin sentiment attaching to the army and 'the Dook,' and the vulgar conception of the battle of Waterloo as a stand-up street fight between an Englishman and a Frenchman, a conception infinitely less respectable than that which led Byron to exclaim, when he heard of Napoleon's defeat, 'I'm damned sorry'?

HENRY JAMES on *An Ideal Husband* by Oscar Wilde in January 1895. His own play, *Guy Domville* (the 'G.D.' referred to), had failed at the same theatre, the St James's, presented by the same actor-manager, Sir George Alexander:

The thing seemed to me so helpless, so crude, so bad, so clumsy, feeble and vulgar, that as I walked away across St James's Square to learn my own fate, the prosperity of what I had seen seemed to me to constitute a dreadful presumption of the shipwreck of *G.D.*, and I stopped in the middle of the Square, paralysed by the terror of this probability – afraid to go on and learn more. 'How *can* my piece do anything with a public with whom *that* is a success?'

SHERIDAN MORLEY (b. 1941), journalist and drama critic, in *Punch*, 1976, on a play by Goldoni:

There is a number of possible explanations for the presence of *Il Campiello* in the repertoire of the National Theatre at the Olivier. The one I like best is that it represents a complete and never-to-be-repeated mental, physical and theatrical breakdown on the part of all concerned.

❦

George Jean Nathan (1882–1958), an American critic, on the 1942 New York production of *Flare Path* by Terence Rattigan:

Flight Lieutenant Teddy Graham's wife, Patricia, a former actress, has, unknown to him, enjoyed protracted premarital sexual experience with a moving-picture idol, Peter Kyle by name. Peter, now at forty-seven passé for screen purposes, pursues her to a provincial hotel where she is staying to be near her husband and tells her that he needs her more than ever. Patricia, it is at once apparent, still is amorously fetched by him but, interrupted only by the periodic rushing in and out of RAF fliers and gunnery noises off stage, for the subsequent hour and a half indulges in the elaborate repertoire of facial contortions commonly employed under such circumstances to indicate, *seriatim*, doubt, hesitation, gradual process of decision, and, finally, resolve. At ten-thirty she accordingly decides that not only her heart but the rest of her anatomy and physiology belong to Peter and is about to give him her all when the door opens and in staggers Teddy just returned from a bombing raid.

Teddy is broken. He senses what is up and confesses to Patricia that he needs her even more than Peter does, since he had lost his nerve and can no longer do his flying duty unless he can lean on her love, rest on her faith, and know when away that she will be waiting for him with receptive arms. Taking a cue from Candida, Patricia concludes that it is the weaker of the two who needs her most, sends Peter packing, and reinspires Teddy to new feats of derring-do against the enemy.

The playwright's brilliant imagination does not, however, end here. Appreciating that there must be some humorous relief, he brings in a Polish flier who has enlisted in the RAF and permits him to induce ten or twelve minutes of wild hilarity in the English characters by pronouncing *peasants* as *pheasants* . . .

George Bernard Shaw from the *Saturday Review*, September 1896:

I confess to a difficulty in feeling civilized just at present. Flying from the country, where the gentlemen of England are in an ecstasy of chicken-butchering, I return to town to find the higher wits assembled at a play 300 years old, in which the sensation scene exhibits a woman waking up to find her husband reposing gorily in her arms with his head cut off . . .

Cymbeline . . . is for the most part stagey trash of the lowest melodramatic order, in parts abominably written, throughout intellectually vulgar and judged in point of thought by modern intellectual standards, vulgar, foolish, offensive, indecent, and exasperating beyond all tolerance.

Bernard Levin in the *Daily Express* on an American comedy, *The Gazebo* by Alec Coppel, 1960:

A gazebo is a kind of summer house, to anticipate your first question.

The etymology of the word is not certain, but the Oxford Dictionary hazards a guess that it may be facetious coinage on the lines of 'placebo'.

A placebo, to anticipate your *second* question, is a pill which looks impressive but is, in fact, quite inefficacious.

It is given by doctors to hypochrondriacs, who need nothing more than reassurance. Its etymology is from the Latin: placebo means 'I will please.'

The Gazebo is a placebo and it doesn't.

A reviewer in the *Manchester Guardian* on the first performance of *The Birthday Party* by Harold Pinter at the Lyric Theatre, Hammersmith, May 1958:

What all this means, only Mr Pinter knows, for as his characters speak in non sequiturs, half-gibberish and lunatic ravings, they are unable to explain their actions, thoughts or feelings. If the author can forget Beckett, Ionesco and Simpson he may do much better next time.

KENNTH TYNAN on *Look Back in Anger* by John Osborne at the Royal Court Theatre, 1956:

That the play needs changes I do not deny: it is twenty minutes too long, and not even Mr Haigh's bravura could blind me to the painful whimsy of the final reconciliation scene. I agree that *Look Back in Anger* is likely to remain a minority taste. What matters, however, is the size of the minority. I estimate it at roughly 6,733,000, which is the number of people in this country between the ages of twenty and thirty. And this figure will doubtless be swelled by refugees from other age-groups who are curious to know precisely what the contemporary young pup is thinking and feeling. I doubt if I could love anyone who did not wish to see *Look Back in Anger*. It is the best young play of its decade.

Sir Harold Hobson (1904–92), drama critic of the *Sunday Times*, May 1953:

The aim of art is to produce desirable states of mind, and the state of mind from which *Guys and Dolls* proceeds can, if it is typical of America, cause only disquiet. Is America really peopled with brutalized half-wits, as this picturization of Damon Runyon's story implies? Is it really witty to bring a Salvation Army girl to the edge of fornication by the not very original trick of putting intoxicants into her milk shake? Is it clever to quote words of Jesus in the melancholy hope of raising a laugh? Let us make clear that I am not protesting against either irreverence of impropriety as such. I only ask that they should attain a certain level of intelligence. I see no reason why religion should not be attacked or even traduced in the theatre. It is, I am sure, quite strong enough to defend itself. But let the attack have some rational intellectual basis. Otherwise it becomes a bore. That, alas, is what *Guys and Dolls* is, despite its striking, incidental merits; an interminable, an overwhelming, and in the end intolerable bore.

Ode by John Keats written in 1820 on the blank page before Beaumont and Fletcher's tragi-comedy, *The Fair Maid of the Inn*:

> Bards of Passion and of Mirth,
> Ye have left your souls on earth!
> Have ye souls in heaven too,
> Double lived in regions new?
> Yes, and those of heaven commune
> With the spheres of sun and moon;
> With the noise of fountains wond'rous,
> And the parle of voices thund'rous;
> With the whisper of heaven's trees
> And one another, in soft ease
> Seated on Elysian lawns
> Brows'd by none but Dian's fawns;
> Underneath large blue-bells tented,
> Where the daisies are rose-scented,

And the rose herself has got
Perfume which on earth is not;
Where the nightingale doth sing
Not a senseless, tranced thing,
But divine melodious truth;
Philosophic numbers smooth;
Tales and golden histories
Of heaven and its mysteries.

    Thus ye live on high, and then
On the earth ye live again;
And the souls ye left behind you
Teach us, here, the way to find you,
Where your other souls are joying,
Never slumber'd, never cloying.
Here, your earth-born souls still speak
To mortals, of their little week;
Of their sorrows and delights;
Of their passions and their spites;
Of their glory and their shame;
What doth strengthen and what maim.
Thus ye teach us, every day
Wisdom, though fled far away.

    Bards of Passion and of Mirth,
Ye have left your souls on earth!
Ye have souls in heaven too,
Double-lived in regions new!

BEN JONSON, 1623:

To the Memory of My Beloved Master William Shakespeare, and What He Hath Left Us

To draw no envy, Shakespeare, on thy name,
Am I thus ample to thy book and fame;

While I confess thy writings to be such,
As neither Man nor Muse can praise too much.
'Tis true, and all men's suffrage. But these ways
Were not the paths I meant unto thy praise;
For seeliest ignorance on these may light,
Which, when it sounds at best, but echoes right;
Or blind affection, which doth ne'er advance
The truth, but gropes, and urgeth all by chance;
Or crafty malice might pretend this praise,
And think to ruin where it seemed to raise.
These are, as some infamous bawd or whore
Should praise a matron; what could hurt her more?
But thou are proof against them, and, indeed,
Above the ill fortune of them, or the need.

I therefore will begin: Soul of the age!
The applause! delight! the wonder of our stage!
My Shakespeare rise! I will not lodge thee by
Chaucer, or Spenser, or bid Beaumont lie
A little further, to make thee a room:
Thou art a monument, without a tomb,
And art alive still while thy book doth live
And we have wits to read, and praise to give.
That I not mix thee so my brain excuses,
I mean with great, but disproportioned Muses:
For if I thought my judgement were of years,
I should commit thee surely with thy peers,
And tell how far thou didst our Lyly outshine,
Or sporting Kyd, or Marlowe's mighty line.

And though thou hadst small Latin and less Greek,
From thence to honour thee, I would not seek
For names: but call forth thund'ring Aeschylus,
Euripides, and Sophocles to us,
Pacuvius, Accius, him of Cordova dead,
To life again, to hear thy buskin tread
And shake a stage; or when thy socks were on,
Leave thee alone for the comparison

Of all that insolent Greece or haughty Rome
Sent forth, or since did from their ashes come.
Triumph, my Britain, thou hast one to show,
To whom all Scenes of Europe homage owe.
He was not of an age, but for all time!
And all the Muses still were in their prime,
When, like Apollo, he came forth to warm
Our ears, or like a Mercury to charm!
Nature herself was proud of his designs,
And joyed to wear the dressing of his lines!
Which were so richly spun, and woven so fit,
As since, she will vouchsafe no other wit.
The merry Greek, tart Aristophanes,
Neat Terence, witty Plautus, now not please;
But antiquated and deserted lie,
As they were not of Nature's family.

Yet must I not give Nature all; thy Art,
My gentle Shakespeare, must enjoy a part.
For though the poet's matter nature be,
His art doth give the fashion: and, that he
Who casts to write a living line, must sweat,
(Such as thine are) and strike the second heat
Upon the Muses' anvil; turn the same,
And himself with it, that he thinks to frame;
Or for the laurel he may gain a scorn;
For a good poet's made as well as born.
And such wert thou! Look how the father's face
Lives in his issue, even so the race
Of Shakespeare's mind and manners brightly shines
In his well turned and true filed lines:
In each of which he seems to shake a lance,
As brandisht at the eyes of ignorance.

Sweet Swan of Avon! what a sight it were
To see thee in our waters yet appear,
And make those flights upon the banks of Thames,
That so did take Eliza and our James!

But stay, I see thee in the hemisphere
Advanced, and made a constellation there!
Shine forth, thou Star of Poets, and with rage,
Or influence, chide or cheer the drooping stage,
Which, since thy flight from hence, hath mourned like night,
And despairs day but for thy volume's light.

OLIVER GOLDSMITH, from *Retaliation*, 1774:

Garrick

Here lies David Garrick, describe him who can,
An abridgement of all that was pleasant in man:
As an actor, confess'd without rival to shine;
As a wit, if not first, in the very first line:
Yet, with talents like these, and an excellent heart,
This man had his failings – a dupe to his art.
Like an ill judging beauty, his colours he spread,
And be-plaster'd with rouge his own natural red.
On the stage he was natural, simple, affecting;
'Twas only that when he was off he was acting.

With no reason on earth to go out of his way,
He turn'd and he varied full ten times a day:
Though secure of our hearts, yet confoundedly sick
If they were not his own by finessing and trick:
He cast off his friends, as a huntsman his pack,
For he knew when he pleased he could whistle them back.
Of praise a mere glutton, he swallow'd what came,
And the puff of a dunce he mistook it for fame;
Till his relish grown callous, almost to disease,
Who pepper'd the highest was surest to please . . .

But peace to his spirit, wherever it flies,
To act as an angel and mix with the skies:
Those poets, who owe their best fame to his skill

Shall still be his flatterers, go where he will;
Old Shakespeare receive him with praise and with love.
And Beaumonts and Bens be his Kellys above.

LAURENCE IRVING (1897–1988), grandson and biographer of Sir Henry, describes the reaction to the great actor's death on 13 October 1905:

The news of Irving's death was carried swiftly to his company in their scattered lodgings; shocked as they were, it seemed to be the climax to a tragedy long rehearsed. A porter brought the news to Tree as he sat with his friends at supper in the Garrick Club; in silence the message was passed round the table and in silence the members rose, and left the Club. His sons journeyed to Bradford through the night. The next day Toole, dazed and broken-hearted by the news of his friend's death, bade his servants recover from the waste-paper basket the last words which Irving had written to him – his address on a wrapper round a newspaper containing an account of the civic reception at Bradford. In Manchester, on the following night, Ellen Terry strove to keep faith with her public. She was playing *Alice Sit-By-the-Fire*. When she came to the lines: 'It's summer done, autumn begun . . . I had a beautiful husband once . . . black as raven was his hair . . .', she broke down. The curtain was lowered and in respectful silence the audience left the theatre. Mrs Aria, hearing that the end had come as he desired, was content; she expended her grief in fashioning a pall of fresh laurel leaves such as she knew would have pleased him.

When the people heard of his death, the expression of their sorrow was akin to that inspired by Nelson, for, like the great sailor, Irving was honoured and respected for his actions and for his nature loved. The flags throughout the kingdom were flown at half mast. The pillars of the desecrated Lyceum were hung with crêpe and every London cab-driver tied a black bow upon his whip. The newspapers of the world published columns of eulogy and appreciation; the humble and the great subscribed their tributes. A few dissentient voices recapitulated the old contentions, but they were scarcely heard. Yet, while Irving's body lay in state in the house of the Baroness Burdett-Coutts, the controversy which had been the background of his life survived his death.

Ellen Terry once had asked him, half in jest, if he thought it possible that he might be buried in Westminster Abbey. 'I should like them to do their duty by me and they will – they will,' was his reply. His confidence in the people was not misplaced. Alexander and a few of Irving's close friends so gauged public feeling that they asked the Dean of St Paul's if they might bury their dead leader in his cathedral. Their request was refused. They waited upon Dr Armytage Robinson, the Dean of Westminster, with a memorial signed by the leaders of their profession and by the great men of literature, art and science and of a society whose intellectual recreation Irving had enriched. The Dean had been threatened with blindness and lay in a darkened upper room attended by his sister, in whom the old prejudices against players and playhouses lingered. When she heard the purpose of the petition she protested vehemently against the burial of any more actors in the Poet's Corner. The members of the deputation were still waiting for an answer when Sir Anderson Critchett, who had become the leading oculist in the country, passed through the room in which they sat, on his way to see his patient. Recognizing several of his friends, he asked what they were waiting for. When he heard the purpose of their mission, he promised that he would do all he could to help them. He reminded the Dean that, when he had saved his sight, he had asked what return he could make as a token of his gratitude. Now, said Critchett, was the time and opportunity to make that return by granting the request of the gentlemen waiting below. The Dean's sister repeated her protest – 'No actors – no actors!' but in vain. The Dean honoured his debt.

On the eve of the funeral, Irving's cremated remains were carried through the streets lined with silent crowds. The people had finished their day's work and were grateful for this opportunity to pay their last tribute to the dead actor – for on the morrow there would be no room for them in the Abbey.

The actors and actresses whose working lives he had dignified, the craftsmen and handymen in the well-found theatres for which the Lyceum had been the model, the generations of patrons, humble and great, in whom he had created a hunger for the higher drama, the troops of friends he had known and those who had been but a blur of faces beyond the footlights – these Alexander and his helpers laboured to accommodate in the nave and transepts of the Abbey where in homage they would accord the great actor an ovation, silent but more eloquent than the applause that had so often thundered in his ears.

During the night, the coffin which contained the ashes of Irving lay in St Faith's Chapel. On October 20th, shrouded with its laurel pall, it was borne upon the shoulders of his friends into the Abbey, where, in the presence of a vast congregation, it was laid at the feet of the statue of his beloved Shakespeare and at the side of his fellow-player, David Garrick.

BEN JONSON, from *Timber: or, Discoveries Made upon Men and Matter*, 1641:

I remember, the players have often mentioned it as an honour to Shakespeare, that in his writing (whatsoever he penned) he never blotted out line. My answer hath been, would he had blotted a thousand. Which they thought a malevolent speech. I had not told posterity this, but for their ignorance, who choose that circumstance to commend their friend by, wherein he most faulted, and to justify mine own candour, for I loved the man, and do honour his memory (on this side idolatry) as much as any. He was indeed honest, and of an open, and free nature; had an excellent phantasy, brave notions, and gentle expressions, wherein he flowed with that facility, that some-times it was necessary he should be stopped: *Sufflaminandus erat*, as Augustus said of Haterius. His wit was in his own power; would the rule of it had been so too. Many times he fell into those things, could not escape laughter, as when he said in the person of Caesar, one speaking to him, 'Caesar thou dost me wrong' – he replied: 'Caesar did never wrong, but with just cause,' and such like, which were ridiculous. But he redeemed his vices, with his virtues. There was ever more in him to be praised, than to be pardoned.

D. J. ENRIGHT (b. 1920), poet, 1973:

All's Well That Ends

OR, SHAKESPEARE UNMASKED

I'm afraid he'll have to go.
He won't pass muster these days.

Black men he didn't like: he made them
Proud and gullible and jealous and black
(Good fighters, but otherwise out of their depth).
He didn't like women, but neither
Was he a frank and manly homosexual.
'Woman delights not me: no, nor man neither . . .'
As for Jews, his complaint was that they were
Interested in money, were not Christians, and
If you pricked them they bled all over the place.
They deserved to have their daughters make
Unsuitable marriages.

(Put like that, Jews sound like a lot of us.
I shall have to rewrite this bit.)

A very dangerous man.
Think of all the trouble caused by that
Thoroughly offensive play of his, *Coriolanus*.
One night it wounded the feelings of the fascists,
The next it wounded the feelings of the communists.

He was anti-Scottish: it took an English army
To settle the hash of that kilted butcher
Macbeth. He made jokes about the Welsh, the
French, the Danes, the Italians and the Spanish.

He accused a West Indian (or possibly Algerian)
Of trying to rape a white girl unsuccessfully.
If it wasn't a base Judean he displayed
As criminally careless with pearls, then
It was an equally base Indian. Thank God
He hadn't heard of the Australians!

To be sure, he was the servant of his public,
A rough unlettered lot, who rarely washed
And dwelt in the polluted alleys of London
Or the corners of slippery palaces. There wasn't
A drama critic of independent mind among them.
Even so, he must bear most of the blame,
He could have stayed in Stratford and led a
Quiet and useful life.

Worst of all, he believed in good and evil,
And mixed them up in a deliberately nasty
And confusing way. A shifty character,
He pictured the human condition as one of
Unending and uneasy struggle, not to be
Resolved in a *haiku* or even a television
Debate. He made difficulties, he made
Much ado about nothing.

Now that we've stripped him clean
Of his poetry, we can see him plain.
Plainly he'll have to go.

WILLIAM HAZLITT (1778–1830) described in the *Examiner* the farewell performance on 4 June 1815 of the actor John Bannister (1760–1836), of whom it was said, 'The stage can point to few men of more solid virtue and unblemished character':

He then came forward to take his leave of the stage, in a farewell address, in which he expressed his thanks for the long and flattering

243

patronage he had received from the public. We do not wonder that his feelings were overpowered on this occasion: our own (we confess it) were nearly so too. We remember him in the first heyday of our youthful spirits, in the Prize – which he played so delightfully with that fine old croaker Suett, and Madame Storace – in the farce of My Grandmother, in the Son-in-Law, in Autolycus, and in Scrub, in which our satisfaction was at its height. At that time, King and Parsons and Dodd and Quick and Edwin, were in the full vigour of their reputation, who are now all gone. We still feel the vivid delight with which we used to see their names in the play-bills, as we went along to the theatre. Bannister was almost the last of these that remained; and we parted with him as we should with one of our oldest and best friends. The most pleasant feature in the profession of a player, and which is peculiar to it, is, that we not only admire the talents of those who adorn it, but we contract a personal intimacy with them. There is no class of society whom so many persons regard with affection as actors. We greet them on the stage; we like to meet them in the streets; they always recall to us pleasant associations; and we feel our gratitude excited, without the uneasiness of a sense of obligation. The very gaiety and popularity, however, which surrounds the life of a favourite performer, makes the retiring from it a very serious business. It glances a mortifying reflection on the shortness of human life, and the vanity of human pleasures. Something reminds us that 'all the world's a stage, and all the men and women merely players.'

SIR JOHN GIELGUD (b. 1904) has been a leading actor for almost seventy years, and the theatre owes as much to him for its richness and standing in this century as to anyone. He has also written well about actors and acting. His book *Distinguished Company* (1972) is a collection of essays, which, as the title suggests, recalls some of his friends, acquaintances and colleagues. Here he is writing about an actress he calls an 'exquisite comedienne', Dame Marie Tempest (1864–1942):

I was with her when she created her last new role, the grandmother in Dodie Smith's *Dear Octopus*, produced on the eve of Munich. She behaved impeccably at rehearsals, though we were all a little afraid of her at first, but the young director, Glen Byam Shaw, handled her with perfect tact, and she listened to him obediently. She had some difficulty in learning her lines, and we were convinced that, except for her own part, she had never even read the play. 'Are those some of my children?' she would inquire doubtfully, as another of the large assembly of characters came forward to greet her. One day she sent us all away while she took a lesson to learn 'The Kerry Dances', two verses of which she was to sing in the nursery scene. When we returned some hours later she had mastered it with apparent ease, and sang it enchantingly at the cottage piano, her voice still sweet and true. In the last act I liked to watch her in the scene when she was folding napkins for a dinner party in the shape of water-lilies. She was supposed to have drunk a cocktail and was a little tipsy, throwing one of the napkins into the air and catching it just in time with a wicked chuckle.

We became great friends during the run. I would be invited every evening to go to her dressing-room during one of my waits. There, with the white drugget on the floor and the patience cards laid out (she always played patience every night when she arrived at the theatre) I would be given French bread and butter and a cup of coffee, served by her dresser-companion with impressive ceremony.

When we were in Newcastle to try out the play, Marie Tempest insisted on coming down every morning in the hotel, always beautifully dressed. Sometimes she wore a big shady straw hat with a gardenia decorating the brim, and she always turned back her white gloves over the wrists as she ate her lunch. Sometimes we would go for a short drive together before her afternoon rest, and it was amusing to watch her choosing a cock-lobster ('not a hen,' she stipulated firmly) after she had climbed in her high heels over a steep step into the little white-washed cottage where the woman who was selling the lobsters had her shop. The creatures were scuttling about all over the stone floor, but Marie Tempest went on calmly chattering to her and seemed to understand what she was saying, despite her very thick Northumbrian accent.

When the War broke out, *Dear Octopus* closed in London. Her

Regent's Park flat was bombed, and she moved for a few weeks to Great Fosters, the hotel near Windsor, where I also happened to be staying for a few nights while I was making a film at Teddington. Here I would encounter her among the other residents, walking impatiently to and fro in the Great Hall during an air raid, impeccable as ever in a suit of blue slacks, and as a particularly loud explosion shook the walls I heard her remark to her companion, 'Quelle vie de dog!' (A rival actress was once heard to remark, 'Do you think Mary speaks what they call working French?')

My contract in *Dear Octopus* had expired and I left the play which had resumed its run after the blitz, but she continued acting in it for many months. Not long afterwards she was taken ill. I went to call on her with books and flowers, but after ten minutes' nervous conversation she caught me surreptitiously looking at my watch. 'It was sweet of you to come, my dear,' she said drily, 'but you think me rather an old bore really, don't you?' I felt deeply ashamed, for I loved and admired her very much. But a few days later, in October 1942, she was dead.

On February 26 1851, William Charles Macready (1793–1873) gave his farewell performance as Macbeth at Drury Lane. ALFRED LORD TENNYSON (1809–1902) paid him tribute:

> Farewell, Macready, since tonight we part;
> Full-handed thunders often have confessed
> Thy power, well-used to move the public breast.
> We thank thee with our voice, and from the heart.
>
> Farewell, Macready, since this night we part.
> Go, take thine honours home! Rank with the best,
> Garrick and statelier Kemble, and the rest
> Who made a nation purer through their art,
> Thine is it that our drama did not die,
> Nor flicker down to brainless pantomime,
> And those gilt gauds men-children swarm to see.

Farewell, Macready; moral, grave, sublime,
Our Shakespeare's bland and universal eye
Dwells pleased, through twice a hundred years, on thee.

WILLIAM MAKEPEACE THACKERAY, (1811–63):

> The play is done; the curtain drops,
>   Slow falling to the prompter's bell:
> A moment yet the actor stops,
>   And looks around to say farewell.
> It is an irksome word and task:
>   And when he's laughed and said his say,
> He shows as he removes his mask,
>   A face that's anything but gay.

Edmund Kean's last performance was given at Covent Garden on 25 March 1833, playing Othello to the Iago of his son, Charles. He collapsed into Charles's arms and moaned, 'I am dying – speak to them for me.' He had announced his retirement three years before in July 1830, and an unknown author writing in the *Morning Herald* reported the event. The scene is the King's Theatre, Haymarket:

Last night, long before the opening of the doors, that part of the Haymarket fronting the King's Theatre, and the Colonnade at the back of it, were densely crowded with persons of respectable appearance, who were desirous to view, for the last time, the performances of this eminent tragedian. Shortly after the opening of the door, which, by the by, was a full twenty minutes after the time mentioned in the bills, the pit and gallery were filled almost to suffocation. In fact, the pit overflowed, and many who were compelled to take their standing on the sides of it, sought relief by getting possession of several of the lower tier of boxes, from which they were afterwards ejected, on the arrival of the parties by whom they had been taken. Although the getting in was effected with much difficulty, and there was occasionally much screaming by the females, who were seemingly very respectable, yet no accident, we believe, beyond the loss of a shoe or two, and the bruises inflicted by lean elbows on fat sides, occurred. The pit and gallery, as before stated, were overflowingly full, as were also the boxes, before the performances commenced, and the stage wings were so choked with eager spectators, as to deny to the performers the privilege of ingress and egress. But amply were the audience compensated for the inconveniences incurred, by the excellence of the performances which consisted of a selection from those plays in which Mr Kean has been most celebrated, and commenced with the fourth act of *Richard the Third*, in which Kean maintained that superiority which has ever distinguished him in this part. All his peculiar points were well made and were greatly applauded. The fourth act of the *Merchant of Venice* succeeded, and never did we hear Kean in better voice, or see him play it throughout with more decided success. The fifth act of *A New Way to Pay Old Debts* followed, which was equally successful. The second act of *Macbeth*, which contains that beautiful soliloquy, 'Is this a dagger,' &c. was marred by the uproarious Gods, who had an affray of their own to settle. But the great treat of the evening which was reserved as a *bonne bouche* wherewith to finish the entertainment was the third act of *Othello*, where Iago – 'honest *Iago*,' first impregnates his mind with jealousy. His celebrated delivery of 'Farewell the tranquil mind' lost none of its original raciness (*sic*), and that harrowing speech, 'If thou dost slander her and torture me,' &c. was never more effectively given; it brought down a unanimous burst of applause which was repeated two or three times for the lapse of some minutes. It would be unjust, and ungallant also, were we to refrain from all notice of the ladies who gave the aid of their talents upon this occasion; but the late hour at which the performances terminated, must necessarily very much abridge our notice of them. Mrs William West, who has been for some time a stranger to the London boards, undertook her usual part of Portia. She was warmly greeted on her entrée, and she acquitted herself with her accustomed success. Mrs Knight, of Drury Lane Theatre, sustained the parts of Duchess of York in *Richard the Third*, and Lady Allworth in *A New Way to Pay Old Debts*, both of which she played with much judgment as did Mrs W. Clifford in the Queen in *Richard the Third*, and Emilia in *Othello*, though in neither had she much to perform. Mrs Bunn kindly sustained the part of Lady Macbeth, and was greatly applauded, as was also Miss Jarman, after a considerable absence from town, in the part of Desdemona. Cooper played the little of Iago which was allotted to him with great judgment. Between the acts, Messrs Harley, Anderson and Miss Betts, sang a variety of songs which met with different degrees of success though most of them were encored. The 'Storm' by the latter gentleman, met with but a *stormy* reception.

At the conclusion of these performances Mr Kean was led on 'in the habit which he wore' as Othello, to make his farewell adieu, but the expressions of regard were of so vehement a character for some time as to deprive him if not of speech at least of the opportunity of being heard. Among other testimonials a laurel wreath was thrown upon the stage, and cries of 'God bless you, Kean,' 'You must not leave us,' and such other expressions as seemed to combine personal regard for the man with admiration for the merits of the actor. Kean possesses these in a far greater degree than any other performer, and in the latter capacity, his greatest enemy cannot deny it to him after the recent evidences which he has given at the Haymarket Theatre, which he filled to the ceiling on every night of his performance. It has been the fashion with some persons and with some actors in particular, to regard Kean's acting as humbug – that there is enough of this it must be admitted, in all professions nowadays; nor is the stage, we suspect, more exempt from it than others, where it may endure for its 'season'; but will the more experienced believe that Kean's acting, if it were humbug, could retain public favour as it has done ever since he first performed in London to the present time, a period we believe of sixteen years? Attended by Messrs Cooper and Harley, and by all who had assisted in the performance, he delivered the following farewell Address, the commencement of which he altered, adapting it to the circumstance of his enthusiastic reception, as before described: –

'Ladies and Gentlemen: You may well guess how much my feelings are corroded in the utterance of that painful word – farewell. The glorious consolation in this my, perhaps, eternal banishment, will be the recollection of your liberality and kindness on this occasion.

Another point will be a solace that my mind's eye only will see – for the tears of the corporeal, I fear, would overflow my heart, – I allude to the fall of that drama, which has been the pride of Britain from the days of Queen Elizabeth to the close of our late lamented Monarch's life – Shakespeare, Massinger, Beaumont and Fletcher, and such-like names are, I understand, to be banished from the theatrical catalogue with me to make room for trans-atlantic experiments, and vaudevilles, melodramas, and second-rate music are to supply their places. How far the British public may succumb to these innovations, would be impertinent in me to prophecy; but in the humble opinion of an honest man, whose sentiments are always undisguised, that public will soon sigh for the restoration of the legitimate drama, and blush to see the grand Temple of the Muses profaned by insignificant and ephemeral abilities. It is a national concern – the nation's honour is at stake; and as the public acts on this occasion so will the names of the present era be handed to posterity – exalted or degraded. I have no longer any individual interest in the British stage; – but in a distant country a man feels more for his own than when is a resident, and it is painful to think I shall not be able to rebut those sarcasms and vituperative invectives, when they tell me the British stage is defunct, the professors are robbed of their dignity, and the only resource the talented part of the community have left is to fly to us foreigners, and be assured of our protection. America has now become if not the cradle, certainly the bed of genius, and rewards its instructors in the histrionic art both with fortune and with friendship – a name much more congenial to the soul of talent than all the riches of the universe. But whatever events may occur, my heart will never cease to feel its attachment to its native soil; and its last pulsation will be with gratitude to its former generosity. At length I summon my resolution to my aid and that, Ladies and Gentlemen, with considerable difficulty, and with prayers and best wishes for your prosperity and happiness, and speedy restoration of your dramatic rights, I bid you a long, a last farewell.'

ANONYMOUS, 1623 (prefaced to the First Folio of Shakespeare's works):

To the Memory of Mr W Shakespeare

We wondered, Shakespeare, that thou went'st so soon
From the world's stage to the grave's tiring-room.
We thought thee dead, but this thy printed worth,
Tells thy spectators that thou went'st but forth
To enter with applause. An actor's art,
Can die, and live, to act a second part.
That's but an exit of mortality;
This, a re-entrance to a plaudite.

D. H. LAWRENCE, 1929:

When I Read Shakespeare –

When I read Shakespeare I am struck with wonder
that such trivial people should muse and thunder
in such lovely language.

Lear, the old buffer, you wonder his daughters
didn't treat him rougher,
the old chough, the old chuffer!

And Hamlet, how boring, how boring to live with,
so mean and self-conscious, blowing and snoring
his wonderful speeches, full of other folks' whoring!

And Macbeth and his Lady, who should have been choring,
such suburban ambition, so messily goring
old Duncan with daggers!

How boring, how small Shakespeare's people are!
Yet the language so lovely! like the dyes from gas-tar.

G. K. CHESTERTON (1874–1936):

The Shakespeare Memorial

Lord Lilac thought it rather rotten
That Shakespeare should be quite forgotten,
And therefore got on a Committee
With several chaps out of the City,
And Shorter and Sir Herbert Tree,
Lord Rothschild and Lord Rosebery,
And FCG and Comyns Carr,
Two dukes and a dramatic star,
Also a clergyman now dead;
And while the vain world careless sped
Unheeding the heroic name –
The souls most fed with Shakespeare's flame
Still sat unconquered in a ring,
Remembering him like anything.

NOËL COWARD's famous advice, 1935:

Mrs Worthington, Don't Put Your Daughter
on the Stage

A SONG

Regarding yours, dear Mrs Worthington,
Of Wednesday the 23rd,
Although your baby,
May be,
Keen on a stage career,
How can I make it clear,
That this is not a good idea.
For her to hope,
Dear Mrs Worthington,
Is on the face of it absurd.

Her personality
Is not in reality
Inviting enough,
Exciting enough
For this particular sphere.

Don't put your daughter on the stage, Mrs Worthington,
Don't put your daughter on the stage,
The profession is overcrowded
And the struggle's pretty tough
And admitting the fact
She's burning to act,
That isn't quite enough.
She has nice hands, to give the wretched girl her due,
But don't you think her bust is too
Developed for her age.
I repeat
Mrs Worthington,
Sweet
Mrs Worthington,
Don't put your daughter on the stage.

Don't put your daughter on the stage,
Mrs Worthington,
Don't put your daughter on the stage,
Though they said at the school of acting
She was lovely as Peer Gynt,
I'm afraid on the whole
An ingénue role
Would emphasize her squint.

She's a big girl, and though her teeth are fairly good
She's not the type I ever would
Be eager to engage,
No more buts,
Mrs Worthington,
NUTS,

Mrs Worthington,
Don't put your daughter on the stage.

Don't put your daughter on the stage, Mrs Worthington,
Don't put your daughter on the stage,
She's a bit of an ugly duckling
You must honestly confess,
And the width of her seat
Would surely defeat
Her chances of success,
It's a loud voice, and though it's not exactly flat,
She'll need a little more than that
To earn a living wage.
On my knees
Mrs Worthington,
Please! Mrs Worthington,
Don't put your daughter on the stage.

Don't put your daughter on the stage, Mrs Worthington,
Don't put your daughter on the stage,
One look at her bandy legs should prove
She hasn't got a chance,
In addition to which
The son of a bitch
Can neither sing nor dance,
She's a *vile* girl and uglier than mortal sin,
One look at her has put me in
A tearing bloody rage,
That sufficed,
Mrs Worthington,
Christ!
Mrs Worthington,
Don't put your daughter on the stage.

WILLIAM SHAKESPEARE, *The Tempest*, Act IV, Scene 1:

> PROSPERO:
>> You do look, my son, in a moved sort,
>> As if you were dismay'd: be cheerful, sir.
>> Our revels now are ended. These our actors,
>> As I foretold you, were all spirits, and
>> Are melted into air, into thin air:
>> And, like the baseless fabric of this vision,
>> The cloud-capp'd towers, the gorgeous palaces,
>> The solemn temples, the great globe itself,
>> Yea, all which it inherit, shall dissolve,
>> And, like this insubstantial pageant faded,
>> Leave not a rack behind. We are such stuff
>> As dreams are made on; and our little life
>> Is rounded with a sleep.

Acknowledgements

The author and publishers wish to thank the following who have kindly given permission for the use of copyright material:

MICHAEL BILLINGTON for an extract from his book *Peggy Ashcroft*, published by John Murray (Publishers) Ltd (1988).

KITTY BLACK for extracts from her book *Upper Circle: A Theatrical Chronicle* (1984).

BLOOMSBURY PUBLISHING LTD for extracts from *Manuscripts Don't Burn: Mikhail Bulgakov, a Life in Letters and Diaries* by Julie Curtis (1991).

THE CALDER EDUCATIONAL TRUST, London, for extracts from *The Theatre and Its Double* by Antonin Artaud, translated by Victor Corti. Translation Copyright © John Calder (Publishers) Ltd, 1970, and Calder Publications Ltd, 1993.

CURTIS BROWN GROUP LTD on behalf of the Estate of Elizabeth Bowen for reviews (1937).

DOUBLEDAY, a division of Bantam, Doubleday, Dell Publishing Group Inc., for an extract from a review by George Jean Nathan included in *No Turn Unstoned* compiled by Diana Rigg. Copyright © 1982 by Declutch Productions Ltd.

The Estate of SIR LAWRENCE OLIVIER for his letter to Archie Nathan.

The Estate of KENNETH TYNAN for extracts from his publications, and from reviews in the *Observer*.

The Estate of P. G. WODEHOUSE for an extract from a letter, and the poem 'Mr. Beerbohm Tree' from *The Green Parrot and Other Poems* published by Hutchinson, an imprint of Random House UK.

FABER AND FABER LTD for an extract from 'Whispers of Immortality' from *Collected Poems 1909–1962* by T. S. Eliot; the poem 'Gus: The Theatre Cat' from *Old Possum's Book of Practical Cats*' by

T. S. Eliot; extract from 'Hamlet' from *Selected Essays* by T. S. Eliot; extract from *Almost a Gentleman* by John Osborne, and an extract from *Collected Poems and Prose* by Harold Pinter.

GUARDIAN NEWSPAPERS LTD for extracts from an article by Ranjit Bolt in the *Guardian*, July 1991, and a review in the *Manchester Guardian*, May 1958.

HARPERCOLLINS PUBLISHERS LTD for an extract from *The Casting Couch: The Uninhibited Memoirs of a Young Actress* by Joan Wood (1975).

DAVID HIGHAM ASSOCIATES on behalf of Simon Gray for an extract from *An Unnatural Pursuit and Other Pieces* (1985).

HODDER & STOUGHTON LTD for an extract from *Distinguished Company* (1972), now republished as *Backward Glances*, by Sir John Gielgud.

MICHAEL IMISON PLAYWRIGHTS LTD on behalf of the Estate of Noël Coward for extracts from *The Noël Coward Diaries* and *Autobiography*, and on behalf of Timberlake Wertenbaker for an extract from *Our Country's Good* (1988) based on the novel *The Playmaker* by Thomas Keneally (1987) Copyright © The Serpentine Publishing Company Pty, published by Hodder & Stoughton, and Sceptre.

PAMELA INGLE-FINCH and JOHN H. B. IRVING for extracts from *Henry Irving: The Actor and His World* by Lawrence Irving.

MACMILLAN PUBLISHING COMPANY, New York, for extracts from *On Directing* by Harold Clurman. Copyright © 1972 by Harold Clurman.

SHERIDAN MORLEY for a review published in *Punch*, 1976.

THE OBSERVER NEWSPAPER for an extract by Sacha Guitry, 1957.

OXFORD UNIVERSITY PRESS for an extract from *Lichtenberg's Visits to England* translated by Mare & Quarrell (1938).

PARAGON HOUSE PUBLISHERS for an extract from *Son and Artist* by Louis Sheagger.

PAVILION BOOKS for extracts from *I, An Actor* by Nicholas Craig (1989).

PETERS FRASER & DUNLOP GROUP LTD, on behalf of The Estate of J. B. Priestley for an extract from a letter; on behalf of The Estate of Hilaire Belloc for an extract from 'The World's a Stage' from

Complete Verse, published by Pimlico, a division of Random Century; and on behalf of Claire Tomalin for an extract from *The Invisible Woman: The Story of Nelly Ternan and Charles Dickens*, published by Penguin Books Ltd.

CASAROTTO RAMSAY LTD on behalf of Alan Ayckbourn for quotes in the *Daily Telegraph* (1986) and the *New York Times* (1979).

REED INTERNATIONAL BOOKS for extracts from *Antigone* by Jean Anouilh and *Playing Shakespeare* by John Barton, published by Methuen London Ltd.

EVA REICHMANN for extracts from *Around Theatres* by Sir Max Beerbohm.

THE SHAKESPEARE GLOBE TRUST for access to archive material in the Shakespeare Globe Museum, Bear Gardens, London.

THE SOCIETY OF AUTHORS on behalf of the Bernard Shaw Estate for extracts from *The Problem Play, Fanny's First Play, The Quintessence of Ibsenism, On Cutting Shakespeare, Dramatic Criticisms*, and a letter to Arthur Clark.

THE STAGE & TELEVISION TODAY NEWSPAPER for a report published in *The Stage*, 4 January 1889.

TIMES NEWSPAPERS LTD for reviews by Sir Harold Hobson and James Agate published in the *Sunday Times*.

MRS. W. E. TREWIN on behalf of The J. C. Trewin Estate for extracts from *The Stratford Festival: A History of the Shakespeare Memorial Theatre* and *Five and Eighty Hamlets*.

WATSON LITTLE LTD on behalf of D. J. Enright for the poem 'All's Well That Ends' from *Collected Poems of D. J. Enright* published by Oxford University Press.

A. P. WATT LTD on behalf of Michael Holroyd for extracts from *The Life of Oscar Wilde* by Hesketh Pearson.

MARGARET WOLFIT for a letter written by Sir Donald Wolfit to Archie Nathan.

Every effort has been made to trace all the copyright holders, but if any have been inadvertently overlooked the publishers will be pleased to make the necessary arrangement at the first opportunity.

Index of Authors

General Index